HOTEL ADLON

HOTEL ADLON

The Life and Death of a Great Hotel

HEDDA ADLON

*Translated from the German and edited
by Norman Denny*

HORIZON PRESS
NEW YORK

First American Edition 1960
HORIZON PRESS, NEW YORK
Library of Congress Catalog Card Number 60-14653

Printed in Great Britain by
Western Printing Services Ltd Bristol

CONTENTS

LIST OF ILLUSTRATIONS

I

The Kaiser's Hotel

THE Adlon was so much a child of good fortune, almost of magic, that I might well begin its story with the words 'Once upon a time'.

Even after the heaviest disasters had fallen upon Germany, when Berlin had been pounded to an almost unrecognizable expanse of rubble, the splendid house at Number One, Unter den Linden, still remained in being. Half-hidden by clouds of smoke, lighted by the glare of neighbouring fires, it was still almost intact, only superficially damaged by bomb-fragments. A world was collapsing, but it seemed that by a mysterious dispensation one gleam at least of the grace and elegance of an earlier age was destined to be preserved.

But the Adlon outlived this miracle by only a few days. Berlin had surrendered, the fighting in the streets had ceased and the guns were silent, when suddenly fire broke out in the building, sweeping through it from cellar to roof. Within a very short time all was over. The fabulous world of the Adlon had vanished, just when it seemed that the worst danger was past.

The fabulous world of the Adlon! There was scarcely a crowned head, during its lifetime, who did not pay it at least one visit. Statesmen and diplomats, bankers and industrialists, legendary maharajahs and world-famous artists, all the great ones of the earth made it their headquarters when business or pleasure brought them to Berlin. It was in the Adlon that they met and mingled, a brilliant, cosmopolitan society adorned with the beauty of women —those whose names shone in lights and those whose only talent was to be beautiful. And it was men and women, their affairs and their vicissitudes, their scandals great and small, which made the Adlon what it remained throughout its history, an admired and

B   I

coveted centre of the great world, and a subject of dreaming to the many who knew it only from the outside. To have dined or danced at the Adlon, to have spent a night there—above all, a bridal night —these were cherished ambitions, tales to be told to the children after many years.

The Adlon—I find myself talking of it as though it were a living creature—was born on the 23rd October 1907, and its godparent was the Kaiser Wilhelm II, who with some justice always spoke of it as 'My Hotel'.

He asked that no other guest should be allowed to enter the hotel before he had done so, and Lorenz Adlon was only too happy to agree. Without the Emperor's help he would never have been able to build it at all.

And so, during the late afternoon of that autumn day, Kaiser Wilhelm drove to Number One, Unter den Linden, accompanied by the Empress, the Princess Victoria Louise, the Princes Adalbert and August Wilhelm, and a large company of ladies and gentlemen. Standing in the doorway to receive him was Lorenz Adlon, ceremonially clad in morning coat and striped trousers.

The Kaiser offered his hand in greeting and then gazed at the handsome doorway, which was flanked by two stone columns bearing large, elaborate lanterns resting on figured stone pedestals. Beneath each lantern was a bronze plate bearing the words, 'Hotel Adlon'.

'Gentlemen, do you note the modesty of our friend, Adlon?' said the Kaiser. 'The nameplates are no bigger than my hand!'

With the Empress and their retinue he then passed into the hotel, in the decoration of which artists such as Reinhold Begas and Adolf von Menzel had collaborated.

'Those venturing inside', so reported a newspaper on the following day, 'will find themselves in a sumptuous hall filled with *objets d'art*, rich, costly materials and expensive stone and metal work. Recollections of the halls of Venetian palaces come to mind, princely reception rooms, formal apartments, half dwelling and half monument. One thinks of the royal palaces of Bavaria.

'Everything is solid and massive. The square pillars of the lobby are of dark-yellow clouded marble, and the stone chimney-piece in the hall is surmounted with a Roman-imperial bust of the Kaiser. Dark and white marbles gleam in every corner. The elaborately ornamented capitals of the pillars are of precious metals. But despite the huge expenditure on rich materials there is no vulgar excess. . . .

'Perhaps some day a new Treaty of Europe will be signed in the green Empire room with its many mirrors, which conjures up a picture of glittering uniforms. Perhaps the masters of finance and industry will determine the commercial future of Germany in the lofty room containing a magnificent Tiepolo, while art-historians meet in the Raphael room, adorned with murals and ornaments after the fashion of Raphaelite grotesques; and in the Goethe garden, the flower-garden of the hotel where old Goethe's bust presides, perhaps men of letters will discuss the future of German literature. . . .'

The Kaiser was brought to a standstill before he had even passed through the lobby, and he beckoned to his Lord Chamlain, Count Robert Zedlitz-Trützschler.

'Trützschler, do you see that marble?'

'But your Majesty has just as fine marble at the palace,' said the Lord Chamberlain.

'Of course my marble is just as fine,' said the Kaiser. 'But look how this has been cleaned! Look how it shines!'

He went on into the vast reception hall and here again stood in amazement.

'What sort of carpets are these, Adlon? They're wonderful. Where did you get them?'

'I bought them in Constantinople,' answered Lorenz Adlon.

'And what did you pay for them?'

Lorenz Adlon told his Majesty the price.

'Trützschler,' cried the Kaiser, 'do you hear that? You once saddled me with two carpets for the Potsdam Palace that were like doormats compared with these, and by God, they cost twice as much!'

Lorenz Adlon knew that from that hour he had one more
enemy in the world. He said afterwards that he would remember
the Lord Chamberlain's expression all his life.

The Kaiser continued to look about him. His glance fell upon
the twenty page-boys lined up in their smart uniforms along one
side of the hall, like a row of toy soldiers. Lorenz Adlon had paid
particular attention to these, knowing his guest.

As he had foreseen, the Kaiser went to the end of the row and
looked along it, like an officer on the parade-ground, to inspect
the dressing.

'Excellent! First-rate discipline!' he said.

After further admiring the decoration of the reception hall, and
pausing a moment before the bronze bust of himself, he pointed to
the magnificent bronze candelabra representing the sun and the
planets.

'Adlon, tell Trützschler where you got this. I want one like it.'

There was indeed scarcely anything that his Majesty did not
want, from the furnishings of Australian Jarrah-mahogany in the
Beethoven room to the chimney-piece of Sienna marble rimmed
with old silver.

'If I left it to my Lord Chamberlain,' he said laughingly to
Lorenz Adlon, 'I should never have a new chair or carpet. I
should still be living with the Frederick the Great's furniture!'

But then, when the exalted party reached the ladies' drawing-
room, decorated in the style of Louis XVI, it was the Empress's
turn to start wanting things.

'Oh, Wilhelm, how delightful this is! I've been meaning to tell
you for ages that my boudoir at Kassel is really beginning to look
very shabby.'

'Nonsense, nonsense!' said the Kaiser in great haste. 'Your
boudoir at Kassel is quite charming.'

After this he almost ran.

There followed a tour of the whole house from the ducal suites
on the first floor to the more modest bedrooms on the fourth. The
Kaiser turned on the hot water in all the bedrooms to make sure
that it really worked. He switched on the lights, and was en-

chanted to learn that there were no bells in the hotel, but that waiters and chambermaids were summoned by light-flashes.

He left the building highly delighted with his round of inspection, while Lorenz Adlon sighed with relief that all had gone so smoothly.

Two days later the Chancellor of the Reich, Prince Bülow, paid his first visit to the Adlon. He led Lorenz Adlon into a quiet corner, and they sipped a glass of sherry together.

'My warmest congratulations,' he said. 'The hotel is truly wonderful. But all the same, Herr Adlon, I have a bone to pick with you. You have simply no idea of the trouble you are causing me. During my audience yesterday with the Kaiser I was scarcely able to get a word in edgeways. He kept interrupting to tell me about your bathrooms! He wanted to know when I intended to give my first dinner-party here and if I was going to invite him. And a minute later he was saying that it was a very long time since the Crown Prince had done any entertaining, and that he ought to invite his brothers and a few members of the Diplomatic Corps to dine at the Adlon. And so it went on throughout the entire audience!'

Presently Lorenz Adlon took him to see the wine-cellar with its huge stock of vintage clarets and burgundies, hocks and champagnes.

'But it's prodigious!' Prince Bülow exclaimed. 'It must have cost a fortune!'

Lorenz Adlon told him that in no case had he laid down less than a hundred bottles of any single wine, and that in all the cellar contained a quarter of a million bottles.

'I beg of you, Herr Adlon,' said the Prince, half-joking and half in earnest, 'don't ever let the Kaiser see this. If he knew you had a quarter of a million bottles he'd be certain to think he ought to have a million!'

In accordance with the wish expressed in that most exalted quarter, the first notable event at the Adlon was the dinner given by the Crown Prince to his brothers. The menu was all that a menu should be, and some of the noblest vintages were served. At the end of the evening the Crown Prince paid the bill with a cheque for three hundred marks.

Lorenz Adlon later told his son, Louis Adlon, of his feelings at that moment.

'I stood for some time in the hall,' he said, 'with that three-hundred-mark cheque in my hand, and as I looked at it I reflected that the hotel had cost twenty millions. I simply hadn't the courage to reckon how many cheques that size would be needed to pay for it. Suddenly, for the first time, the thought really came home to me—Adlon, my lad, you're twenty millions in the red!'

2

Birthpangs of a Remarkable Enterprise

TWENTY million marks. It may seem no very enormous sum by present standards. But these were gold marks at a time when the mark had a parity of about twenty to the pound. A million pounds in the year 1907! The reader may reckon for himself its equivalent today.

How did it come about that Lorenz Adlon, a self-made man born in humble circumstances, was able to lay out this huge sum in building an hotel of such luxury that it was a world sensation? As I think of it, now that I write this memoir, it still seems to me like a fairy-tale.

To begin with I must give some account of how I myself live at the present time. My dwelling is in a house, near the Kurfürstendamm in Berlin, which was formerly the property of my late sister. Before the 'Reichsmark period', that is to say, the last currency conversion, the rooms I occupy formed part of a much larger apartment. Mine is far from being a luxury flat, nevertheless I love these few rooms for the sake of the mementoes with which I have filled them.

The room in which I sit writing is more like a museum than a work-room. On the walls hang portraits in oils of my husband, Louis Adlon, my sisters and myself; and the tables and every available space are covered with silver-framed, signed photographs of princes, statesmen, actors, actresses and other persons of note. I cherish these and much else that belonged to my former life—furniture, rugs, chests, vases. And there are piles of old letters, Adlon menu-cards, old legal documents and newspaper cuttings.

From among these papers, which I have thumbed through so many times, I have retrieved an item which may serve as an

7

introduction to the story of Lorenz Adlon's debts. It is the libretto of a Berlin revue produced at the Metropole Theatre in 1905.

There is a scene in which the ghost of Count Redern, the former chief administrator of the Royal Playhouse in Berlin, appears on the stage. The ghost laments the fact that the family mansion, the Palais Redern in Unter den Linden, is to be pulled down, and mournfully proclaims that it wishes 'To shed a last tear for my beloved old Berlin.'

Then, this being a revue, the ghost breaks into song:

> *The new era brings new fashions,*
> *Berlin puts on another dress,*
> *Things that once charmed us with their beauty*
> *Are now considered only fit for peasants.*
> *First they drove out of the Playhouse*
> *The style of acting of the good old days,*
> *And now with a heavy heart I see*
> *That my splendid palace is going.*
> *That which Schinkel built and the plane-trees adorned*
> *Is to become a hotel for the use of foreigners.*
> *Thus do you vanish, my old Berlin!*

The back-cloth depicting the Palais Redern is then raised, and in its place an impression of the Hotel Adlon appears, and the ghost sings:

> *The old Berliners mourn*
> *The passing of the old-time resorts*
> *Where in the steamy, smoky air men ate in comfort,*
> *Often six together round the foam-capped glasses.*
> *No white-haired host to jest with us in greeting,*
> *No boy to serve the claret;*
> *The* Bierstube *that suited old Berlin*
> *Has turned into a Beer Palace,*
> *With all the menu written down in French*
> *And all the furnishings brought new from England,*
> *Hungarian orchestra and waiters from Vienna—*
> *Thus do you vanish, my old Berlin!*

The song arose out of the fact that my father-in-law, Lorenz Adlon, had succeeded in persuading Kaiser Wilhelm II to allow him to buy and demolish the Palais Redern, which had been protected as an historic monument, in order to set up in its place, on the finest site in Berlin, a luxury hotel such as Europe had never seen.

Lorenz Adlon was a remarkable man. The son of an artisan, he was born in Mainz, but there is some doubt as to where the Adlon family originated. The French name has led most of its members to believe that their forebears were Huguenots, but this seems to be contradicted by the fact that the later generations were all Roman Catholic. I think it more probable that the family was of Wallonian descent.

Lorenz Adlon was born in Mainz in 1849, and his father had him apprenticed as a carpenter. He devoted a great deal of his spare time to gymnastics and was a member of a *Turnverein*, or sports club. It was this which led him suddenly to abandon his carpenter's calling and, as he put it later, 'go in for making money in a big way'. His club paid a visit to Coblenz, and his fellow-members asked him to take charge of the catering for the excursion. This small enterprise showed a profit, and it gave him a taste for the business. He invested in a tent which he took round to sports meetings, and which brought in so much money that before long he was able to set up a more permanent establishment in Mainz.

His success grew, and in the years that followed he amassed a considerable sum in Dutch gilder by setting up tent restaurants at all the principal fairs in Holland.

Soon the tents were not enough. He had more ambitious plans. His journeyings had enabled him to see something of those upper strata of society which patronized the better restaurants. He studied their habits with great interest, taking careful note of their especial fads and fancies. Above all he studied the elaborate menus and the expensive wine-lists.

And presently, when the World Exhibition in Amsterdam was

in preparation, he put in a tender for the principal restaurant. He secured the concession, and this enterprise alone brought him a profit of a hundred thousand gilder.

Berlin was his next stop. He bought a share in the Hotel Continental and also acquired the Restaurant Hiller, on Unter den Linden, which under his management became the best restaurant in Germany. He got the concession for the leading restaurant at the big Arts and Crafts Exhibition, held at the turn of the century, and with this established himself in the capital as a person of consequence.

Berlin at the end of the nineteenth century was still far from being a town that attracted foreigners. Of the nations whose well-to-do upper class were given to European travel, the most important were Russia and England. The Americans were also just beginning to discover Europe. But the countries most commonly visited by those travellers were France and Italy, and the towns which attracted the wealthy public were Paris, Rome, Biarritz and Monte Carlo.

The Russians did indeed visit Germany a good deal, but their ports of call were Dresden, for its opera and art-galleries, and Baden-Baden for its hot springs. English and American gentry might once in a lifetime make the journey up the Rhine as far as Baden-Baden, but Berlin did not tempt them. Under Kaiser Wilhelm I the Court and the capital of the Reich possessed few splendours worthy to be witnessed. The opera was no more than adequate and the art-galleries offered nothing sensational. The hotels were insufficient in size and number, and could in no way compete with those of France and Italy, particularly those on the Riviera.

But it was precisely this that had brought Lorenz Adlon so early to Berlin. He was convinced that Berlin was destined to become a *Weltstadt*, one of the world's great capitals, although in those days it was little more than a respectable, middle-class provincial garrison town. He based his belief most particularly on the impression made upon him, during his youth, by Prince Wilhelm, afterwards Kaiser Wilhelm II, for whom he always had a profound esteem.

'I would give a great deal to know the Prince personally,' he said to one of his friends; and when the latter showed little understanding for this singular aspiration, he added roundly: 'When he becomes Kaiser the Prince will make me a millionaire.'

His friend inquired sceptically how this was to come about, but Lorenz Adlon did not answer. He had definite projects in mind, but he was not yet ready to discuss them with anyone.

That he did in fact become acquainted with Prince Wilhelm shortly after this was owing to an exceptional chance, a case of good fortune in misfortune, as he said.

The misfortune was the fire at the Hotel Continental, in the Inner Town of Berlin. Lorenz Adlon, who was part-owner of the hotel, was the first of the directors to be on the spot. A big crowd of sightseers surrounded the burning building, which, as one of them admiringly exclaimed, was a magnificent spectacle, affording the Berlin fire-brigade and several parties of pioneer troops from the garrison an opportunity of going into action with the utmost clamour and display.

The managing director of the company, Rudolf Sendig, who owned a number of hotels in different parts of Germany, was in Dresden at the time. He came with all speed on receiving a telegram from Lorenz Adlon, and reached the scene of the disaster just in time to see the whole building collapse in flames. As he was trying to force his way through the crowd a policeman stopped him.

'I'm the general manager of the hotel,' he cried.

'You should have got here sooner,' said the policeman. 'It doesn't need a manager any more.'

In the meantime Prince Wilhelm had arrived on the scene. Lorenz Adlon did the honours of the burning house, and in doing so made a most favourable impression. The two men stood side by side with the fire-brigades at work around them, while officers shouted orders to the pioneer squads. Everyone in any way concerned in the proceedings made a point of reporting to the Prince exactly what was going on. This gratified Prince Wilhelm, but he was even more interested in what Lorenz Adlon had to

say. Adlon was telling him that the devastated hotel must be replaced by a new one which would be truly representative of the
capital of the Reich and would make Berlin a worthy objective for
rich and eminent cosmopolitan travellers.

This was exactly the right line to take with Prince Wilhelm.

'Do you really believe it can be done?' he asked.

Lorenz Adlon plunged with passionate enthusiasm into an
account of his plans. With arms outstretched against the background of flames he sketched a new hotel to overshadow all others,
so huge and luxurious that the most distinguished foreigners
would come to Berlin for the mere pleasure of staying in it. The
project so fascinated Prince Wilhelm that he lost all interest in
the fire.

'We must talk it over thoroughly,' he said. 'I am determined
that such a hotel shall be built.'

This conversation took place at the time when the Berlin Zoo-
logical Garden was being greatly extended. Big new restaurant
sites and broad terraces were being constructed, and the Berlin
restaurateurs and hotel proprietors were fiercely competing for
the right to set up establishments on them. Lorenz Adlon had put
in his bid, but in this matter he laboured under a severe handicap
—he was not a native of Berlin. Local patriotism loomed large in
the town in those days. And here his encounter with Prince
Wilhelm worked wonders. He renewed his efforts, referring
to his acquaintanceship with the Prince, and, securing the concession, realized a profit of about two million marks within a few
years.

This immense success did not come of its own accord. It was
the fruit of intelligent planning. Apart from Hiller's, which
already belonged to Lorenz Adlon and was very exclusive, there
was no restaurant in Berlin where French cooking could be
obtained, and indeed no establishment of any kind where the
dishes had an international flavour. The Berlin food was charac-
terless. Even the leading hotels did not ordinarily serve *hors
d'œuvres*. Soup, fish, roast and sweets were all that the menus

offered, well-cooked and nourishing dishes, but finally no different from what people got in their own homes.

Lorenz Adlon opened an establishment on the so-called 'Red Terrace' of the Zoo, which did not merely follow the Parisian style but was, for all intents and purposes, a Parisian restaurant. The chef came from Paris and the waiters were all polyglot, as well able to understand Russian and Italian as English and German.

For the first time Berlin tasted *bouillabaisse*, cooked by an expert whom Lorenz Adlon had brought from 'Chez Basso' in Marseilles. In another of his terrace restaurants the cooking was international—soused cuttlefish, Rhine mussels, English lobster pie, shark-fin soup and other exotic delicacies.

All Berlin thronged to the Zoo restaurants for afternoon coffee, and consumed ices such as they had never tasted before. Vanilla, chocolate and lemon had been the accepted flavours, served on a plate with a spoonful of whipped cream as the height of luxury. Lorenz Adlon caused them to be served on silver or cut glass— and what ices they were! A specialist had been brought from Naples to astonish the Berliners with the Neapolitan ice known as a 'cassate'. There were ices in which stoned frozen cherries reposed on a bed of snow tasting of lemons, champagne sorbets and coffee ices with a flavour quite unlike the coffee one got at home; and with them went small, delicious pastries prepared by a pastry-cook brought from Budapest.

The lady cashier with whom, every evening, Lorenz Adlon checked the day's takings, is still alive and living in Berlin. It fascinates me to hear her complain of the labour of carrying the heavy bags of money from the table to the safe. People paid in gold and silver in those days.

The daily turnover of the terrace restaurants during the summer averaged 60,000 marks. Anyone familiar with the catering trade, who knows the margin on such things as coffee and, above all, ices, can estimate the profit this figure represents. Adlon built his business on the revolution in taste which he himself brought about. His menus consisted, not of four courses, as had hitherto been universal, but of six or seven.

When I show those menus to young people nowadays they are apt to cry out in consternation, 'How could people possibly eat so much?' But of course the notion of quantity is quite mistaken. People did not eat an undue amount but in greater variety, the portions being quite small, after the French pattern. When the diner has finished his meal he must feel ready to start all over again. That was the secret and the reason for Lorenz Adlon's success.

And this success was crowned when one day Prince Wilhelm came quite unexpectedly to lunch on one of the Zoo terraces with a party of officers and members of his suite. To Berlin society this was an event as startling as it was unusual. The Prussian princes were not at all in the habit of patronizing public restaurants in Berlin. If they were not expressly forbidden to do so it was only because those who prescribed the formal rules governing their conduct had never thought it possible that a son of the Royal House, still less a future Kaiser, would so far forget himself as to mingle in this free and easy fashion with ordinary citizens.

The news of the prince's visit to Adlon's restaurant swept through Berlin like a whirlwind, and thereafter every Guards officer with any social pretensions made a point of visiting the Zoo, not to look at the monkeys but to dine at the board of Lorenz Adlon.

The years passed, Prince Wilhelm became Kaiser, and then one day the Palais Redern, at Number One, Unter den Linden, was put up for sale. Lorenz Adlon, who had long cherished the idea of building his projected hotel on that unique site, went to work immediately.

He had to overcome two great difficulties. In the first place, the mansion was protected as an historic monument and could not be pulled down except with royal permission. Secondly, according to the existing estimates, the hotel he wanted to build would cost fifteen millions. It was a colossal sum for those days. He would have to borrow from the banks, and it was by no means certain that they would be disposed to invest on such a scale in so extraordinary a venture.

Nevertheless, Lorenz Adlon had high hopes. He requested an audience of the Kaiser, and Wilhelm II, who had not forgotten their first meeting, at once received him. The Kaiser had an especial liking for the tall, elegant man. In a very little while the first problem had been solved and the necessary permission granted.

Seeing the Kaiser thus favourably disposed, the banks turned a more friendly eye upon the enterprise, and credits to the extent of fifteen million marks were made available. It seemed that Lorenz Adlon had been brilliantly successful in surmounting the two major obstacles.

But before he had begun the demolition of the Palais Redern he found himself confronted by a powerful and dangerous adversary who threatened to wreck the entire project—the *Berliner Hotel-Betriebs AG*, or Berlin Hotel Syndicate.

This concern owned the Central Hotel and the Wintergarten; it had a large share in the Aschinger Hotel, owned breweries and numerous other establishments, and in the course of decades had become so wealthy and powerful that it was very well able to bring pressure to bear on the Berlin banks. The Hotel Bristol had also recently been acquired by the Syndicate, and when the word went round that a Hotel Adlon was to be built at Number One, Unter den Linden, it at once joined battle.

The head of the syndicate was a certain Herr Koppel, a man of immense wealth, a millionaire many times over, who had no need of further profits but whose singular ambition it was to be the leading hotel proprietor in Berlin. For a long time past he had been closely following Lorenz Adlon's activities, and he had bitterly reproached the representatives of his own concern for failing to secure the Zoo concessions. Now, beside himself with apprehension, he plotted counter-measures.

He, too, had friends at Court, and before the demolition of the Palais Redern was begun he prevailed upon them to seek to dissuade his Majesty from the destruction of that historic building. But Wilhelm II was not the man to change his mind once it was made up. To their tactful approaches he replied:

'Thank God that old eyesore is to be pulled down at last! It was a disgrace! It ruined my Unter den Linden. Adlon has promised to build something much more handsome, and then perhaps my capital will begin to look like a modern city. Don't you agree?'

What else could they do?

When the Palais Redern was half-demolished Herr Koppel gleaned further details of Lorenz Adlon's plans.

The new hotel was to have about 300 bedrooms and 250 bathrooms. With the best will in the world, not more than 60 to 70 bathrooms could be built into the Bristol. Furthermore the Adlon was to have from 100 to 150 suites with sitting-rooms and even dressing-rooms, in the case of the most expensive.

But even more alarming was the degree of elegance and luxury that was to characterize the entire building. It seemed that the main stairway was to be built of Carrera marble, that all the decorations were to be executed by leading artists and that only the very finest woods were to be used for the panelling. Moreover all the beds were to be made of artistically worked bronze, costing unbelievable prices. The liveries, the linen and towels were being ordered from the house of Rudolf Herzog, and it was said that this distinguished firm was being required to submit sketches of all uniforms to leading experts who would ensure that they were consistent in style.

These terrifying reports caused Herr Koppel to resolve upon desperate measures. Surely financial pressure could be used to nip the project in the bud? He estimated Lorenz Adlon's private fortune at about two million marks, but he had heard that the cost of the hotel was estimated at fifteen millions. Therefore, reasoned Herr Koppel, Adlon must be borrowing a very large sum of money, and since it was a question of long-term credits he could only get it from the mortgage-banks. Herr Koppel was on particularly good terms with these institutions owing to his earlier purchase of development sites to the west of Berlin, which had enormously increased in value. But to his intense indignation he learned that someone had already spoken to the mortgage-banks —no less a person than the Kaiser himself.

The directors of these banks, to their astonishment and extreme delight, had been invited to a *Bierabend im Schloss*, a beer-evening at the Palace, at which they had been personally presented to his Majesty, who had then delivered an address in which he told them that it was his most earnest desire to make Berlin a world-capital, and that he looked to them to assist him in this work. He had even gone so far as absent-mindedly to address one of their number as 'Herr Kommerzienrat',[1] a dignity which the gentleman did not then possess; and he had referred in passing to Lorenz Adlon and the hotel which he proposed to build.

After this Lorenz Adlon had no need to go to the bankers, they came to him! So it was clear to Herr Koppel that financial pressure would not work.

Accordingly he tried the use of charm and persuasion. He got in touch with Lorenz Adlon, and the two very dissimilar men went for a stroll together in the Tiergarten, Adlon tall and elegant, always dressed in the latest fashion, Koppel small by comparison, walking with short, hurried steps, and clad in a black frock-coat which, according to his friends, he wore even in bed.

Herr Koppel came to the point at once. Without any beating about the bush he said that his syndicate was disturbed by what it had heard of Herr Adlon's projects, and he made an offer:

'We are prepared to repay, with full interest, everything that you personally may have invested in this undertaking. You shall suffer no loss on our account.'

Lorenz Adlon replied briefly that he was not interested.

'Very well,' said Herr Koppel, and raised his bid. 'We will not only repay your money, we will engage you as general manager of the Berlin Hotel Syndicate with a salary of two hundred thousand marks. Will you consider that?'

'No,' said Lorenz Adlon, 'I have no need to consider it. I intend to build my own hotel.'

[1] Honorary title conferred by Government on successful businessmen.

C

Herr Koppel walked on for a time in silence, and then his self-restraint gave way.

'This will break you, Adlon. I know your financial position and I also know what the building will cost. You'll never even get the structure completed, to say nothing of all the extravagant trimmings!'

'Well, if you know all that,' said Lorenz Adlon, 'I don't understand why your company should be making me this handsome offer. You'll be able to get what you want much more cheaply later on.'

This brought the negotiations to an end.

'Very well,' said Koppel. 'If you insist on ruining yourself, go ahead. But later on perhaps you'll remember this conversation.'

He drove off in a cab, resolved to pursue his campaign by other means.

His first step was to put his statistical department to work, and with their aid, after careful calculation, he reached a conclusion which gave him great pleasure.

The figures showed that if the hotel was to cost fifteen millions, the number of rooms planned for would not be enough to cover the capital outlay. Despite the improving prospects for the tourist traffic in Berlin, Adlon could not count upon having all his rooms occupied all the time. He needed a considerably larger number of rooms in order to make the largest possible profit at the peak seasons and thus balance his takings over the year.

As it happened, however, Lorenz Adlon had at the same time been making similar calculations and had reached the same conclusion, which, as he afterwards admitted, brought the perspiration to his forehead. Standing contemplating his growing building, he saw that he would have to buy the adjoining plot of land, on the corner of Unter den Linden and the Wilhelmstrasse, in order to extend it. This would cost additional millions, but he could see no other way out of his dilemma.

Once again he had to turn to the banks. He found them ready to grant him increased credits on mortgage, but with some reluctance. They were clearly less favourably disposed than they had been.

And in this difficult situation there descended upon him the fearful blow which Koppel had been secretly preparing. Koppel had bought the Wilhelmstrasse–Unter den Linden site from under his nose! Moreover Lorenz Adlon also learned that the syndicate was trying to secure the next site along the Wilhelmstrasse. He succeeded at the last moment in 'beating them to the punch' and buying this site himself; but he now knew that it was war to the knife.

Looking back on it, and considering Lorenz Adlon's position, it seems almost inconceivable that he should have run such risks. By the standards of that time he was already a very wealthy man. He had a fortune of two million marks, and the businesses which he controlled brought him in several hundred thousand a year. But all this did not suffice him. He wanted a hotel of his own, and the finest in the world. He plunged monstrously into debt, forsaking the life of a carefree man for that of one who could scarcely sleep at nights.

When at length the Adlon was completed it cost not fifteen but well over twenty million marks. He had sunk every penny he possessed in it, and he still owed twenty millions. Moreover the last loans he had been forced to raise represented a deadly peril, since they were of very short duration.

When Rudolf Herzog had delivered all the goods ordered by the hotel his bill was found to amount to six hundred thousand marks. Reckoning up his commitments in the sleepless nights, my father-in-law was faced by the grim, inescapable fact that he owed tradesmen in Berlin alone more than a million.

The things he had ordered or had specially made! He had spent his days increasing the gamble by his particularity in such trifles as the size of a face-towel! The glass was all made to his own design, manufactured exclusively for the Adlon. The cords on the uniforms of the porters and coachmen, the lighting fixtures, everything down to the last detail had been sketched by himself, and in consequence cost very much more than the stock equivalents would have done.

He saw with dismay that the Berlin tradesmen were growing increasingly impatient. It was out of the question for him to pay them anything until the hotel began to earn a sufficient income, but this time was still a long way off. In the meantime he had to make provision for salaries and wages.

He had no money left, but not for an instant did he think of turning to the Kaiser for help. For one thing Lorenz Adlon was in certain respects a reserved man who kept his troubles to himself; but apart from this he had a sound understanding of men in general and the Kaiser in particular. He knew very well that although one might approach Wilhelm II in the matter of pulling down an historic monument, one must in no circumstances go to him for money.

These developments were being followed, naturally with great satisfaction, by Herr Leopold Koppel.

The tale of Adlon's difficulties soon got abroad in Berlin commercial circles, and the amount of his debts became known. Koppel was able to get exact figures from the agitated tradesmen, and he passed these triumphantly on to the banks which had advanced the last millions on mortgages that could be foreclosed at short notice.

The bankers were naturally highly alarmed, and when Koppel offered to take over the mortgages they were only too delighted. A representative of the Berlin Hotel Syndicate then called upon Rudolf Herzog and all the other Berlin concerns to whom Adlon owed money. Koppel offered to cover all their claims on Adlon, paying the full amount in cash.

It was Rudolf Herzog himself who came to Lorenz Adlon's rescue in this desperate situation. Without Lorenz's knowledge he called a meeting of his Berlin creditors, at which he expounded the situation and urged that a man of so much courage and enterprise deserved their support, and that at least they should hold their hands a little longer before selling out to his bitterest rival.

When certain of them protested that they were in urgent need of the money, Herzog offered to settle with them himself, and did so forthwith. After these smaller concerns had been satisfied, the larger creditors resolved to wait, and they informed Lorenz Adlon of the fact. It was wonderful news!

But Adlon's troubles were not yet over. With the hotel still unopened, notice was served on him, on Koppel's behalf, of the foreclosure of the mortgages. He passed a week in a state of utter despair, and then something remarkable happened; something, moreover, that gave him grounds for revising his judgment of men, in general and in particular. By some means which was never discovered the Kaiser had learnt of his difficulties. He helped him in a way that cost no money but merely drew upon the authority of the Crown and human vanity.

The Kaiser Wilhelm Institut, in Dahlem, was a centre of scientific research which was always in need of money; and it was held in high esteem by wealthy citizens desiring dignities and titles, since these were to be acquired by conferring endowments upon it. Such distinctions only followed, however, if the royal permission had been granted for the donation to be made. It so happened that at the very time when Lorenz Adlon was in the toils Leopold Koppel addressed a plea to the Kaiser, respectfully requesting to be allowed to endow the Institut with a million marks. The Kaiser gathered from the Lord Chamberlain's office that Herr Koppel was hoping in return to receive the Prussian Order of the Crown.

William II handled the matter very shrewdly. He staged a little comedy such as he often resorted to when High Finance failed to fall in with his wishes. A small announcement appeared with his authorization in the press, merely stating that Herr Leopold Koppel had asked to be allowed to contribute a million to the Kaiser Wilhelm Institut. But the Kaiser did not give the aspiring gentleman permission to hand over his money. He waited.

And after keeping him on tenterhooks for a fortnight he summoned Herr Koppel to the palace, where he received him coldly.

'Is it really true', he asked, 'that certain people are trying to interfere with my plans?'

Koppel at first tried to pretend not to understand, but the

Kaiser gave him little chance to say anything. He burst out into a tirade. For years he had been striving to make Berlin one of the great capitals of the world, and he had taken it for granted that Herr Koppel, who had been granted the title of *Kommerzienrat* by the King of Prussia, would do everything in his power to help him. Yet it now seemed that he had to regard Herr Koppel as an adversary. Or was he mistaken?

Herr Koppel began to quiver. The Kaiser went on:

'And now you want to present a large sum of money to the Kaiser Wilhelm Institut. It would be unfortunate if a public announcement had to be made to the effect that you have been refused permission to do so. By God it would!'

After a little more conversation on these lines the Kaiser had the cheque for a million in his pocket, together with Koppel's promise that the mortgages on the Hotel Adlon would be placed on a fifteen-year basis at a moderate rate of interest.

And so it came about that the new hotel on Unter den Linden was opened without further hitch on the prescribed date, and that the official blessing was bestowed on it by the Kaiser's own inaugural visit.

'It all worked out splendidly,' his Majesty said later to Lorenz Adlon. 'And it was damned funny, by God it was!'

3

Climax of an Epoch

THE Adlon knew its most brilliant years in the gaily lighted but ominous period preceding the First World War. The tales of a wonderful future with which Wilhelm II, its godfather, beguiled his subjects, were no longer taken literally. But the growing doubts and the portents could be forgotten in the outward splendour of the Court, until the day came when peace was seen to be hanging by a thread—no doubt, appropriately, a thread of gold.

But it was in those last days, a little more than a year before the war, that the magnificence of the Wilhelm II epoch blazed up in the festivity of a royal wedding, the marriage of the Kaiser's only daughter, the twenty-year-old Princess Victoria Louise, to Prince Ernst August of Cumberland, Duke of Brunswick and of Luneburg.

It was said at the time that the match, at the best, was one of love at second sight, being at first sight a matter of politics. The bridegroom was a prince of the House of Guelf, which until then had been on anything but friendly terms with the House of Hohenzollern.

The crowned heads of Europe came in a body to Berlin for the wedding celebrations. Even the ultra-cautious Czar of Russia, who travelled abroad only with the greatest reluctance, came in state from St. Petersburg. And in the presence of this noble company Berlin staged what might be described as a glorious finale to an era, with brilliant uniforms, ceremonial trains, gold lorgnettes and waltz music. It was a time of carnival, with dancing everywhere, and especially at the Adlon.

The date of the wedding, the 24th May 1913, had been scarcely announced before the telegrams and express letters came streaming in to the Adlon, while the telephone rang incessantly,

23

all with requests for accommodation. But nearly every bed was already reserved for the Kaiser's guests, and telegrams of regret had to be sent out in almost equal numbers.

The housing of the Kaiser's guests was a ticklish business about which Lorenz Adlon had many tales to tell. Royal etiquette required that a visiting sovereign should be accommodated in one of the palaces of the monarch whose guest he was. The leading monarchs, such as the kings of England, would often sooner have gone to the Adlon, if they had had any choice in the matter. It was the minor royalties who clung most firmly to protocol, although Wilhelm II did his best to dissuade them.

'My dears,' he was accustomed to say on these occasions, 'why don't you go to the Adlon? It's perfectly beastly at the palace— cold and draughty, and no hot water in the few bathrooms we possess. You'd be far better off with Lorenz Adlon.'

But it was never any use. They preferred cold feet at the palace to the Adlon's hot baths.

And now accommodation had to be found for all the many guests invited to the wedding, together with the members of their entourage. The Adlon had some four hundred rooms, including the sitting-rooms in the suites, and could at the very utmost take no more than eight hundred people. To find shelter for this huge company called for a miracle of contrivance.

Lorenz Adlon was a man who did not easily lose his self-control, but during the weeks preceding that wedding he came very near to doing so. To judge by his subsequent accounts, the house at this time must have been more like an agitated nursery school than a luxury hotel.

After much pressing, the Lord Chamberlain's office finally produced a list of the guests to be accommodated at the Adlon. But this was only a beginning, because there were constant changes in the allocation of rooms and suites. And about a week before the commencement of the festivities an alteration had to be made which caused an immense upheaval.

It was suddenly announced that one of the Empress's brothers and his wife, the Duke and Duchess of Schleswig-Holstein, were not to be housed in a suite on the third floor, although this had been arranged at the Duke's express wish, since the third-floor balconies commanded the best view of Unter den Linden. It now had to be altered. The Lord Chamberlain gave instructions that the Duke and Duchess were to be brought down to a suite on the first floor. And the reason was that the Czar of all the Russias was not able to travel in a lift!

The Czar had arranged to pay the Duke a courtesy visit the day before the wedding, but it was clearly out of the question that he should walk up three flights of stairs. On the other hand, the very strict code of etiquette governing every movement of the Czar and his Court, which dated from the time of Catherine the Great, did not envisage the possibility of lifts. No one knew how the Czar and his suite should conduct themselves in such circumstances. Should his Majesty be the first to step into the lift? Should he remove his hat? And so on.

Lorenz Adlon pointed out that motor-cars had also not existed in the days of Catherine the Great, but that nevertheless the Czar used one. To this the reply was given that the rules merely referred to his Majesty's 'carriage', a word that could apply equally to a horse-drawn or horseless vehicle; but that they contained no reference to anything analogous to a lift.

It need hardly be said that Lorenz did not believe a word of this talk about Catherine the Great. The real reason for the agitation was probably the fear that a lift with the Czar inside it would make things too easy for a possible assassin. In any event, a suite on the first floor had to be prepared for the Duke and Duchess of Schleswig-Holstein.

The next noteworthy occurrence was the arrival of officials from the Berlin Political Police who came to examine the whole hotel and its staff as a security measure. They tramped through the building from top to bottom, peered under every bed, looked into cupboards and drawers. They would suddenly vanish and no less suddenly reappear in the cellar, the larders, anywhere. They seemed to be constantly tripping over one another.

And to make things worse the Kaiser chose this time to pay the hotel a surprise visit. He appeared one rainy evening in the reception hall and said, 'Adlon, I've come in to get warm. It's too cold and draughty in the palace. Bring us something decent to drink.'

Being there he naturally wanted to be shown round, so that he could see for himself how the preparations were going. He was in an expansive mood that evening and he complained ruefully to Lorenz Adlon of the dullness of his own dwellings. Certainly the Adlon was not dull. While they were inspecting the Duke of Schleswig-Holstein's suite his Majesty had a shock. A dark-clad figure suddenly backed out of a wardrobe, to vanish swiftly through the doorway; and then a pair of large feet came into view under a sofa. It was a relief to the Kaiser to learn that this was only evidence of the thoroughness with which everything was done in Germany, even by the police.

'Perhaps,' he said, 'we had better withdraw to the bar.'

Three or four days before the arrival of the first guests two gentlemen, for whom accommodation had been reserved in the hotel by the Russian Embassy, called upon Lorenz Adlon. They explained their business in his private office.

They were officials of the Russian Secret Police who had been entrusted with the task of watching over the safety of the Czar during his visit to the Duke of Schleswig-Holstein. The visit would probably not last longer than half an hour, but they had nevertheless come all the way from St. Petersburg especially for this purpose, and they asked to be given all possible assistance.

Lorenz Adlon disposed of them by passing them on to the German police-officials who were still combing the building for anything suspicious, without, however, having thus far found anything.

The Russians naturally possessed no authority on German territory, but their German colleagues did everything they could to help them in their task. The policemen of both countries, in Lorenz Adlon's opinion, conducted themselves very much better than did the statesmen during those days.

To Lorenz Adlon all this police business seemed farcical. It was inconceivable to him that any potential assassin could be sheltering in his hotel. All the guests then stopping in the hotel were known to him personally, and there was certainly not one who had any designs on the Czar's life.

The hotel staff, from the hall-porter to the youngest chambermaid, was subjected to the most rigorous scrutiny and interrogation. The police examined each one separately, including the hotel manager, who was responsible for the whole establishment, and the assistant manager, whose name, I think, was Jansen.

Herr Jansen during those days was the most harassed man in the hotel. He was in charge of the intricate and complex room-arrangements on all floors. This was his especial task, and in view of all the complications it can have been no light one. He had to organize the room-service, oversee the condition of the rooms, and provide against the thousand and one contingencies that may arise in any hotel. The police, moreover, summoned him at all hours of the day and night, demanding floor-plans and even architects' designs, and wanting to know about secret passages and other possible hiding-places. The unhappy man scarcely knew which way to turn. From his pallid, distraught appearance, he might not have slept for days. No one could blame Herr Jansen if he took a poor view of the Czar's forthcoming half-hour visit to the Adlon.

Unter den Linden on the morning of the 21st May must have been a wonderful sight.

The hotel was decked with flags. Wonderful Persian rugs hung from the balconies, and the public rooms were like a flower-garden.

Along the rest of the splendid avenue the house-fronts were almost hidden by flowers and flags, and the old trees were truly in blossom, as depicted in the song with which, years later, Walter Kollo won the hearts of the Berlin public.

The guests at the Adlon, like the whole town, were awakened out of sleep in the early hours of the morning by the strains of martial music echoing up and down the street. Shortly afterwards the Kaiser's bodyguard passed by on the first of its visits to the various railway stations to act as escort to the arriving royalties.

Its route lay from the palace past the Adlon and under the Brandenburger Tor by way of the central archway, which was at all
times exclusively reserved for the carriage and escort of the
Emperor and Empress.

The weather was wonderfully clear and fine—'royal weather'.

Towards eleven o'clock the Kaiser passed by, escorted by a
squadron of the *Garde du Corps* regiment, on his way to the
Lehrter railway station. King George V and Queen Mary of
England, two of the most exalted guests, were expected at this
time.

They were escorted with all honour through the town. The gay
procession—shining breastplates, pennoned lances, gleaming
sabres and high-stepping chargers—again passed under the central archway of the Brandenburger Tor, past the Adlon to the
palace.

The ladies and gentlemen belonging to the entourage of the
English Royal Pair were lodged in the Adlon. Lorenz Adlon stood
awaiting them in the reception hall and handed each lady an
enormous bunch of roses. This was another detail for which the
unfortunate Herr Jansen was responsible. Looking horribly pale,
he stood just behind Lorenz Adlon and passed him the bunches.

On the following morning—I am trying to keep things in
chronological order—the Emperor and Empress paid another
visit to the railway station, this time to welcome the Empress's
brother, the Duke of Schleswig-Holstein, and his wife. On this
occasion, however, the returning procession did not go as far as
the palace but stopped outside the Adlon, where the first-floor
suite was in readiness.

The Duke, an elegant, good-looking man, had naturally arrived in uniform, but half an hour later he came down to the
lobby in civilian clothes. He made a telephone call, which must
have seemed a little odd; and then, evidently somewhat put out,
he paced up and down the lobby until he saw Lorenz Adlon.

'Herr Adlon,' he said, 'may I please have a car immediately?
I mean, an ordinary taxi. And would you be so good as to lend
me five hundred marks?'

Lorenz Adlon got the money from his office and handed it unobtrusively to the Duke. The taxi was already waiting.

Less than an hour later the Duke was again seen in the hotel, carrying a small package in his hand. After that Lorenz Adlon lost sight of him.

That afternoon the Czar's special train arrived in Berlin. Contrary to expectation, the Czar had come without the Czarina, a fact which gave rise to a great deal of political comment. He was received with the same honours as the King of England, but people who witnessed the occasion maintain that the procession moved considerably faster, and that never had so many policemen and detectives been gathered along one stretch of road.

The guests had now all arrived and the rejoicings could begin. The Grand Court Ball was to be held on the following evening, and the wedding on the day after. Three hundred guests had been invited to dine at the palace, more than half of whom were stopping at the Adlon.

That same evening, two days before the ceremony, the public rooms at the Adlon presented a spectacle of matchless elegance— the scented, rustling evening gowns, the bright uniforms and immaculately cut evening coats. There was not a vacant place in the dining-room, where nearly two thousand dinners were served.

The Kaiser's guests diverted themselves in company with a large number of young army officers dancing with their fiancées, sisters, cousins, or with any other pretty girl, of which there was no shortage. It would have been contrary to the spirit of the time if any youthful Guards officer, on such an occasion, had had any thought in his head except for girls and waltzes.

The merrymaking went on all night. At two in the morning a cavalry captain in a brilliant blue uniform strode on to the platform and took charge of the orchestra. He caused them to play a passage from 'Der Freischutz':

> *We'll wind for you your maiden-wreath*
> *Of silk as blue as violets . . .*

And suddenly the air was filled with violets scattered like sweet-scented confetti. It was the notion of certain high-spirited young lieutenants, who went from table to table offering every lady a bunch with a deep bow. They had discovered the violets on the flower-stands in the lobby and had bought whole baskets-full.

But they also took a fancy to the carefully chosen flower-girls —Lorenz Adlon was a man who did things properly or not at all. These pretty young things, in their smart black-and-white dresses, had stayed in the hotel to get a glimpse of high life, and now they found themselves dragged into the party. The whole company— evening dresses, gala uniforms, flower-girl costumes—danced through the rooms in a lively polonaise, while everyone sang:

> *We lead you on to play and dance,*
> *To joy and lovers' rapture!*

Lorenz Adlon stood leaning against a pillar in the hall, enjoying the vivid, carefree spectacle.

But suddenly two new guests appeared in the lobby, two gentlemen in long evening-coats. After handing their cloaks and top-hats to a page they went hurriedly up to Lorenz Adlon. They greeted him with smiles, but he said afterwards, when telling the story, that he had an instant feeling that the smiles were somewhat forced.

The gentlemen were a superintendent and inspector from the Berlin Political Police. They announced that they had something of pressing importance to say, and Lorenz Adlon took them into his office.

'Herr Adlon,' said the superintendent, without any beating about the bush, 'we have had word from a reliable source in Switzerland that Russian anarchists have prepared an attempt on the Czar's life. I repeat—*have prepared!*'

He paused, and went on in tones which made it clear that his word was not to be doubted:

'A bomb has already been hidden in this building!'

4

The Story of the Bomb

'A BOMB in my hotel?' repeated Lorenz Adlon.

He gazed in stupefaction at the two police officers, unable to doubt their earnestness but no less unable to believe that the information from Switzerland could be correct. The thing was impossible! And then there passed through his mind the recollection of something the Kaiser had said on the occasion of the hotel's opening:

'Adlon, your hotel has absolutely everything!'

'Even bombs . . .' reflected Lorenz Adlon.

He must unwittingly have smiled, because the superintendent said sharply:

'Herr Adlon, you don't seem to realize the seriousness of the situation. Even if the political consequences of the Czar's assassination on German soil mean nothing to you, you might at least consider what will happen to your hotel if the bomb explodes!'

'One moment, gentlemen,' said Lorenz Adlon, now becoming very matter-of-fact. 'You talk of a bomb in this hotel as though you had actually seen it. How do you know that the whole story is not an elaborate mystification, an attempt by political intriguers to start a scare for some reason of their own?'

The superintendent pursed his lips, and it was clear that he was trying to come to a decision. High police officials are never precisely talkative when it is a question of disclosing sources of information, still less when their work lies in the political field. The superintendent hesitated. But on the other hand he could not overlook the fact that Lorenz Adlon had friendly relations in the very highest circles, and might even, in an extreme case, carry a complaint to the Kaiser himself. He decided upon frankness.

The information, he said, had been passed as a matter of

extreme urgency to the German police by a secret agent in whom they had the utmost confidence. Switzerland, as Herr Adlon doubtless knew, was the resort of Russian anarchists of all denominations. According to the agent's report, one of these anarchist groups, having bribed a member of the Adlon staff, had sent him a bomb with a time-fuse, to be set to coincide with the Czar's visit to the hotel.

'In fact,' concluded the superintendent, 'it's very likely ticking away somewhere at this moment!'

He paused to observe the effect of his words, but Lorenz Adlon still did not seem to be unduly impressed. He was, indeed, thoroughly sceptical of the whole melodramatic story, and he found it particularly hard to believe that any member of the Adlon staff, all of whom he knew and trusted, could have been suborned for so monstrous a purpose. However, if there was any truth in it at all, the matter was one of the utmost gravity. At least they had a little time in which to identify the culprit and locate the bomb, if it was not due to go off until the Czar's visit. The German officers wished to consult instantly with their Russian colleagues, who were still in the building, and Lorenz Adlon was about to go in search of them when there was an interruption.

The door of the office was flung open and a page-boy rushed in. I may remark that this in itself was something unprecedented in the Adlon. My father-in-law, a very composed man, who valued calm and good manners above all things, would in the ordinary way have dealt drastically with anyone who dared to enter a room without knocking. Only an extreme emergency could have caused the boy to do so. But such it proved to be.

'Herr Adlon,' he burst out, 'there's a dead man at the bottom of the light-well!'

The two policemen started up. Lorenz Adlon pulled himself together.

'Max,' he said, kindly, 'you must never panic. You know quite well that there are police all over the place. When the Kaiser and I were inspecting the Duke of Schleswig-Holstein's suite we saw a pair of legs under a sofa, but they turned out to be quite alive.'

Ignoring this, the superintendent grabbed the boy by the arm and demanded to be taken at once to the scene. The two policemen vanished without another word.

Lorenz, now really shaken, stood hesitating for some moments. Then he hurried out to look for the hotel manager and above all for Herr Jansen, who had been assisting the police in their security measures. He remembered, however, that he himself had sent Herr Jansen to bed a short time before, because the poor man looked as though his nerves would stand the strain no longer. The sight of a corpse would probably cause him to collapse.

He ran into the manager in the lobby, and the latter said excitedly:

'Herr Adlon, some important news!'

Lorenz Adlon nearly collapsed himself. He had had enough news for one night. Before he could ask, the manager said in a dramatic whisper:

'The Crown Prince has just arrived!'

As though to underline this pronouncement, they heard the sound of a long-drawn fanfare played by the orchestra in the ballroom, followed by a great burst of clapping. It was by now three o'clock, and the revelry was at its height.

'I can't come at present,' said Lorenz Adlon. 'I'll make my bow to the Crown Prince later. Something has happened which upsets all our arrangements and may have disastrous consequences for the hotel. I must ask you to go instantly and try to find the two Russian secret police.'

'The Russians? During the last hour or two I've only seen one of them. He was searching everywhere for the other.'

The one Russian turned up a minute later, still searching. Before he could say anything Lorenz Adlon made a sign to him and the manager, and then led the way through the various rooms to the narrow doorway leading to the light-well.

The scene that met their eyes was like something in a thriller. In the Adlon's history there had been many dark moments mingled with the highlights, but Lorenz Adlon declared, years afterwards, that this was the worst of all.

D

On the narrow floor of the light-well, with its high, sheer walls broken only by small windows, the superintendent, the inspector, and Max the page-boy were silently standing. At their feet, motionless and with shattered limbs, lay the body of a man in a dark suit with his face to the ground.

The Russian bent over him and uttered a little cry as he saw that it was his colleague. He presently stood upright, facing the other men.

'No one must know of this,' he said in his harsh, laborious German. 'Everything must be kept secret—no doctors and no police. He must be taken at once to the Russian Embassy.'

Lorenz Adlon glanced questioningly at the German police superintendent, who merely shrugged his shoulders. It was left to my father-in-law to decide upon the best way of dealing with the matter in the interests of all concerned, including those of the hotel.

Everything had to be done by those present, the two German police officers, the Russian secret agent, Lorenz Adlon and his manager, and the page-boy. An ordinary hand-cart was hastily dragged out into the back-yard of the hotel. It was all that was needed, for the Russian Embassy was only a hundred yards away.

And presently, with the first gleam of dawn showing in the sky, the cart with its burden was trundled down the yard towards the back entrance, on the Wilhelmstrasse. There was not much risk of meeting anyone in that place at that time of day. It was the part of the wide-spreading building which we called the 'courier's wing', where the outdoor servants—chauffeurs, coachmen, grooms and so on—of our wealthier patrons were housed. The dead man had most rigorously examined these premises only the day before, and had caused much laughter by remarking, when he saw the accommodation provided, You aren't servants, you live like lords!'

Now he lay on the creaking boards of the cart, covered with a white tablecloth. Had he been thrust through one of the windows of the light-well by one of those same servants, because he suspected him of being a hired assassin?

The iron wheels rattled over the cobbles, while Lorenz Adlon kept an anxious eye on the boy, Max, who, pale and shaken, was helping the Russian and the German police inspector to push the cart out into the Wilhelmstrasse. The strange funeral cortège was accompanied by the strains of music from the hotel ballroom, and of voices joining in the refrain of a popular song of the moment:

Slumber sweetly, slumber sweetly—
Dream as though in Paradise . . .

Directly the cart had vanished the superintendent turned to Lorenz Adlon and his manager.

'As I am sure you realize, after what has happened I shall have to ask for a large number of extra men. The whole hotel will have to be searched again, and the bomb discovered, before daybreak.'

The manager made a gesture of despair.

'And I suppose the Russians will also ask their Embassy for reinforcements!'

Oddly enough the superintendent was doubtful of this. He was even of the opinion that they would hear nothing more from the Russians—above all, nothing about the murdered secret agent. In his view the Russian Embassy would simply keep a more close watch than ever on the measures taken by the German police.

In this he turned out to be right. Nothing concerning the apparent murder was ever made public. The other Russian agent vanished from that moment, and was not seen again. Neither was anything said on the German side, although, of course, the superintendent made a full report to his superiors. The whole thing was hushed up. There was never any 'sensational murder mystery', then or later. . . .

'May I telephone from your office?' asked the superintendent.

'Of course,' said Lorenz Adlon. 'But I think I should tell you that his Royal Highness, the Crown Prince, is at present in the hotel, with a great many other eminent guests.'

The superintendent seemed not to hear this. He walked silently beside the two men.

Lorenz Adlon now reflected that the time had come to fetch the assistant manager, Herr Jansen, from his bed, since he had been principally concerned with the inspection of the hotel that had already taken place. At least he would have had a few hours' sleep. Lorenz sent the manager up to tell him what had happened and to arrange with him for such steps as could be taken to ensure that the forthcoming, more intensive search would not trouble the hotel visitors—so far as the thing was possible.

He took the superintendent back to his office to telephone and then at once withdrew. Slowly and plunged in thought he walked out into the lobby.

Here he was caught a minute later by the Crown Prince, who greeted him jovially, and after asking where he had been and remarking that he looked as though he had just come from a funeral, seized him by the arm and dragged him along to the ballroom.

The festivities were still in full swing—light and laughter and music, bright eyes, flushed cheeks, and dresses and uniforms all colours of the rainbow. Lorenz Adlon sighed and called for a double brandy. But he had scarcely raised it to his lips when the manager came up and whispered in his ear.

'Herr Jansen wants to speak to you. I really think you should see him. I'm afraid he's going out of his mind.'

With a feeling that nothing could now surprise him, Lorenz Adlon put down his glass and making his excuses to the Crown Prince, went to the assistant manager's office. Herr Jansen was seated at his desk, in such a state as to be almost unrecognizable. Normally a well-groomed man, punctilious in his manners, he seemed to have gone utterly to pieces. He was unshaven, and his hair struggled over his forehead. His tie hung loose from his unbuttoned collar. His quivering hands were fingering a packet, wrapped in tissue paper, which lay on the desk in front of him. The steel safe at his back stood open.

'I can't go on any longer, Herr Adlon,' he said, rising slowly from his chair and supporting himself against the desk. 'After all that has happened I'm at the end of my strength.'

Lorenz Adlon was sorry for the man. What with the bomb

business, and now the murder, it was small wonder if those concerned felt that they were taking leave of their senses. At the same
time he was exasperated and he did not disguise the fact. A man
in Herr Jansen's position had no right to lose his nerve like this.
That he should have dragged him away from the company of the
Crown Prince, simply in order to tell him that he was at the end
of his strength, was nothing less than disgraceful.

'Why on earth didn't you get to bed when I told you to?' he
asked sharply. 'What we have to think about now is how we're
to deal with the fresh disturbance the police are going to inflict
on us.'

Herr Jansen hung his head. Then with shaky movement he
picked up the small packet from the desk and handed it to his
employer.

'What's this?' asked Lorenz Adlon. 'What's inside it?'

'The bomb,' said Herr Jansen.

It was Lorenz Adlon's turn to start shaking. He could understand his assistant manager's agitation, and he heartily wished he
had had time to finish his brandy. His first impulse was to throw
the packet straight out of the window.

'When is it due to explode?'

'It isn't. The time-fuse hasn't been set.'

Greatly relieved, Lorenz Adlon examined the package more
closely.

'So this is the bomb,' he said meditatively, 'and the superintendent's information from Switzerland was right after all. It's
almost unbelievable. Where did you find it?'

'I didn't find it. I've had it here in my safe for the past week.
I was going to hide it in a basket of flowers in the Duke of
Schleswig-Holstein's suite, in time for the Czar's visit.'

Lorenz Adlon was so dumbfounded that all he could find to say
was:

'Why?'

The wretched Jansen explained that he had heavy gambling
debts and was being threatened with exposure. So he had
accepted the bomb and a large sum of money. Then he had found

that one of the Russian agents suspected him. There had been a struggle, and the Russian had fallen through a window down the light-well. This had broken Jansen's nerve completely.

And that was the climax of this thriller that had been enacted behind the scenes at the Adlon, the villain being none other than the representative of the management appointed to co-operate with the police in safeguarding the Czar's life. It all hung together.

'And now what are we going to do?' Lorenz Adlon asked.

Herr Jansen looked at him and said:

'Will you allow me one minute? I was once an officer.'

Lorenz Adlon went silently out and after a very short interval heard the sound of a muffled explosion. He returned quickly to the room and found Herr Jansen lying across his desk with the blood pouring from a big wound in his head. Beside him lay a large-bore revolver, its barrel wrapped in a hand-towel. Hence the muffled sound. After a lifetime spent in the hotel business, Herr Jansen's last thought had been to avoid disturbing the guests.

A few minutes later Lorenz Adlon and the superintendent stood together in the lobby, while the departing guests, mostly young couples flushed with dancing and champagne, streamed past them and out through the revolving doors. The party was ending at last. In the emptying ballroom the orchestra was playing its farewell piece:

> *Come with me to my bower of love,*
> *Come to our Paradise . . .*

The Crown Prince appeared, surrounded by a bevy of chattering young ladies. He held out both hands to Lorenz Adlon.

'It has been a wonderful night. So many delightful surprises! I hope you'll arrange another before long, my dear Adlon.'

'Your Highness,' said Lorenz Adlon decidedly, 'at the Hotel Adlon anything can happen!'

The weather on the next day, the 23rd, was again perfect, and by early morning a large and cheerful crowd was assembled outside the hotel to watch the Czar's arrival. I have been told that during those days of the wedding festivities a great many Berliners never went to bed at all, or even to their homes, but installed themselves permanently on the Pariser Platz, between the Brandenburger Tor and the Adlon, in order to be sure of missing nothing.

The Czar's visit went exactly according to plan. When he entered the hotel he was greeted by Lorenz Adlon amid a sea of flowers, and escorted by him and the manager to the Duke of Schleswig-Holstein's suite. Only Herr Jansen was lacking. The relatively small number of secret police in attendance had no need to go into action, and since they kept discreetly in the background their presence was not noticed by anyone.

Exactly thirty-seven minutes later the Czar departed, and when the last of his retinue had left the hotel Lorenz Adlon felt an urgent need to sit down. He sank into a chair behind the elaborate screen of flowers, and presently overheard a conversation between two pages.

'Gosh!' said one. 'Fancy the coppers thinking they were going to find a bomb in our house!'

'They nearly blew up themselves when they didn't!' said the other.

The affair of the bomb was in fact kept secret for a long time. But after the First World War, when there was no longer any need for secrecy, all kinds of versions got into circulation. Truth and poetry were intermingled, many new details being invented, until at last the story was again forgotten.

The bomb itself was taken to police headquarters the same day and dissected by experts. Only the highest ranking officials, under oath of strict secrecy, were allowed to see it.

But there was a brief sequel which was told to my husband in the twenties by Superintendent Gennat of the Berlin Police. It seems that in 1919, after the Czar's life had been brutally ended by other means, the bomb was exhibited in a glass case in the Berlin Criminal Museum, there to be admired by numerous sightseers. In 1925, however, Gennat instructed the officer in charge of the museum—the present Superintendent Paul Kuckenburg, who still lives in West Germany—to remove that 'old-fashioned infernal machine', as it had come to be called, and replace it with something more exciting.

The historic bomb, that never exploded but caused so much commotion at the Adlon, had ceased to be of interest even as a museum piece. And later there were far better things to be seen. Anyone who wanted bombs had only to step out on to the hotel balcony to watch them falling.

Another strange story, which might well have had a tragic ending, is also connected with the Czar's visit, although only indirectly.

It will be remembered that at the beginning I told how the Duke of Schleswig-Holstein reappeared in the lobby in civilian clothes, half an hour after his arrival, and mysteriously borrowed 500 marks from my father-in-law.

Some days later, when the wedding festivities were over and most of the guests had departed, Lorenz Adlon saw the Duke seated by himself in a corner of the lounge looking strangely despondent. He had in a sense been connected with the bomb affair, since he had been the reason for the Czar's visit to the hotel; but this could scarcely account for his dejected aspect, since he no more knew what had happened than did any of the other distinguished visitors.

Not liking to approach him directly, Lorenz Adlon asked the hall-porter if anything had occurred to upset the Duke. Hotel porters, as everyone knows, are always remarkably well informed about the guests. This one was no exception. Although he did not know what lay behind them he knew a number of interesting details, and these gave Lorenz Adlon much food for thought.

The hall-porter had learnt from a taxi-driver that for some days past the Duke had been driven almost every day to a somewhat shabby district at the northern end of the Friedrichstrasse, where he spent some time in a house of disreputable appearance. Each time, according to the taxi-driver, he came out looking more miserable than before and was driven back to the Adlon.

Lorenz Adlon now resolved to speak to the Duke. After a few remarks about the weather he passed on to the subject of the recent celebrations, which had greatly fatigued everyone who took part in them.

'That's true enough,' said the Duke absently. 'But if it were no more than that . . .'

Lorenz Adlon went a step further.

'Can I be of any assistance to your Highness?'

The Duke shook his head.

'Don't worry yourself, Herr Adlon. No one can help me any more.'

With these words he got up and went slowly towards the lift.

It seemed to Lorenz Adlon that there was a new misfortune to be prevented if possible. He went at once to the telephone and, calling police headquarters, asked for an officer to be sent round who was accustomed to handling ticklish affairs in the highest circles.

It thus came about that a quarter of an hour later the two officers who had been involved in the bomb affair again entered the Adlon. But that is the beginning of another story.

5

A Duke in Trouble

THE superintendent appeared this time in a highly jovial mood. Lorenz Adlon learned the reason for his high spirits from the inspector, who was looking a good deal less cheerful.

'The Russians have given him the Order of Stanislaus, First Class,' he murmured while the superintendent was taking off his overcoat.

'What for?' asked Lorenz Adlon.

'Because the Czar's visit to the Adlon went off without a hitch,' murmured the inspector.

'And you got nothing? But that seems unfair. After all, you were the one who wheeled the body along to the Embassy.'

'Exactly,' said the inspector, and he sighed.

'Well now,' said the superintendent, returning, 'let's get to business. What is it this time?'

Lorenz Adlon told him of the Duke of Schleswig-Holstein's strange demeanour, and of his daily visits to the sinister-looking house near the Friedrichstrasse. The superintendent spent some moments in thought and then said:

'I think I know that house.'

He nodded to the inspector, and the two of them left the hotel.

It must be recorded to the superintendent's credit that this time he did some real work. When he returned that afternoon he said, 'We've arrested him.'

Lorenz Adlon started back in horror.

'The Duke?'

'No. The man he's been visiting.'

The superintendent fished a pile of letters and documents out of his brief-case and displayed them in triumph.

'I must see his Highness at once and tell him the good news.'

But the hall-porter said that the Duke had just left the hotel, his aspect that of a man plunged in the depths of despair.

'Did he take a taxi?'

'No, he said he didn't need one this time.'

'Did you notice which way he went?'

'He walked across the Pariser Platz towards the Brandenburger Tor. It looked as though he was going into the Tiergarten.'

'Send a couple of messengers to try to find him and keep an eye on him, in case anything happens. I'll telephone headquarters and have some plain-clothes men sent out.'

While they waited the superintendent told Lorenz Adlon what had happened. They sat in that quiet corner of the hotel bar where a low table stood between a leather settee and red leather armchairs.

That famous corner! My father-in-law could never pass it without pausing for an instant to glance at it, for in the course of the years it was the scene of many conversations that influenced the course of history. Here the men of power sat quietly and unobtrusively, statesmen and ambassadors, bankers and industrialists, discussing their problems and concerting their plans. And here the leading newspaper men came to talk over events and concoct stories to startle the breakfast-tables of the world. At a later stage, towards the end of the Republic and the beginning of the Third Reich, Louis Adlon said more than once that he must get that worn leather upholstery renewed. But the journalists protested that in doing so he would destroy the character of the place, the aura of crisis and scandal, of true and false report. They threatened to go elsewhere if he did not leave it as it was, and so he did.

Here Lorenz Adlon and the superintendent sat while the latter recounted the events of the past few hours.

He had at once guessed the address of the house near the northern end of the Friedrichstrasse. It was one that had been known to the police for some time. There was a small plate on the door bearing the legend, 'Heinrich Pariser—Wholesale Leather

Goods', but it was known to be visited by members of the nobility and army officers in particular. The police could guess what they went for, but they had no proof. They had no grounds for searching the place because no charge had been brought against the occupier.

But in view of what Lorenz Adlon had told them, the superintendent and his colleague resolved to try a bluff. They forced their way into the house, announcing that they had come to investigate a charge brought by the Duke of Schleswig-Holstein.

The man, Heinrich Pariser, threatened to go at once to the Kaiser. He claimed to have letters in his possession, written by the Empress to her brother, the Duke, in which she said things about her husband that were far from complimentary. The superintendent replied that his Majesty had no dealings with blackmailers, but at this Pariser only laughed.

'Who's accusing me of blackmail? I'm a reputable money-lender, advancing loans on note of hand. What business is that of the police?'

While this argument was going on the inspector had been examining the contents of the safe. He had found enough evidence to warrant a prosecution for usury. And then the man's secretary broke down under the threat of arrest, and divulged information which would enable more serious charges to be preferred.

'Did you find anything directly concerning the Duke?' asked Lorenz Adlon.

The superintendent indicated the papers he had brought with him.

'As you probably know, the Duke is not very wealthy in his own right. That does not prevent him from living extravagantly, paying incognito visits to Paris and the Riviera, and gambling for high stakes. The Duchess is richer than he is, but very careful with her money and by no means sympathetic to her husband's escapades. The sum represented by the Duke's notes-of-hand runs into six figures, but it has been doubled by interest and other charges. They were all very short-term loans, and he has had to pay through the nose to get them renewed. He has had to mort-gage large parcels of land to this man. He also handed over a great many letters which Pariser was particularly anxious to get hold of, for obvious reasons, and in addition to this he let him have, among other things, his Order of the Black Eagle.'

'The Order of the Black Eagle? But that's almost worthless.'

'Not to Herr Pariser. The Duke was obliged to wear it when he received the Czar, and so he had to borrow it back for the occasion, at a price of five hundred marks.'

'So that explains it!' said Lorenz Adlon.

'Explains what?'

'Nothing. I was only thinking that I can now understand the Duke's state of mind. But how can any man fall so easily into the hands of a money-lender?'

'My dear Herr Adlon, you know how extraordinarily ignorant of business matters people in those circles often are. The shock of awakening is apt to be painful. All I hope is that nothing disastrous has happened to him.'

There followed several hours of anxious suspense. Lorenz Adlon was frequently called away on business, but he always came back to the bar, where the superintendent sat nervously watching the clock. At length, when dusk was beginning to fall, one of the page-boys appeared, very much out of breath, and blurted out an incoherent sentence in which the words 'duke' and 'lake' brought the two gentlemen instantly to their feet.

'Pull yourself together, boy,' said Lorenz Adler sharply, 'and say what you have to say properly.'

'I found the Duke sitting by the lake—the Neu See. He——'

'Did you say, sitting?'

'Yes. He was feeding the fishes.'

The gentlemen relaxed.

'A man who contemplates suicide,' remarked the superintendent, 'is unlikely to waste time feeding fishes. What did you say to him?'

'I said he was urgently wanted at the hotel. But he said he had any amount of time and he would walk back.'

It was in fact nearly an hour before the Duke appeared. When the superintendent went up to him and respectfully introduced himself, he turned very pale. Speaking in a low but carefully controlled voice he invited him up to his room.

The rest can be quickly told. It was announced some twenty minutes later that the Duke intended to leave Berlin immediately. When he came downstairs again, in company with the superintendent, he was a man transformed. He patted his companion affably on the shoulder.

'The Berlin police are wonderful,' he said. 'The superintendent has just brought me some splendid news from home. But it's an official secret, isn't it, my dear fellow?' Then, turning to Lorenz Adlon, he asked: 'How much do I owe you?'

It was a purely rhetorical question. The Duke knew very well that he had nothing to pay. He was the guest of the Palace. The Kaiser paid the Adlon a round sum of 150,000 marks a year for the entertainment of his personal guests. In return for this rooms had to be kept available at any time for members of the aristocracy who had been invited to Court but could not be lodged at the palace. If the yearly account exceeded this sum the difference was made good; and in theory, if the total was not reached, the hotel was entitled to retain the balance. I may add that this case never arose.

When, therefore, Lorenz Adlon replied, bowing, that the account was already settled, and that his Highness had done him great honour in patronizing his house, the Duke strode smiling past the rows of bowing page-boys and out to the waiting car.

'I still don't quite understand the change in him,' Lorenz Adlon said to the superintendent. 'How did you manage it? You got those letters back, but debts are still debts.'

The superintendent wagged his head.

'In the first place we worked it out that he has already paid so much in interest, renewal charges, blackmail and whatever else you like to call it, that the amount of the original loans has been very nearly covered. And secondly I removed the sword of

Damocles from over his head by promising him that the business would be handled with the utmost delicacy and discretion.'

'Is he so terrified of the Kaiser?'

'No—of his wife.'

A week later the superintendent's assistant, the inspector, paid another visit to the Adlon. He brought Lorenz Adlon a sealed envelope from his superior which turned out to contain the five hundred marks borrowed by the Duke of Schleswig-Holstein.

Lorenz Adlon accepted it with a chuckle. He was about to return to his work when he was struck by the inspector's gloomy countenance.

'Are you still worrying about that Order of Stanislaus?'

'The Russian star? Oh, no, I'd forgotten all about that. But the superintendent has just received another decoration.'

'Really? Who from?'

'From the Duke of Schleswig-Holstein—for special services.'

Lorenz Adlon suppressed a chuckle.

'Cheer up,' he said. 'It's the same with me. I'm always out when it hails, but never when the decorations come floating down.'

The inspector shrugged his shoulders.

'Personally I wouldn't care in the least, but——'

'I know,' said Lorenz. 'You suffer from the Duke's trouble—your wife.'

The inspector nodded and went sadly out through the revolving door.

6

La Belle Otéro

THUS far the tale has been all of crowned heads, princes and uniformed officers, as though we had no other kind of guest at the Adlon. . . .

And when I say 'we' I must ask the reader's indulgence. It was only at a later stage that I made the acquaintance of the only son and heir of the house, Louis Adlon, whom I married. I was not a witness of any of the events I am at present describing. But my husband told these tales of the 'good old days' so often that they are vivid in my mind. Naturally I have a first-hand knowledge of the events of later years, when my husband and I managed the hotel together. Then it was truly 'we'—up to the time when the proud building vanished in the flames, and Louis Adlon, surely the most innocent of war-victims, was taken away by the Russians.

But we are back in the year 1914, when, although those behind the scenes could see the storm-clouds gathering, the majority of people lived as heedlessly as they had done ever since the hotel was founded. During this year two very great artistes visited the Adlon—Enrico Caruso and the ravishing dancer who was known to all the world as 'La Belle Otéro'.

Otéro swept in like a duchess and at once stood the whole establishment on its head. She brought with her a parrot, two pug-dogs, a guinea-fowl, a Siamese cat, thirty-eight trunks, a maid, and her own almost unbelievable beauty. Lorenz Adlon described her as the most exquisitely lovely woman he had ever seen.

I think I should here explain to the present generation who La Belle Otéro really was.

Her father, a young man of a well-to-do Greek family named Carasso, fell in love in Spain with a gipsy who had a child by him, baptized Carolina. Soon afterwards the young man's love affair

48

involved him in a duel in which he was killed. The gipsy then placed her daughter in a convent, where she was brought up by Catholic nuns.

All went well until the girl was fourteen, when she climbed over the convent wall for love of a certain Señor Pacco, who took her to Lisbon and had her trained as a dancer. Within a year she had achieved a sensational success with her extraordinary beauty and the entirely novel freedom and grace that she brought to the performance of Spanish dances. She used the name of Carolina Otéro, and a French journalist wrote of her in the *Figaro*:

'She is supple as a snake, her golden skin as warm and smooth as a panther's coat. Her hips sway distractingly, while her eyes speak promises and her hands offer enticements . . .'

Heralded by paeans of this sort she embarked upon a triumphal progress through all the world's great cities, captivating every man who set eyes on her. She was the Lolobrigida plus Marilyn Monroe of her day. She stayed at the Adlon while fulfilling an engagement at the Berlin Wintergarten Theatre. It was customary for artistes appearing at this theatre, the biggest and best of the variety houses, to stay at the Central Hotel, which was practically under the same roof. But only the Adlon, where the dukes and princes stayed, was good enough for Otéro. She had recently paid a triumphant visit to St. Petersburg, where, it was whispered, she had been carried naked on a silver platter borne on the shoulders of a dozen Russian grand dukes.

One day the Kaiser paid an informal visit to the hotel. It was early afternoon and the lounge was very quiet. His Majesty came accompanied by only one or two gentlemen, but he left these behind while he strolled with Lorenz Adlon in the Goethe garden.

'I just dropped in to take a glass of wine with you,' he said.

Lorenz Adlon called for a bottle of the best the house could offer. The Kaiser sipped and murmured, and then for a while was silent, stroking his moustache. Then he remarked casually:

'I understand you have a dancer stopping here whom everyone is talking about. Is she really as talented as they say?'

E

'Not only extraordinarily talented, your Majesty, but also extremely beautiful.'

'It's a pity I can't see her. I can't possibly go to the Wintergarten, it wouldn't look at all well . . .'

His Majesty fell silent again.

Lorenz Adlon cleared his throat and said.

'There's another way. If she were to appear at some sort of charity performance your Majesty could attend with the entire Court.'

The Kaiser shook his head.

'That won't do, I'm afraid. Trützschler thought of it. But the Empress strongly disapproves because someone has told her that the lady is always being carried round naked on trays.'

'I see,' said Lorenz Adlon gravely. 'Well, in that case—if your Majesty would not mind waiting a moment . . .'

He hurried to his office and made use of the telephone. A few minutes later La Belle Otéro appeared quite by chance in the Goethe garden, but did not fail to make a most elegant curtsy when she saw the Kaiser. His Majesty was most gracious and talked to her for some minutes. She answered him in broken but intelligible German, and finally withdrew as gracefully as she had come.

'Wonderful!' said the Kaiser to Lorenz Adlon. 'Truly superb!' He emptied his glass and rose. 'Well, I must be going. But your wine was first-rate, my dear Adlon—quite delicious!'

The next day a portrait-painter appeared at the hotel, having been commissioned on the Kaiser's behalf to paint the dancer, life-size and in oils.

Alas, things did not go smoothly. At the very first sitting one of the pug-dogs bit the painter's leg, and the hotel doctor had to dress the wound. But this was not the worst. There arose, only the day before the portrait was due to be completed, a threat of scandal which might have had serious consequences for everyone concerned. It came about in the following manner.

La Belle Otéro was in the habit of rising at about midday, and, being a dancer, she was accustomed to start the day with a few breathing exercises at the open window. Naturally enough, she performed these exercises very lightly clad. As ill-luck would have it, her suite did not look out on to Unter den Linden, but over-looked the Goethe garden, so that it was possible to see into her bedroom from the windows opposite.

On the day in question, while she stood at her window in her usual state of undress, she saw something gleam in one of the opposite rooms which she instantly suspected to be a camera-lens.

'It was a press-photographer!' she cried in huge excitement. 'If the photograph is published it will ruin my reputation!'

She sent for the manager, who did all that could be done in the circumstances. He went to the occupant of the room and asked him point-blank if he had been taking photographs from his win-dow at that time. The gentleman, a Frenchman from Paris, ad-mitted that he had, and, further, that he was connected with the press.

'But,' he went on, 'I did not know that there was any rule against taking photographs of the Goethe garden at midday. I'm doing an article for my paper on the world-famous Hotel Adlon. Surely there is nothing wrong in that?'

The manager replied that the taking of photographs might cause inconvenience to the guests and must therefore be subject to the permission of the management.

'Forgive me,' said the Frenchman, 'but if a lady shows herself at her window at midday insufficiently clad, she may be guilty of something more than merely inconveniencing the guests. She may be charged with indecent exposure, which is a punishable offence under German law.'

The manager had no answer to this. He could only return to Otéro to report his failure. She promptly smashed a costly vase against the wall, greatly upsetting the pug-dogs, the Siamese cat, the parrot and the guinea-fowl. She then demanded that the police should be summoned and the picture confiscated, since the man obviously intended to blackmail her. And when the manager declared this to be impossible, she said calmly:

'Then I shall go to the palace and appeal to the Kaiser. He is a chivalrous gentleman who will understand and protect me.'

Whether in fact she did this is not known. She left the hotel a few days later, having completed her engagement at the Wintergarten, and the painter had to finish the picture without her.

But it never reached the Kaiser. Two of the Empress's more influential ladies-in-waiting, Countess Brockdorf and Countess Keller, cunningly contrived to divert it. Later it was sent on to La Belle Otéro as a present, and she kept it for many years. I heard that she sold it comparatively recently in Nice, where she still lives, a very old lady.

Wilhelm II was never able to collect a gallery of beauties like that of Ludwig of Bavaria.

7

The Great Escoffier

THAT any guest at the Adlon should be in any way incommoded, as happened in the case of the beautiful Otéro, was almost unknown. For the most part they were so well content with the food, service and amenities of the hotel that they quite often preferred to give up their private dwellings in order to install themselves permanently with us.

An hotel is a little world of its own, in which the guest can feel himself a king. Although he may possess the biggest and most luxurious of houses, nowhere else are there so many agreeable possibilities at his command.

Lorenz Adlon's recipe for ensuring a sense of the utmost well-being in his patrons was a very simple one. When the Kaiser once asked him what he regarded as the most important items in the running of an hotel, he answered briefly:

'Bed and breakfast.'

'No more than that?' asked the Kaiser in astonishment.

'It's a great deal, your Majesty. The bed, for instance, must be so designed and arranged as to ensure absolute repose. Nothing must disturb the sleeper. That is why there are no bells in my house, but only light-signals, and thick carpets in all the corridors and stairways. It must be possible for every room to be completely darkened, and the very look of the bed, with its pillows and coverlets, should convey a feeling of comfort. The whole thing must give the visitor the impression of sheltering in a secure retreat where nothing can enter to disturb him.'

'Just so,' said the Kaiser. 'And what about breakfast?'

In the first place, said Lorenz Adlon, the very smell of breakfast was highly important. It was not enough that the tea and coffee should taste good, their aroma alone should have a reviving and fortifying effect. The visitor who took breakfast in his room, as most of those at the Adlon did, should be brought to such a contented frame of mind that he hated to leave it.

'All the same,' said the Kaiser, 'I should have thought that luncheon and dinner were even more important.'

'No, your Majesty. The guest who has slept and breakfasted well is ready to overlook a trifling hitch at luncheon. He has made a good start to the day. And the same applies even more to dinner. I still maintain, your Majesty, that bed and breakfast are the most important things of all.'

'I shall have to make a note of it,' said Wilhelm II. 'Perhaps someday I shall start a hotel myself.'

'God forbid!' said Lorenz Adlon.

'Why? Have you such a low opinion of my ability? Are you afraid I'd ruin myself?'

Lorenz Adlon executed a courtly bow.

'Your Majesty,' he said, 'I'm afraid you'd ruin *me*.'

But that is not to say that the kitchens and cellars of the Adlon were in any way neglected. The restaurant plays far too large a part in the general economy of any hotel the size of ours. Bar and restaurant attract a great many patrons in addition to the room-guests, and big receptions, gala dinners and private dances, to say nothing of *rendez-vous* in the bar, are among the most important sources of revenue.

I shall not attempt to estimate how many special menus the hotel was accustomed to prepare, or capable of preparing, on days of public festivity, such as New Year's Eve. Neither do I wish to go into financial details. These are arid matters, of little interest except to those professionally connected with the hotel business.

Our first chef was Escoffier, on whom Wilhelm II bestowed the title, 'The King of Cooks'. There is certainly no chef today with a reputation that equals his. His big cookery-book is to be found in every first-class hotel and restaurant. His recipes are classics. He was unquestionably one of the greatest cooks in the world.

Before going on to describe our kitchens in some detail I will tell a story of Escoffier by way of illustrating the financial value, to a hotel, of a chef of his quality.

King Edward VII, of England, was due to visit Berlin. He had expressed a wish to see the new Hotel Adlon, and knowing that Escoffier, whom he had met in Monte Carlo, was our chef, he wanted to have a meal there.

The Kaiser came to the Adlon in a state of high excitement, saying that something special must be done to mark this occasion. He did not doubt that the dinner would be all that it should be, but it must contain something original, an entirely new dish of some kind.

This discussion took place in the private office. Both the Kaiser and Lorenz Adlon remained on their feet, pacing earnestly up and down the room. At length Lorenz Adlon said:

'Your Majesty, this is very difficult. Edward VII is a famous gastronome and judge of cookery. There is very little about the subject that he doesn't know. I think we should consult Monsieur Escoffier.'

'*Zum Teufel!*' exclaimed the Kaiser, who was much given to using this expression. 'Devil take it! You mustn't let me down, Adlon. But by all means send for Escoffier.'

A page-boy was sent, and after ten minutes had passed the Kaiser growled:

'Devil take it! What's keeping the fellow?'

Finally the page-boy returned and reported, standing stiffly to atention:

'Monsieur Escoffier says he can't come at present. He's making a bouillabaisse.'

'By God, what a man!' said the Kaiser. 'In that case, my dear Adlon, we had better go down to the kitchen. I shall be interested to see how my colleague, the King of Cooks, makes bouillabaisse.'

Various equerries and gentlemen-in-attendance were waiting in the lobby. His Majesty, now in a high good-humour, waved them aside, explaining that he was going to consult with his colleague, and Lorenz Adlon led the way to the kitchen. No sooner had they entered the vast, lofty place than an under-chef, hurrying past with a saucepan in his hand, recognized the Kaiser and shouted:

'Attention everyone! His Majesty!'

There was then a great clatter of pots and pans followed by a dead silence, and the startled Lorenz Adlon beheld the majority of the kitchen staff standing rigidly to attention, facing their Emperor.

The silence was broken by two voices speaking together. The Kaiser exclaimed:

'For heaven's sake, children, what are you doing? You mustn't let the food burn!'

At the same time Escoffier poured out a flood of indignant words in French, to the general effect that no one except himself gave orders in his kitchen, and that the whole staff would be dismissed if they did not instantly resume their duties.

The Kaiser, still in the happiest of moods, burst into loud laughter. He went over to Escoffier. The chef was standing at a big stove, intently stirring the contents of a large saucepan. Near by were hot-plates and dishes containing lobster, mussels and portions of soft fish. The soup he was stirring was yellow with saffron.

'Good morning, Monsieur Escoffier,' said the Kaiser. 'Forgive me for disturbing you. I need your advice in an important matter of State.'

Escoffier was at once mollified.

'Your Majesty must excuse me for a few minutes,' he said. 'I am already engaged on a matter of importance. Some very eminent visitors to the hotel have ordered bouillabaisse. They are connoisseurs, and I am just approaching the most crucial moment in the preparation of the dish.'

'I would not hinder you for the world,' said the Kaiser. 'You are the King of Cooks, as I have always said, and I am the Emperor of Germany. We must work together. What exactly are you doing?'

'Your Majesty,' said the flattered Escoffier, 'this is highly secret.'

He called out something in French, and the other chefs all turned their heads away. Escoffier was famous for the stringency with which he guarded his secrets.

'The soup,' he said in a whisper, 'must have just the slightest accent of garlic, scarcely enough to taste, a mere hint to the palate.'

Looking round to make sure that no one else was watching, he spiked a clove of garlic with a fork, sniffed it and then carefully waved it three times through the steam. But it seemed that the aroma he had thus created was not quite sufficient. He took a small fan out of his pocket, opened it and fanned the garlic over the pot. Then he hastily put it away and began to stir.

'Remarkable!' said the Kaiser.

'Isn't it, your Majesty!' said Escoffier.

Then he very quickly threw the lobsters, mussels and other fish into the soup. After stirring a little more he took a bottle and a tea-spoon, poured a bright green fluid into the spoon, emptied it into the soup, stirred again, tasted the soup and finally offered a spoonful to the Kaiser.

'But this is marvellous!' cried the Kaiser. 'Adlon, I shall lunch here today, and I want some of this soup. But tell me, Escoffier, what was that last thing you put in?'

Escoffier again looked cautiously about him and then whispered:

'That is the greatest secret of all, your Majesty. I had to go to endless trouble in Marseilles before I was able to arrive at it. The last ingredient was absinthe, a small teaspoonful, no more, to a pan of soup this size.'

'Extraordinary!' said the Kaiser.

'It's the key to the whole thing,' said Escoffier. 'And your Majesty is the only man, besides Herr Adlon and myself, who knows it.'

After luncheon a conference was held to decide upon the menu for the King of England, the participants being the Kaiser, Lorenz Adlon and Monsieur Escoffier.

'Devil take it!' exclaimed the Kaiser. 'This chap Edward is

terrible. He seems to know everything. What are we to do about it, Monsieur Escoffier?'

The King of Cooks reflected.

'Sole is the dish that King Edward likes best of all,' he said. 'I have often wondered whether it would not be possible to serve sole with an entirely new sauce, something that has never been done before, with a flavour that no one has ever tasted.'

'Damn it, Escoffier!' cried the Kaiser. 'This isn't just a matter of concocting a new sauce. It's a question of an entirely new dish!'

Escoffier apologetically shook his head.

'Allow me to tell your Majesty a story. The chef of King Louis XIV one day found himself in great trouble. The master of the King's Household had told him that far too much money was being spent in the kitchen. Since they could not agree about this the King himself sent for his chef and questioned him. He had spent 100,000 livres in a single month. The Master of the Household had reckoned up the cost of wages and raw materials, and he did not understand how the figure could exceed 30,000 livres. "But, Sire," cried the chef, "his Excellency has not counted the cost of the sauces! They are the most expensive thing of all!"'

There seemed to be no answer to this. It was accordingly agreed that Escoffier should have twenty-four hours in which to meditate upon an entirely new and original sauce to be served with the sole for King Edward VII.

'Devil take it!' said the Kaiser in conclusion. 'You see what a lot of problems I have to solve, my dear Adlon.'

'Your Majesty certainly seems very anxious to consign them to the devil,' Lorenz Adlon remarked.

'The devil I do!' said the Kaiser. 'I should have an uncomfortable evening at the palace if the ladies heard me.'

The Adlon people relate that life with Escoffier was by no means easy the next day. He sat brooding in the kitchen. Contrary to his usual practice, he did not busy himself with anything. He wandered about, tasting dishes here and there, pulling a long face and constantly muttering the Kaiser's favourite expletive, '*Zum Teufel!*—Devil take it!'

Then his eye happened to alight upon a box of fresh dates that had been brought in for dessert. He picked it up and gazed meditatively at the dates, smelt them and put one in his mouth. And suddenly he cried:

'Devil take it!—I've got it!'

He told his assistant, the sauce-chef, that he was going out for a walk to compose the sauce for Edward VII, and then he vanished.

By the time he returned to the kitchen, not only had Lorenz Adlon been informed that the great man was on the track of a new sauce, but the glad news had been passed on to the Kaiser, who sent word back to Lorenz asking him to try to find out what kind of sauce it was.

A poet does not like to be questioned about the poem that he is in the act of writing. Neither did Escoffier like to be cross-examined when he was in the act of composing a new dish. When Lorenz Adlon came into the kitchen, where he was pacing restlessly up and down, and asked what the sauce was to be made of, he answered tersely and irritably:

'Dates.'

Lorenz Adlon was horrified and so was the Kaiser.

At eleven o'clock that night Escoffier came to Lorenz Adlon and said that he had now finally composed the sauce in his head. Dates were to be the main ingredient, but there was another item which must be procured with all possible speed, because without it the sauce could not be made. He must have some Indian mangoes.

At this Lorenz Adlon nearly gave way to despair. Mangoes were quite unobtainable in Germany. Finally he went to the palace. Upon hearing that Herr Adlon had called to see him the Kaiser deserted his company and came to hear what the matter was. Lorenz Adler reported that his exotic chef insisted upon having an exotic fruit.

The Kaiser recalled that mangoes had been among the favourite fruits of Queen Victoria. A telegram was instantly sent to the

German Embassy in London, asking that some might be procured and brought with all speed by special messenger to Berlin. The Embassy messenger reached the Adlon at ten o'clock on the morning of the day on which Edward VII, who had in the meantime arrived in Berlin, was to dine at the hotel. It was to be a dinner for gentlemen only.

Monsieur Escoffier had arranged a corner of the kitchen especially for the production of his sauce. Lorenz Adlon had no idea how it was to taste or look, or what its ingredients were to be; neither had the Kaiser.

Eight or ten gentlemen sat down to dine, and at first everything passed off quite uneventfully. The dishes served were, it need hardly be said, of the utmost excellence, but the King of England made no comment.

And presently the sole was brought in. Lorenz Adlon was himself present to supervise the service. Escoffier now entered, but he passed behind King Edward, who did not notice him. He wore a frock-coat and bore himself with great dignity. He carried a large gold sauce-dish. The whole dinner-service, it may be said, was of gold.

As the waiter placed the big sole before King Edward he made his first comment on the meal:

'This looks excellent!'

Escoffier then came forward with the sauce-dish, and the King exclaimed:

'Hullo, Escoffier! So you're here, are you!'

Escoffier made a slight bow and then dressed the fish with the sauce, while King Edward gazed at it in some astonishment. It was brown and thick, with a fragrant but quite unfamiliar odour. When all the gentlemen had been served the King began to eat.

'Escoffier,' he cried, 'what is this sauce? I've never had anything like it. It's superb! You must tell me at once what it's made of.'

The Kaiser was no less delighted.

'A sauce worthy of the occasion,' he said. 'But may the devil take you, Escoffier, if you betray the secret to his Majesty!'

King Edward laughed.

'Well, at least, Escoffier, tell me what it's called.'

'Sauce diable,' answered Escoffier.

No other chef at the Adlon was ever able to imitate Escoffier's *sauce diable*. Naturally the ingredients became known. It was compounded of dates, mangoes, raisins, tomatoes, sugar, vinegar and tamarinds, together with various spices. But the exact proportions in which these numerous ingredients were mixed remained Escoffier's secret.

The next day the newspapers printed a full account of the event, and that night every table in the restaurant was occupied by diners eating sole with *sauce diable*. People still came, years afterwards, especially to taste it. Lorenz Adlon said that it would be impossible to compute how much custom this 'date sauce', as the hotel people called it, had brought to the restaurant. 'The devil of a lot,' he concluded.

8

Caruso

ESCOFFIER'S kingdom, with his 'brigade', as the kitchen-staff
was called, was often the scene of momentous events. The kitchen
of a big hotel can almost be likened to a seismograph, a sensitive
instrument registering every shock that occurs in the establishment, even when it takes place in some remote part. A watchful
observer might discern from the aspect of the Adlon kitchen whenever any especially important, or troublesome, guest had arrived
at the hotel.

Things were particularly lively in our kitchen when Enrico
Caruso was stopping at the Adlon.

The great tenor, who at that time—it was in 1914—was at the
peak of his success, brought with him a secretary and his own cook.

The *maestro* himself was seldom seen, since he only left his
suite to go to the theatre. Only the world-renowned voice was
sometimes to be heard, generally between ten and eleven in the
morning, bursting through the thick door and rolling down the
corridor, not in arias but in those loosening-up exercises—mi-mi-
mi-mi-mi—which are necessary to all tenors.

However, while Caruso was only to be heard, the secretary and
cook became familiar figures in the hotel, the secretary long and
thin, the cook short and fat, like a comedy-film team.

When the cook made his first appearance in the kitchen he at
once proclaimed with a flourish:

'Me only cook for *maestro*. Capito?'

Our cooks had been warned. They welcomed the little man in
the friendliest manner and took him under their wing. A space
was cleared for him in the kitchen, and everyone watched with the
greatest interest to see what he would first cook for his master. It
was a great disappointment when, after so much display, he
cooked nothing but a dish of plain spaghetti.

'Midday spaghetti,' he explained. 'Grand supper evening.'

He laid the long strands gravely on a silver dish, as though he were performing a religious rite, and then put the dish on a huge tray.

He insisted upon himself carrying the tray at a trot up to the *maestro's* room. Despite his plumpness he never moved at anything less than a trot, in the kitchen and elsewhere, so that one of our cooks, who had worked in Italy, remarked:

'He must certainly have served in the Bersaglieri!'

However that may be, the little Italian explained to his colleagues, in halting German supplemented with words of French, that the brilliance of his illustrious master's voice was entirely owing to his cookery. It was the carefully measured quantity of olive oil that caused the smoothness of his melodic line, the meticulously compounded vegetable sauce that strengthened his vocal cords, and the exactly calculated portion of meat that brought to his *bel canto* its unequalled lustre.

'In that case,' said one of our cooks, 'I must try the same diet. It may start me on a new career.'

The Italian, not understanding a word and seeing himself surrounded by friendly grins, bowed his acknowledgements.

Caruso was to sing the part of the Duke in 'Rigoletto' at a gala performance at the State Opera. All Berlin was talking of the event, and thousands of applications for seats had had to be refused. A gala performance meant that royalty was to attend with a full retinue. There were no such impediments as had frustrated the Kaiser in the case of La Belle Otéro. The Empress was most anxious to be present.

But on the morning of that day another great crisis occurred at the Adlon.

It began when the *maestro's* lean secretary, who was always clad in ceremonial black, came running in extreme agitation to the reception desk and announced that his master was unwell. He had a sore throat, and a doctor must be sent for immediately if the performance that evening was not to be cancelled.

The reception-clerks fully realized the seriousness of the situation.

A gala performance with royalty attending was something that simply could not be cancelled. But before anything could be done the secretary was joined by the cook, in an even greater state of excitement, and the effect produced by the gesticulating pair—the tall, thin, black-clad secretary, and the short, rotund, white-clad cook—was so comical that the clerks had great difficulty in keeping straight faces.

And then, as though sent by Heaven, the hotel's house-doctor appeared on the scene, Dr. Küttner.

Dr. Küttner was a notable character. His forthrightness and dry, sarcastic humour were famous in the hotel. Whenever his well-groomed, portly figure appeared in the hall, members of the staff who happened to be on duty would gather round to listen to his conversation with the chief receptionist.

He was accustomed to start by asking if anyone was ill, and, being apologetically informed that everyone was in good health, would utter loud complaints, saying that nobody ever got ill in these days and that he would end up in the workhouse. On this occasion, however, he was more fortunate. The chief reception-clerk, with a glance at the two Italians, drew him hastily to one side and told him of the crisis, impressing upon him that his prospective patient was none other than the great Caruso.

'Business is looking up,' said the doctor.

When the two Italians learned who he was they seized hold of him, one on either side, and dragged him to the lift and up to the *maestro's* room. Caruso, his expression one of the utmost gloom, was seated in an armchair with a thick woollen shawl wrapped round his neck and a hat on his head.

'*Dottore!*' cried the secretary and the cook together, thrusting their captive forward in triumph.

'Well, now,' said Dr. Küttner, 'what seems to be the trouble?'

The singer, who understood very little German, made a theatrical gesture of despair and then opened his mouth and pointed down his throat. The doctor got a throat-mirror out of his bag and said:

'Say "ah".'

The Kaiser's Hotel

The 'botched-up remnant of a ruin'

The Founder

(*Left*) LORENZ ADLON

(*Top*) WITH THE CROWN PRINCE

This request, which the Italians failed to understand, led to some confusion. The secretary rushed into the next room and came back with a tuning-fork with which he sounded the note A. Finally the doctor took Caruso by the jaw, opened his mouth, and, not knowing the Italian for 'say', instructed him:

'Cantare, maestro! Cantare A!'

Caruso understood this at once. Thrusting aside the doctor's hand, and sustaining the note as long as his breath held out, he sang a high A of such exquisite purity that any concert hall would have been moved to rapturous applause.

The doctor was able to look down his throat and form his opinion. He saw nothing but a slight redness which was certainly not serious; and in any case the quality of the voice had been enough to tell him that there was nothing much amiss. However, since the patient was an illustrious singer he felt that he must be handled with particular care.

He tried to explain that the *maestro* should apply a cold compress to his throat, and when this was not understood he went to the bathroom and came back with a wet towel which he offered to Caruso, indicating with gestures that he should wrap it round and go back to bed.

'Sera returno,' he said, by which he intended to convey that he would come back that evening.

At this the secretary rounded upon him, flourishing a newspaper containing an announcement of the gala performance and crying out in Italian that all this was nonsense. The doctor had been sent for to cure the *maestro* forthwith, so that he would be able to sing that evening.

The doctor caught his drift although he did not understand the words. Pointing in his turn to the newspaper announcement he shook his head vigorously and said:

'Niente cantare! Niente Opera!'

Whereupon he was furiously assailed by all three Italians. The cook shook his fist under his nose and the secretary brandished the tuning-fork as though it were a dagger.

'Nix dottore!' they cried and thrust him towards the door. And

F

when he was out in the corridor they hurled a last insult after him
—'Ignorante!'

The door was then slammed.

Towards midday, the whole hotel having in the meantime
heard of the doctor's adventure, the cook was seen to come down
the stairs, at the trot as usual, and vanish into the kitchen. Here
he set the entire staff in an uproar. One of the French chefs
managed to elicit the purpose of his excited preparations. He had
thought of a dish that would surely cure his master's indisposition
and save the gala performance.

'*Tagliolini!*' he said in triumph.

He made a *pasta*, rolled it, cut it into finger-thick strips, cooked
it and dressed it particularly richly with butter and parmesan
cheese. All the time he worked he sang—naturally—the tenor's
aria from 'Rigoletto'.

When it was ready he put the *pasta* on a big silver dish, covered
it with thick tomato sauce, put the dish on an even bigger tray,
and took it, with his Bersaglieri stride, up to the *maestro*.

When Lorenz Adlon entered the kitchen a short time afterwards, he was astonished to find the entire staff, with beaming
faces, singing 'La donna e mobile . . .'

In fact, the gala performance was held that evening according
to schedule and everything went without a hitch, just as the cook
had said. The critics were unanimous in declaring that Caruso
had never sung so magnificently as he did on that occasion in the
presence of the German Emperor.

Dr. Küttner was also present, in Lorenz Adlon's box, and when
the performance was over Lorenz asked him:

'Was it really the *tagliolini* that worked the miracle?'

The old doctor laughed.

'Well, perhaps. But just to be on the safe side I went to see
Caruso again this afternoon. He was obediently lying in bed with
a thick compress round his neck, sweating hard and looking
utterly miserable. He asked me to write a certificate saying that
he was not fit to appear.'

'And did you?'

'Certainly.'

'Then what did he say?'

'He looked more miserable than ever and said, '*Tutto perduto*', evidently considering that without him the entire occasion would be ruined and the Kaiser's evening spoilt. But I told him not to worry. I said that the *Staatsoper* had some excellent tenors of its own, and that I was sure the Kaiser would thoroughly enjoy his evening.'

'And then,' said Lorenz Adlon chuckling, 'I suppose he threw you out again?'

'Well, more or less. Anyway, he was cured instantly. The day in bed may have helped, to say nothing of the *tagliolini*. How can one ever be sure with these performers?' As he took his leave Dr. Küttner pulled his customary long face. 'So you see, my dear Adlon, I'm out of luck again. There's never anybody ill!'

9

The 1914 War

THE strains of 'Rigoletto' were quickly forgotten, for very soon after Caruso's visit, which took place in the late summer of 1914, a new, plaintive little song was to be heard in Berlin which came to have a deeper and increasingly tragic significance as the weeks went by:

> *Upon a day of August roses*
> *The Guards were marched away...*

The Guards! So many brilliant occasions were bound up with the name, so many balls and society entertainments at the Adlon dominated by the proud uniforms of Guards officers. As they marched singing and flower-bestrewn past the hotel, during those weeks of August roses, few can have had any inkling of what the future held in store for them.

Years later more than one lieutenant of the Guards, who had once danced in our ballroom with princesses and ladies of the Court, came privately to our personnel-manager in search of employment as a professional dancing-partner; and danced to the hit-songs of the 'twenties—'Pretty gigolo, poor gigolo, think no more of your sorrows . . .'

I have no need to dwell upon the events of 1914. It is no history book that I am trying to write, but a book of memories reflecting the times and having a direct connection with the hotel.

In the critical hours of July nearly all the leading personalities came regularly to the Adlon, and the gravity of the situation might be judged from their preoccupied expressions and earnest conversations. Count Moltke, the Chief of the General Staff, came very often for a meal, seeming ever more melancholy as the crisis approached its climax. He nearly always sat alone, keeping his eyes fixed sombrely on the damask tablecloth. He spoke to no one, not even to Lorenz Adlon. The more frivolous members of society called him Cassandra and steered clear of him.

68

Albert Ballin, the shipping magnate, was rather more talkative. As a friend of the Kaiser, and a man to whom his Majesty would sometimes listen, he came to Berlin during those fateful days and stopped at the Adlon in the uncertain hope of seeing him. He wanted to urge him to do everything in his power to preserve peace. But the Kaiser was not to be seen. He did not return from his northern cruise until the 27th July.

On the evening of that day the Chancellor, Count Bethmann Hollweg, also came to the Adlon, where he met Count Moltke. The two gentlemen made use of the sitting-room of one of the royal suites, where for an hour they talked undisturbed. Both were in a state of extreme agitation when they left.

Later the story of what had happened went round the lounge and the bar. The Chancellor had been at the railway station to meet the Kaiser's special train. Wilhelm II, beside himself with consternation at the imminent threat of war, had said to the Chancellor, speaking so loudly that those in attendance could hear:

'You've cooked this infernal hash, now you must damned well eat it!'

But it was not only Bethmann Hollweg who had to eat the hash, it was the German people.

When war was declared the troops marched past the Adlon singing, 'Gloria Victoria, with Heart and Hand for the Fatherland!' It was a wonderful army, gallant and sure of victory. And no less confident were the wives and sweethearts, the brothers and sisters, who accompanied the departing soldiers as they passed under the Brandenburger Tor. But there was little gaiety in the faces of the influential men who stood on the hotel balconies looking down upon this lively scene. Perhaps they already knew in their hearts that the world in which they had lived was doomed to be destroyed.

When Lorenz Adlon and those who worked with him at that time came later to tell of the years 1914 to 1918, their tale was of the slow agony and death of Imperial Germany.

Black-clad, weeping women brought the first mourning into the hotel. Industrialists visiting Berlin, who talked without restraint in the hearing of the hotel staff, scornfully condemning official incompetence in such matters at the wastage of raw materials, brought the first fear.

Throughout the entire war no room in the hotel was ever unoccupied. Countless new Government Departments sprang up in Berlin, and their leading functionaries rented suites with us by the year. Many old members of our staff went off to the war. They never failed to visit the hotel when they came home on leave, and they told us stories of events at the front which grew ever more ominous.

The years passed and the disaster approached. Prince Max of Baden came as the last Chancellor of the Empire to stop at the Adlon. His official residence was the Chancellery in the Wilhelmstrasse, but conditions in Berlin during the final stage of the war were so hectic that it was difficult to keep that huge house going. He found it more convenient to take a suite at the hotel.

His coming was a sign to everyone at the Adlon that revolution must soon follow, and they viewed the future with great alarm.

The first bullets to visit the Adlon, upon the outbreak of revolution, shattered the windows of the famous corner suite which so many distinguished guests had occupied. They were fired from the Brandenburger Tor across the Pariser Platz, and they heralded a series of turbulent and frightening events in our normally tranquil, smooth-running establishment.

The staff stood about in groups in all the rooms discussing the latest happenings. The waiters and *chefs du rang*, like the chefs in the kitchen, were nearly all Swiss or Dutch, for their German colleagues had long ago been drafted into the army. The remaining members of the staff were either too old for military service or else had been so badly wounded in the early stages of the war as to be of no further use.

On the day of the bullets Lorenz Adlon and his son Louis, who as his eventual successor was already taking a large part in the management of the hotel, waited anxiously for prompt and decisive counter-measures by the Prussian general who was responsible for the maintenance of law and order in Berlin. Their astonishment and consternation were the greater when they learned that Wilhelm II had crossed the frontier into Holland. The Kaiser, who had been so closely connected with the story of the Adlon, and whom Lorenz Adlon had always looked upon as a personal friend, had abdicated.

After Scheidemann (the leader of the Social Democrats) had proclaimed the Republic from the steps of the Reichstag, revolutionary troops entered the Adlon to proclaim the Republic here as well, and to search the house for 'war-mongers and weapons'. The soldiers had removed all insignia from their caps and carried their rifles at the ready.

They first rounded up the entire staff in the hall and stood facing them with their rifles cocked. Their leader, a youth wearing a sailor's cap, mounted on a chair and announced in a loud voice: 'When I give the word everyone is to shout "Long live the Republic!" three times, at the same time raising his right arm with the fist clenched. Go!'

Having no option, the staff glumly executed this order.

It now transpired that there was one person connected with the hotel who was not a Royalist but a Communist. The girl in charge of the newspaper-stand in the hall, evidently greatly stirred by this improvised ceremony, sprang on to a table and began to sing the 'Red Flag'. Although she got little support, because no one except the revolutionaries knew the words, she sang the whole of it, every verse and line.

And when she had finished Louis Adlon was thrust forward into the presence of the revolutionary leader. He was asked to say where the officers and capitalists who lived in the hotel were hidden.

The fact was that it was a long time since any generals had stayed at the Adlon. The aristocracy had retired to their country houses and estates in order to save what they could from the wreck, and the industrialists were at their factories, striving to avert the worst disasters. Louis Adlon declared, quite truthfully as he believed, that among the few guests remaining in the hotel there was none who came within the categories named.

No sooner had he said this, however, than he remembered with consternation that there was still one officer in the hotel, a certain Captain von Bergen, who was recovering from a severe wound. He could get about painfully on crutches, but spent most of his time in bed. Was he to be handed over?

'No one?' asked the revolutionary leader. 'No one at all?'

'No,' said Louis Adlon.

The young man looked grimly at him.

'I am now going to have the building searched. If any weapon is discovered, or a single officer, you will be shot for counter-revolutionary activities. Do you understand?'

In order to stress the gravity of his situation Louis Adlon was taken out into the Palm Court and made to stand in front of a statue of the youthful Hercules. The demi-god held a serpent grasped in either hand, their heads with long, forked tongues pointing downwards. As it happened, this was, of all the works of art in the hotel, the one which Louis Adlon least cared for, and he was particularly put out at the thought that he might be shot in front of it.

However, it did not come to that.

The hotel's chief staff-supervisor, Fräulein Hartmann, was able to slip away from the hall without being noticed. She ran to Captain von Bergen's room, stuffed his uniform hastily into a trunk, dragged him out of bed, set him on his crutches and helped him to the laundry-lift, which by good fortune was close at hand. She got into it with him and they travelled up and down, dodging the searchers as they went from floor to floor.

After this had gone on for some time the captain, whose sense of humour had not deserted him, began to find it tedious. He stopped the lift at the second floor and said:

'My dear young lady, go and find a bottle of Hennessy and we will then continue our travels.'

The poor girl had no choice but to go and fetch the brandy. An hour or so later, when the search of the building had ended without result and Louis Adlon was released from his unhappy post in front of the Hercules statue, two swaying figures were seen to emerge from the laundry-lift.

It was subsequently affirmed that they were singing the song which begins, 'I stand in deepest midnight', when they returned to Captain von Bergen's room, where Fräulein Hartmann got the captain back into bed before retiring with all speed to her own room for a spell of well-earned repose.

IO

The Turbulent Time

ON THE 11th December 1918 the Adlon was occupied by the police.

Friedrich Ebert, chairman of the Committee of People's Representatives, and later President of the new German Republic, was paying his first visit to Berlin, to receive a number of generals and high-ranking staff-officers and bid them welcome to the capital. In addition to this the regiments of the old Prussian Guard were marching from Doberitz to Berlin, and Ebert wanted to greet them at the Brandenburger Tor.

He was wearing a frock-coat and top-hat when he entered the hotel and walked through the hall to meet the assembled officers.

Louis Adlon often recalled his impressions as he witnessed this first meeting between two such utterly different worlds. It was as though in that moment all the uncertainty was manifest which was later to be discerned in the evolution of the Republic.

Ebert approached with a natural, easy dignity. The officers, on the other hand, were ill-at-ease, and their attitude betrayed their mixed feelings. They all felt that they had been let down by the Monarch, whom they loved; but on the other hand Ebert, whom they approached with profound mistrust, made an unexpectedly good impression on them. They had difficulty in knowing how to bear themselves.

The scene in the Adlon was a brief one; then Ebert and the officers left the hotel, and the spectators also departed. The two Adlons, Lorenz and Louis, remained thoughtfully behind, concerned with a future which to them was shrouded in darkness. The hotel was empty, the restaurant without customers. Now that the Kaiser's Germany had vanished, with its elegance and its love

74

of luxury, would there be any place for a hotel such as theirs? Would the new kind of society be such as would enable it to pay its way? Or was the house, which for father and son represented the whole world, doomed to fail and disappear?

While they were brooding over these matters they suddenly, and to their great astonishment, heard the strains of an old Prussian military march. They hurried up to a first-floor balcony, and looking across the Pariser Platz towards the Brandenburger Tor saw a sight which seemed to come from another world.

The officers of the Royal Prussian Guard were giving the order 'eyes right' to their men as with a stiff parade-ground step they marched past Friedrich Ebert, the representative of the Revolution and the German Republic.

One can well imagine that the two Adlons, having so recently been visited by the revolutionaries, should have found the new world not easy to understand. The generals and staff-officers, when they returned to the Adlon after the parade, to warm themselves and drink a glass of burgundy in their accustomed fashion, were no less puzzled. They still found it hard to believe that Ebert, the Social Democrat, had cried out warmly to the homecoming troops:

'You have returned undefeated!'

But a few days later Lorenz Adlon and his son, in whose hearts the meeting with Ebert had aroused a gleam of hope, met with a new disillusionment. On the Pariser Platz, just outside the hotel, a large body of Spartacists, the extreme revolutionaries, came into collision with a body of the Republican 'Freikorps'.

Rifle and machine-gun bullets swept from the Tiergarten across the Platz and down Unter den Linden. The Adlon was suddenly between two fires as 'Whites' and 'Reds' engaged in violent conflict.

In the evening, when the noise of battle had died down and the broad square lay seemingly exhausted in the early dusk, a large party of Reds marched unexpectedly into the hall of the hotel. They were for the most part reckless-looking young men, some in civilian clothes and others in tattered uniforms. They all wore broad red arm-bands on their left arms.

Louis Adlon went to meet them and asked them what they wanted.

Their leader flourished a crumpled scrap of paper.

'By Order of the Soldiers' Committee. All your food is requisitioned.'

By way of underlining the authority of this 'order', the revolutionaries flourished their weapons in the faces of Louis Adlon and the other leading members of the staff who were present. It was clearly useless to invoke the Law in the face of so many rifles and hand-grenades, and so they were shown into the kitchen.

Fortunately the head wine-waiter, who had been present when they arrived, had very quickly summed up the situation in so far as it affected him. He feared for his bottles, of which there were something like a million laid down in the cellar, feeling instinctively that the whole future of the house might depend on this valuable property. The cellar doors were swiftly locked and so skilfully hidden with pieces of furniture that they went unnoticed.

In the meantime a scene was being played in the kitchen so grotesque in its nature that no writer of comedies would have been able to improve on it.

Scarcely had the Reds begun to clear out the larders, the cold-rooms and the store-rooms, than one of their sentries, posted at the kitchen door, gave the alarm:

'Watch out! Enemy troops approaching!'

A body of Republican soldiers appeared at the big doorway. Unlike the revolutionaries, they were all correctly clad in uniform. They belonged to one of the Freikorps. At their head was a young lieutenant with a service revolver in his hand.

With great presence of mind Louis Adlon went up to him to restrain him from any act of violence. The lieutenant extended his left hand, in which there was a scrap of paper.

'By order of the Republican Military Command. Your food is requisitioned for the security forces.'

There was an instant cry from the revolutionaries—'Traitors! Betrayers of the working-class!'

And from the men of the Freikorps came the answer—'Spartacist louts! Looters!'

Rifles were raised on both side, while the terrified kitchen staff made hastily for the exits. In this highly critical situation Louis Adlon acted as arbiter.

'Gentlemen,' he said with a masterly composure, 'if you begin shooting nobody will get anything. Since both sides have Requisition Orders it is clear that everything is legal. All you have to do is to share and share alike—there's plenty for everyone.'

These words sufficed. Both sides could appreciate the force of the argument. After a rapid discussion the division of the spoils began.

'A basket of eggs for the Whites, a basket of eggs for the Reds. A pot of jam for the Reds, a pot of jam for the Whites . . .'

The matter was thus settled to the satisfaction of both parties, and Louis Adlon and the hotel staff could breathe again. The soldiers of the Revolution departed with their share of the swag by way of the tradesmen's entrance, while the Freikorps lieutenant led his men out by the front door.

A few days later, when quiet had been temporarily restored to Unter den Linden, the young lieutenant of the Freikorps returned to the Adlon in strange circumstances. He was soon afterwards promoted to the honorary rank of 'house officer' and remained billeted in the hotel for a considerable time.

All this was directly connected with a curious individual, a Count, who came to the hotel one evening to reserve 'a few rooms'. The Count was well known to our chief reception-clerk, having often stopped at the Adlon before the war. A member of that circle of society which never allowed itself to be bored, he was to be seen at all the race-meetings, and his name had figured constantly in the society columns of the newspapers.

This gentleman, then, had himself taken up the first floor, inspected a number of suites and finally took six rooms, only one of which was to be a bedroom, with bath, the others being reception and conference rooms. Our receptionist was somewhat astonished at this, but the Count had a ready explanation:

'I always feel so lonely in the evenings. Everything's so unsettled nowadays. I like to be able to ask a few people in now and then, just to take my mind off things.'

He then got out his wallet, produced a thick bundle of notes, and paid a month's rent in advance for all six rooms. Before going away he gave notice that he would be returning at about eleven, but that his guests would not be coming until midnight, and were to be shown straight up to his suite.

At eleven o'clock he was back again, bringing with him, rather to the concern of the reception officer, a number of strange-looking individuals whom he described as his 'indoor servants'. And when, shortly after this, the Freikorps lieutenant turned up with fifteen soldiers, all armed to the teeth, the reception-clerk began to feel decidedly uneasy.

The Count did his best to reassure him.

'No need to worry,' he said airily. 'Just a little philosophical discussion—Socrates, Plato, Schopenhauer and such like. We don't want to be disturbed, that's all.'

He then went upstairs with his 'indoor servants' and his body-guard. The soldiers took up their posts outside his doors, or else seated themselves in the armchairs that were to be found in the corridor; but the indoor servants carried large baskets into the suite, regarding which it was apparent that their contents were cold meat and bottled beer.

The guests, who soon appeared in large numbers, at first only asked for ice and soda-water, but later called for wine, brandy, and champagne. But the waiters who brought these were not allowed into the rooms. They had to hand them at the door to the indoor servants.

The management became increasingly perturbed. The most obvious explanation was that this was some sort of political conspiracy, which could be very dangerous for the hotel, since affairs in Berlin were still in a highly critical state.

The Count's guests continued to arrive until three o'clock in the morning. For the most part they were men, but there were a few women among them. They were taken up to the first floor by the hotel servants. The lieutenant then informed the Count of their arrival, and he came out, greeted them warmly, and escorted them into his suite. Not until seven in the morning did the company depart—that is to say, the guests, the 'indoor servants' and the lieutenant with his men. The Count went to bed.

A sigh of relief went up in the hotel when in the course of the day the answer to the riddle was discovered. The Adlon waiters learnt it from the waiters at the Restaurant Hiller.

It seemed that the police had closed the elegant gambling club which had its premises above the restaurant. There had been a complaint about the infringement of food regulations. So the proprietor of the club, the Count, had moved his entire establishment over to the Adlon; and being afraid that he might be disturbed by Spartacist troops he had paid the Freikorps lieutenant and his men a high price to protect him.

The games of baccarat went on uninterrupted for about a fortnight, before the hotel management, by passing on hints of imminent police action, were able to persuade the Count to give up his suite and take his guests elsewhere. His departure was mourned principally by the young Freikorps lieutenant, who said sadly that he had been getting a thousand marks a night for the job.

'I was even thinking of approaching the Count in the matter of an old-age pension,' he said. 'Ah, well. I shall have to look out for something else, that's all.'

The 'something else' which the lieutenant hoped for was not long in coming.

Shortly before Christmas in that eventful year of 1918 a gentleman came to stop at the hotel who gave his name as Baron Winterfeld. He was a tall, thin man with black hair and an imperial beard, reserved in manner and apparently well-to-do.

His luggage consisted of a few suitcases and an exceptionally large cabin-trunk which he caused to be immediately taken up to his suite on the first floor, under his personal supervision.

Baron Winterfeld received no mail except on the day after his arrival, when the special-delivery postman[1] brought him a single letter.

At this time Lorenz and Louis Adlon were in a state of some perturbation owing to a very curious letter which Lorenz had received. It ran as follows:

'The Spartacists intend to overthrow the present Government on the 4th January 1919, and to occupy all the leading banks, including the Post Office Savings Bank. If you do not wish to lose your money you should instruct your bank to send you cash, by special delivery, for the amount standing to your credit. It is in your own interest to keep this information strictly secret.'

The letter was signed: 'A Business Acquaintance who, for obvious reasons, desires to remain anonymous.'

Similar letters had been received by a number of well-to-do people, some of whom, being guests at the hotel, discussed the matter with Lorenz Adlon. Many considered that the whole thing was simply a shabby manœuvre designed to embarrass the Government.

A copy of the letter was published in the newspaper *BZ am Mittag*, with an editorial comment which suggested, among other things, that it might be the work of criminals who intended to assault and rob the special-delivery postmen. According to this report the letters had only been received by persons living in the 8th, 9th and 68th postal districts.

Most people, however, did not share the paper's views. There was a general conviction that the Spartacists did indeed intend to try to overthrow the Government by violence on the 4th January. This belief was supported by the fact that the extremists were everywhere being organized in armed groups which were causing an increasing amount of disorder.

In the bar that evening the two Adlons saw a young man in

[1] *Geldbriefträger*—lit. 'money-postman'. Trs. note.

Welcoming Smiles
LAVAL AND BRIAND ON THE BALCONY OF THE ADLON, 1931

Tables in Waiting

The Proof of the Pudding

civilian clothes whose face seemed familiar. He was sitting on a high stool telling the bar-tender war-stories, and after a second glance at him Louis Adlon recognized the Freikorps lieutenant. He greeted him and, in view of that ominous letter, asked him whether it would not be possible for him to come back to the hotel for a few days with his 'security squad'.

The young man said in his light-hearted fashion that, much as he would have liked to do so, this was impossible.

'We're under orders to be in a state of readiness as from midnight tonight. We're rather expecting a spot of bother with our political competitors in the course of the next few days—a small private war, so to speak. I'm sorry.'

New Year's Eve arrived.

The lieutenant, who dropped into the Adlon bar whenever he could spare the time and had become very friendly with the barman, had promised to ring him up directly there was any trouble. But he told him that, contrary to expectation, an armistice had been declared for New Year's Eve, because both sides wanted to celebrate.

The barman, recalling Louis Adlon's suggestion, asked him whether he would care to bring along a party of his men and celebrate at the hotel, and to this the lieutenant promptly agreed.

He turned up that evening with his men and a suitcase. There were scarcely a hundred visitors stopping in the hotel at the time, and so he was shown up to a room and invited to make use of it as the guest of the management. This gave him great pleasure. Half an hour later he came down to the bar in immaculate evening dress, with medals. He clapped his friend, the barman, on the shoulder and said:

'Pretty natty, don't you think? I bought it out of my gamblers' protection money.'

The soldiers were evidently pleased with their elegant commander. He installed them in the messengers' room, where they made themselves at home, grateful for warmth, food and drink. But parties of four took it in turns to mount guard in the hall, fully armed and wearing their steel helmets. This, as it turned out,

G

had its advantages. At a little before midnight a party of Spartacists tried to force their way in, but promptly withdrew at the
sight of the guard.

It must be said that it was a most dismal New Year's Eve.
Naturally there was music, and it goes without saying that the
cooking was as good as it could be. The interior of the hotel was
as brilliantly lighted as ever, for we had our own generating plant.
But our guests were not a party. There were very few of the old
habitués, and such as appeared were all personal friends, living in
Berlin, who had come to celebrate with us.

The rest were the 'new people'. I do not mean revolutionaries
or political leaders, but the new rich. Certainly their evening dress
left nothing to be desired; their ladies came arrayed in costly
furs, and they had learnt the use of lobster-crackers and oyster-
forks. But they bore themselves differently at table. I do not say
worse, but differently. They talked differently to their women,
and their way of treating the waiters was not such as our people
were accustomed to.

After dinner there was dancing, and at midnight everyone
pulled crackers! This was something new in the history of the
Adlon, as were the paper streamers and the confetti scattered over
the carpets. But amid all this frivolity everyone seemed to be
listening with half an ear for the sound of shooting outside.

Long after midnight the lieutenant came into the bar to drink
a New Year's toast with his friend the barman.

'You'll need good luck more than I will,' the barman said.

The lieutenant shrugged his shoulders. He exchanged greetings
with one or two gentlemen at the bar, and then his eye fell upon
a man in a dark lounge suit—a conspicuous figure because all
the other men were in long evening-coats or dinner-jackets. He
had a black beard and seemed to be taking no part in the jollifica-
tion.

'Who's that?' asked the lieutenant.

The barman had to make inquiries before he could answer the
question. He then said that the gentleman was a Baron Winterfeld, who was stopping in the hotel.

'A sinister-looking cove,' said the lieutenant. 'He looks to me like something out of Dostoievsky.'

The barman laughed.

'I've read some of Dostoievsky's novels. They're pretty gloomy, aren't they?—all crime and murder.'

'Yes,' said the lieutenant. 'And you'll have trouble with your Baron Dostoievsky, you mark my words!'

The barman forgot them at the time, but he had cause to remember them later.

On New Year's Day the lieutenant departed with his men, and on the following day the struggle began between the Freikorps and the Spartacists.

Shots were sounding in Unter den Linden as the special-delivery postman, whose name was Lange, entered the Adlon.

Postman Lange was a well-known figure in the hotel. He was aged about fifty, lived in the Paulstrasse, and for the past ten years had been delivering the specially registered letters, containing money, that were distributed from Post Office W 8. He was accustomed to have a chat with the hall-porter when he entered, after which the persons for whom he had letters were notified by telephone. As a rule they came down to the lobby to collect them.

On this morning he told the porter that he had a letter for Baron Winterfeld.

'I'll fetch him down,' said the hall-porter, but Lange protested.

'I know the Baron already. I had a letter for him once before, and I took it upstairs to him. Do you know what he gave me? Some cigars and a packet of ham-sandwiches. It was a nice surprise for the missus and kid, seeing the way rationing is at present. So you give him a ring and say I'm coming up.'

'You'd do better to wait for him down here,' said the hall-porter, grinning. 'You know what it said in the *BZ am Mittag* about special-delivery letters. He might cut your throat!'

At this moment there was a burst of machine-gun fire immediately outside the hotel. The street-fighting had begun in earnest.

Postman Lange went up to the first floor to deliver Baron

Winterfeld's letter, his mind occupied with thoughts of cigars and ham-sandwiches.

On that day the Adlon entirely lost its normal aspect. The whole town seemed to be in a state of uproar. The lieutenant had rung up the bar early in the morning to warn everyone to stay indoors because it looked as though things were going to get lively. He also particularly asked the barman to lock up his bottles, so that their contents might not be drunk by persons holding the wrong political opinions.

Only half the hotel-staff reported for duty, because the Spartacists had immobilized all forms of transport. There were placards at every street corner calling for a General Strike. Even people living close to the hotel were unable to reach it owing to the barbed-wire entanglements, road-blocks and machine-gun nests that had sprung up everywhere.

At midday the lieutenant again rang up the barman and in a rather hoarse voice exhorted him to stand firm. He asked how things were going on Unter den Linden and complained of feeling thirsty.

At about the same time Post Office W 8 rang up the Adlon to ask at what time Postman Lange had entered the hotel. They were told, 'At about ten.' But when they asked when he had left the hall-porter could give no definite answer.

Owing to the general confusion a misunderstanding arose. One of the clerks at the reception-desk said that he thought Lange had left at about 10.30. This was later found to be a mistake. In any event, late that afternoon two police officers visited the hotel.

By the time they arrived, however, the hall-porter who had spoken to Lange was no longer there, having gone off duty. As ill-luck would have it, he did not come at all the next day, being prevented from doing so by the street-fighting. Thus it happened that the name of Baron Winterfeld was not mentioned.

While the police officers were pursuing their investigations in the hotel, to the sound of machine-gun bursts and exploding hand-grenades, an official from the Berlin Central Post Office came in search of them. It had been established that Lange had had an enormous sum of money on him, no fewer than forty-one special-delivery letters whose contents amounted to over 270,000 marks in thousand-mark notes. Those anonymous letters, which later came to be known as the 'Spartacist letters', had done their work well.

Who was the person at the Adlon to whom Lange had to deliver a letter? This could not at once be discovered immediately owing to the failure of the telephone. Nor could the police officers or the Post Office official leave the building. The Spartacists, who had barricaded themselves in the Kaffee Viktoria, where they had set up a strongpoint manned by sailors, were shooting at anyone who showed himself on Unter den Linden.

To crown everything, the police officers later received a most alarming piece of news. An officer who managed to reach the Adlon under cover of darkness told them that police headquarters, on the Alexanderplatz, was being besieged by the Spartacists.

By the morning of the 3rd January the Adlon was in No Man's Land. The Government troops only had a secure hold of the western districts of Berlin, and the situation along the Wilhelmstrasse was constantly changing. The part of Unter den Linden on which the hotel stood had become neutral territory, shot over by both sides.

This was why the hall-porter who had sent Postman Lange up to Baron Winterfeld was unable to come to work, and it also explains why the police officers were marooned in the building, entirely cut off from the outside world. As I was told later, not a single chamber-maid belonging to the first floor came on duty that day. There were also very few waiters because a waiters' strike had been declared and armed pickets were posted outside the hotel.

The police officers, in short, had a difficult task. But they did their best. They painstakingly examined every available person who had been in the building the previous day, among others the hotel barber.

It was no doubt owing to the general disorder that the barber had heard nothing about the presence of police in the hotel, on the previous day, or the search for the missing postman. Directly the question was put to him he supplied the clue that had been lacking. He had seen Lange the previous morning going into the suite which was generally occupied by Herr Heinicke, the managing director of the Norddeutscher Lloyd Steamship Company.

The police hurried upstairs. The door of the suite was locked, and the key had not been left at the desk. A master-key was hastily produced, and when they cautiously entered they saw an appalling sight.

The dead body of the unfortunate postman was seated in a chair to which he had been lashed with ropes. He had a thick cord tied tightly round his throat, a bath-towel wrapped round his head and a gag, made of a face-towel, in his mouth. There was nothing to be done, where he was concerned, except to take note of the fact that death had been caused by strangulation.

The contents of his mail-bag were all gone. In the bedroom the police found Baron Winterfeld's big cabin-trunk, standing open. It would have been quite large enough to contain the body of a good-sized man. Evidently the murderer had toyed with the idea of disposing of his victim in this way, for in the bath-tub was a great pile of papers which had probably come out of the trunk.

There was no other luggage. The occupant of the room had disappeared.

II

'The Curse of Retribution'

THE news of this terrible event spread like wildfire through the hotel, still further depressing spirits that were already low enough in all conscience. The few guests occupying rooms spent most of their time in the bar, since it afforded better protection against rifle-fire than anywhere else. They felt like prisoners, being quite unable to leave the building. Even if they had taken advantage of a lull in the fighting to cross the road, they would certainly not have been able to get out of Berlin, for all the railway-lines had been cut.

Despite the noise of fighting that resounded through the closed shutters from the Pariser Platz and the Wilhelmstrasse, the police examined the rooms occupied by the murderer with their customary thoroughness. They found nothing which afforded any clue to his identity. The man had evidently carried out his plan with great care. And owing to the state of agitation prevailing among the staff, there was no one who could give a reliable description of the so-called Baron Winterfeld.

During the afternoon there was a burst of heavy machine-gun fire from the Brandenburger Tor, and shortly afterwards the Freikorps lieutenant, who was now known to everyone in the hotel as 'our house-officer', came rushing in accompanied by about fifteen soldiers.

The men were plastered with mud, and some wore bloodstained bandages. The lieutenant raced with them right through the house, from the Unter den Linden to the Wilhelmstrasse side. Here they set up machine-guns and emptied their magazines over the Pariser Platz.

Having completed this operation he again came running

through the hotel, put his head in at the bar and shouted to his friend, the barman:

'Mix me a whisky and soda.'

He then vanished once more and presently returned with an army doctor and some hospital orderlies who brought with them instruments, dressings and stretchers. The doctor at once set up a dressing-station in one of the back rooms.

The lieutenant returned to the bar. His face was coated with dirt. He had a carbine in one hand and his belt was stuffed with hand-grenades. Propping himself against the counter, he thrust his steel helmet on to the back of his neck, grinned and said to the barman:

'Mars in person, what?'

Having drunk his whisky he gazed about him. The room was full of people, but he seemed to be looking for one in particular.

'What's become of the Baron Dostoievsky?' he asked. 'Has he started anything yet?'

The barman blinked. Until then he had forgotten the lieutenant's earlier remarks about Baron Winterfeld. He slipped out and had a word with the police officers, and one of these came unobtrusively up to the lieutenant and said:

'I understand you saw Baron Winterfeld, and that you said something about——'

But this was as far as he got. There was a renewed burst of machine-gun fire from outside. An N.C.O. rushed into the bar with a message, and the lieutenant jumped down from his stool and said cheerfully to the policeman:

'Is old man Dostoievsky offended by what I said? He can challenge me to a duel if he likes, but just now I've no time for a private fight. I've got a battle to attend to.'

Without waiting to hear any more he vanished from the bar with the N.C.O.

He never came back, anxiously though the police and everyone in the hotel awaited him. The bar-tender, who had an especial affection for him, went to great trouble to find out what had become of the gallant young man. All he could discover was that he had gone out on patrol and had not returned. Presumably the Spartacists caught him and shot him out of hand.

Within a few days Berlin was quiet again. The Government troops had suppressed the insurrection and restored order. Police headquarters was recaptured from the revolutionaries on the night of the 11th January, and by the 13th the Homicide Department was again functioning. But although the full resources of the police could now be employed, it was a very long time before the mystery of the murder was solved.

In the meantime the ghastly event lay like a shadow upon the hotel. The suite in which it occurred was renovated throughout, the furniture given away, the wallpaper torn down, the rooms rearranged. In short, everything possible was done to wash out the memory of what had happened.

The matter was not finally cleared up until several years later.

On the evening of the 31st July 1922, news was received in the Adlon that a man named Blume had been arrested in Dresden on suspicion of having murdered Postman Lange. That same evening Superintendent Gennat, of the Criminal Police, sent for the reception-clerk who had registered the so-called Baron Winterfeld and took him to Dresden. This development naturally caused intense excitement in the hotel, not only among the management and staff but also among the permanent residents, who followed events with a breathless interest.

This is what had happened.

On the morning of the 31st July a special-delivery postman entered an apartment house in the Topferstrasse, Dresden. He had to climb a great many stairs in order to deliver a letter to a tenant on the stop storey.

He was brought to a stop on one of the landings by the sight of a bank-note lying on the floor. But just as he was stooping to pick it up he caught a glimpse of a man behind him with a heavy blacksmith's hammer in his hands. The postman managed to dodge the hammer and shouted for help at the top of his voice.

Doors opened and other occupants of the house came to the

rescue. The postman's assailant was forced to take to his heels. But as he was rushing wildly down the stairs a policeman entered the house in response to cries from people on the ground floor. The man flung the hammer at him and then wounded him with a revolver shot, but before he could get away he was grabbed from behind. In the ensuing scrimmage he was thrust over the banister and fell to the bottom of the stair-well, where he lay unconscious.

By the time he recovered consciousness he was securely bound, and in this condition was handed over to the police emergency squad which arrived on the scene a few minutes later. With considerable presence of mind the man pretended to be suffering from an injury to his back, and he was therefore taken to the prison-ward of the Friedrichstadt Hospital in Dresden.

Before questioning him the Dresden police got in touch by telephone with the Homicide Department in Berlin. The departmental files contained details of two similar unsolved crimes—the murder of Postman Lange at the Adlon, and the murder of another postman, in September 1918, on the third floor of a house in the Spandauerstrasse, Berlin. The owner of this house, a certain Frau Ruhle, who had let one of her apartments to the murderer, had also been murdered by him, evidently because she had chanced to witness the murder of the postman. The Dresden police rightly concluded that their man was in all likelihood the author of all three crimes.

The rest of the story does not directly concern the Adlon, but it is perhaps worth briefly recounting because of the interest the case aroused.

Superintendent Gennat found the prisoner in bed in the hospital, guarded by two officers of the Saxony Criminal Police. He brought in the clerk from our reception-office, who at once said:

'That's him, all right!'

The clerk then formally declared that this was the man who had occupied a suite at the Adlon during the end of the year 1918 and the beginning of 1919, registering under the name of Baron Winterfeld. He had brought a very large cabin-trunk with him.

After the murder of Postman Lange, in his suite, he had left the hotel unobserved without paying his bill.

After he had testified the clerk was allowed to return to Berlin, and Superintendent Gennat proceeded to inquire into the man, Blume's, past history.

He had been born in Amsterdam in 1876. His father, a tobacco manufacturer, later moved to Berlin. The son had gone to grammar-school and passed his matriculation. He had inherited a modest fortune from his parents, but had soon abandoned his studies. He had various jobs, but was so unreliable that he never kept one for long. Moreover he constantly became involved in love-affairs with the women in the places where he worked.

The most noteworthy thing about him was that he was a would-be writer. He wrote a number of plays, among them a drama entitled 'Simili', set in a hotel in New York, in which a postman was murdered.

When the police came to visit his apartment in Lichterfelde, a Berlin suburb, they found that it was furnished with care and taste, and contained a large library of serious books.

Blume left this apartment in September 1918 to take up temporary lodging in the house in the Spandauerstrasse owned by Frau Ruhle. Here he carried out his first murders, and then, having netted a haul of two thousand marks, returned undetected to his books in Lichterfelde.

The smallness of the loot evidently prompted him to plan his next operation with greater care. He wrote the 'Spartacist letters' in order to ensure that Postman Lange should have plenty of money on him.

A member of the hotel staff who was on friendly terms with the Criminal Police was later able to procure a copy of Blume's formal statement, in which he describes in detail how he went about the Adlon murder.

Having decided that 2,000 marks was altogether too small a return for the risk he had run, his next thought was that a special-delivery postman whose round included Unter den Linden would be likely to be carrying much more money than one working in the less wealthy district of the Spandauerstrasse. But in those days there were no furnished rooms or flats to be rented on Unter den Linden. He would have to go to an hotel.

He devoted careful thought to the question of what sort of hotel he should go to. There were plenty of small, respectable establishments in the side-streets. He visited them all, inquiring after an imaginary acquaintance, and was forced to the conclusion that none was suitable for his purpose. Everything was known and everyone was noticed in a small hotel. The special-delivery-postman would be seen to enter, and questions would very quickly be asked if he did not reappear.

It had to be a big hotel. He visited the reception-halls and lounges of the Adlon and the Bristol. The latter seemed to him the more suitable of the two. There was more coming and going in its ground-floor rooms so that he could hope to slip through the crowd unnoticed after murdering the postman in his bedroom.

He fully realized that the murder must be carried out without the slightest noise, and he meticulously wrote down on a sheet of paper the various means whereby a man might be 'soundlessly' done to death. He wrote the word 'strangulation' and underlined it. He bought a length of rope and a bronze bust of Bismarck, and practised the art of lassooing, surrounded by his bookshelves containing the cream of the world's literature, and perhaps—who knows?—with a volume of Dostoievsky open on the table.

One December morning he saw a classified advertisement in the paper to the effect that a gentleman in the Brandenburgerstrasse had a large cabin-trunk for sale. He bought it for 157 marks, and also a couple of small suitcases. He filled the trunk with bags of sand, and packing his linen and a second suit in the suitcases, he drove with his luggage from Berlin to Velten—a small town northwest of Berlin. There he took the train back to Berlin and deposited the luggage in the cloakroom at the Stettiner Bahnhof. He drove in a cab from the station to the Bristol, registered as 'Baron Gassen, from Stettin' and handed the cloakroom-tickets to the porter.

Then he sat in his room waiting for his luggage. But when at length it was brought up to him something happened which caused him to leave the Bristol the next day, although he had arranged for a letter to be sent to him at the hotel two days later. The hotel servants told him that during the journey from the station to the hotel the cabin-trunk had burst open. It had been found to contain nothing but bags of sand. They had got the trunk shut again, but, said the messenger, with formal apologies, some of the bags had been damaged and part of the contents lost.

This was something Herr Blume had not foreseen.

'Fear overwhelmed me,' he said in his statement. 'My mind was by no means clear. My imagination so ran away with me that for a moment I almost believed I had already committed the murder and was on the verge of being detected. However, I regained my self-control. I tipped the men generously and said with a laugh, "I can assure you that isn't sand. It's a chemical compound of some value." But I could see from their expressions that they did not believe me. I had to leave the hotel at once.'

The next morning he telephoned the lottery-agent from whom he had bought a ticket in the Prussian State Lottery which was to be posted to him at the Bristol. Fortunately the letter had not yet been posted, otherwise the hotel might have forwarded it to Stettin, where nothing would be known of Baron Gassen. A trail might thus have been laid which could have proved fatal to him.

Changing his name to Baron Winterfeld he moved with his luggage to the Adlon.

With the very large sum of money which he acquired by the Adlon murder, Blume went first to Hamburg, where he exchanged marks for sterling on the black market, and then to London, where he set up in business as a bookseller.

But luck was not with him, and finally, having run through the money, he returned to Germany and planned his third crime, changing his scene of operations from Berlin to Dresden. This time he was not as clever, or as fortunate, as he had been on the previous occasions.

Superintendent Gennat, who had charge of the case, was a very experienced officer whom almost nothing could surprise; but there were aspects of the Blume story which astonished him very much.

After committing the Adlon murder Blume had written a gay and elegant comedy which was successfully produced in Dresden in May 1922, at the Neustädter Theatre. He did so under the name of Eilers. And shortly before the piece opened he submitted another play to the management of the theatre, with the title, 'The Curse of Retribution'. The plot of this play—and it was this that so startled Gennat—centred round the murder of the postman in the Adlon. The event was depicted in full detail, exactly as it happened. Then the play went on to show how retribution overtook the murderer, who ended on the scaffold.

Superintendent Gennat went to Blume with the manuscript and said:

'You really did write this, didn't you?'

The author looked up proudly.

'Have you read it? Isn't it a wonderful play? All I hope is that it will be put on before my execution. If it is a success I shall feel that I have not lived in vain.'

Hardened though he was, the superintendent was so flabbergasted by this that he could find nothing to say. He said afterwards that he had never got out of a prison-cell so quickly.

Blume managed to commit suicide before the trial by opening his veins with a smuggled razor-blade. The story was front-page news for days on end; but to the Adlon it meant that at last the memory of that most grisly event could be buried.

12

Hugo Stinnes, Karl Radek,
the Goose-dripping and the Cat-burglar

BUT I must go back to that turbulent year of 1919, during which so many remarkable things happened in our hotel.

Although life in Berlin became somewhat quieter, conditions were still far from normal. For a long time certain streets and quarters of the town remained closed, and could only be entered with a special permit.

The most important of these was the area of Government offices, which included the Wilhelmstrasse, Unter den Linden, the Pariser Platz and the Brandenburger Tor. And right in the middle of this 'closed quarter' stood the Adlon. It was regarded as a 'strategic point of the highest importance', and was very often visited by the police in consequence.

There was little to be bought in those days. All the necessities of life were in short supply and extremely dear. Because of this strikes were of almost daily occurrence. The extremists particularly advocated stoppages of work affecting the public services, so that electricity, gas and water were cut off for long periods. Oil-burning lamps and cookers, and even candles, were brought back into use in private households, just as happened during the Second World War, and there were often queues of people waiting to get water at the public drinking-fountains which were still a feature of the Berlin streets.

At these times the Adlon was the resort of everyone who could get to the hotel, irrespective of nationality, age or social standing. Lorenz Adlon, when he built it, had attached great importance to having his own artesian wells. The house was therefore unaffected by any failure in the city's water-supply, a state of affairs which

95

was always of great value during hot, dry summers. People said: 'At the Adlon it isn't only the waiters who come running—so does the water!'

The hotel also had its own generating plant, as I have already mentioned. Our voltage differed from that of the municipality, being 110 volts, which meant that our electric light bulbs had to be specially ordered. But it had the advantage that in times of shortage we were less likely to be robbed by 'souvenir hunters'.

A hotel in which light and water never failed, and which could even produce ice, was in those days something of a sensation. It is no wonder that the Adlon never lacked custom.

In the matter of guests the hotel's policy had always been one of great exclusiveness, and this was the guiding principle in later years. But at that time we could not pick and choose. Life had suddenly become too disorderly, and its turbulence showed itself in the character of the guests, their habits, their callings and the many objectives which they pursued or were driven to pursue.

They were a strangely contrasting lot. But although the outward appearances were so different, in one respect the hotel retained its former character. Even in those hard times the big reception hall, the lounges, public rooms and kitchens, all presented a picture of cosmopolitan life. English, French and Italian names were to be seen in the visitors' book. German diplomats of the old school still frequented the hotel, together with the leaders of the young Republic, who were having to fight hard for international recognition. And members of the former Russian aristocracy, now living in Berlin in very altered circumstances, rubbed shoulders with the representatives of Soviet Russia, when these came from their Embassy, at No. 11 Unter den Linden, to confer informally with the representatives of other countries.

The Adlon was neutral ground. People met here between the different fronts, to talk and to spy, to exchange a handshake, to make contacts and tentative approaches. Many opportunists also came, seeking to profit by the state of universal insecurity, and many adventurers who in more normal times would have been speedily exposed.

During 1919 there was a cat-burglar at work in Berlin who constantly attracted notice both by his expertness and by the discrimination with which he selected his victims. He burgled only the wealthier private houses, and nearly always got away with valuable jewellery

But where he did not find what he had come for he was accustomed to revenge himself in a peculiarly unpleasant manner. This happened in the case of a banker in the Tiergartenstrasse. Finding nothing worth taking, the burglar in his resentment slashed several valuable paintings and the Gobelin upholstery of several chairs. On the other hand, it seemed that he never disturbed a sleeping woman in her bed. If she showed signs of waking he would creep silently away.

His exploits were much talked about. Legends grew up around him and later a novel was written about him. Many people claimed to have seen him, wearing a mask and black silk tights, but none could offer any clue to his identity. The police were baffled, and Berlin, always noted for its sarcasm, was full of jokes about their unsuccess and the burglar's chivalry towards women. One night he paid the Adlon a visit.

Two days previously a small man of unimpressive appearance had come to the hotel and engaged a suite for his wife and himself. After allotting him one on the first floor, on the Unter den Linden side, the head reception-clerk glanced at the signature in the visitor's book and then looked with a particular interest at the new arrival's knobbly head, his stiffly brushed hair and black, pointed beard. The gentleman seemed unconscious of his gaze. There was no change in the expression of his sallow-skinned face as he went with his wife to the lift.

The receptionist past the book to his colleague at the desk, who read:

'Hugo Stinnes. Mülheim/Ruhr, Schlossstrasse 50.'

H

He was at that time the greatest industrialist, and one of the greatest powers, in Germany.

'He must have come to Berlin in connection with the Peace Treaty,' the receptionist said, and went to tell Louis Adlon the news of his arrival. Hugo Stinnes always stayed at the Adlon when he came to Berlin, but since he never showed himself in the restaurant or the lounges, very few members of the staff knew him by sight. He spent his time holding conferences in his suite or working alone until late at night.

He was much in the news in those days, and his prestige with the public was very great. It was said that his industrial empire was composed of sixty separate concerns. He nevertheless lived a spartan life in the hotel, and his public manner was quite unassuming. But he had about him the air of a man of the great world, and was highly respected by those of the staff who came in contact with him, although not for the size of his tips. I well remember the excitement when, in 1923, at the height of the inflation, he at length doubled his strictly calculated scale of tipping. The cost of living, reckoned in marks, had then risen ten-thousand-fold or more. Louis Adlon said:

'Hugo Stinnes has now recognized the inflation!'

It was Louis Adlon's custom to welcome the more distinguished guests personally, but Stinnes' foibles were naturally respected. So Louis did not go to see him when he arrived but waited for an opportunity of meeting him. It came more quickly than he expected, and in a very different fashion.

Shortly after getting up in the morning Hugo Stinnes missed his gold pocket-watch, which he was accustomed to put on the bedside table. He called to his wife, in the next room, to ask if she had seen it.

Frau Stinnes was one of those wives who look after their husbands' things themselves, without the aid of servants. She was used to questions of this sort, knowing his absent-mindedness and absorption in his work. After searching her own room, without finding the watch, she came into her husband's room, where Herr Stinnes was engaged in putting a stud in his shirt. She glanced at the table in the middle of the room and at once perceived that something else was missing—an aluminium butter-dish with a lid. It must be remembered that in those days butter and other fats were a luxury not easy to come by, and it was not unusual for travellers to carry a supply with them. She had herself filled the dish and packed it before they left Mülheim. So her first question was not about the watch but about what was, to her, even more valuable.

'Where's the butter-dish, Hugo? Did you have something more to eat last night?'

Hugo Stinnes absently shook his head and said:

'Where are my cuff-links?'

These, too, were not to be found, and now they began to suspect that something was wrong. While Stinnes opened his suitcases and the drawers in his room, his wife ran back into her own room and looked in her jewel-case. Her jewels were gone. But this was not all. In addition to the jewels, the gold watch and the cuff-links, the thief had taken Hugo Stinnes' wallet and even his cheque-books.

There was nothing to indicate how the thief had entered. The door of the suite had been locked on the inside. Herr Stinnes at once telephoned the hotel-manager, who came running upstairs. After a cursory examination he felt sure that it was the work of the cat-burglar.

The police were at once notified, but at that time nothing was simple. Police headquarters had only recently been freed from the Spartacists and was still in a state of considerable disorder. Some time elapsed before the call was answered.

Louis Adlon took advantage of the interval to pay Herr Stinnes a visit of condolence, and also to tell him something of the difficulties by which hotel managements were beset in those days. Hugo Stinnes listened in silence, tugging at his beard. Finally he produced a list of the stolen objects which he had already prepared. He valued the jewellery at 50,000 gold marks. The last object on the list was an aluminium butter-dish.

Louis Adlon contemplated this final item with interest.

'Quite worth taking,' he remarked, 'if there was butter in it.'

'It wasn't butter,' said Herr Stinnes. 'It was goose-dripping. My wife ran it off herself.' He then walked a few paces, still tugging at his beard, and turned round with a deprecating smile. 'The man took all my small change. I haven't even the money for a tip. I shall have to borrow from you, Herr Adlon.'

Another hour went by before two police officers entered the hotel and presented their credentials. They had come on foot from the Alexanderplatz, and had been forced by the roadblocks to make numerous detours. They asked first to be shown the visitors' list and inquired if there were any residents in the hotel whom the management could not vouch for. The manager replied, shrugging his shoulders, that in these days things were not what they had been.

They studied the list, and one of them asked:

'Countess Kleinmichel—who's she?'

'A former lady-in-waiting to the Czarina who stayed here several times before the war. She managed to save a good deal of her own jewellery and in any case can scarcely be suspected.'

They made no comment but continued to pore over the list. The senior of the two officers, who had introduced himself as Müller, presently pointed to the name of Countess Hetta Treuberg.

The manager smiled.

'The "red" Countess!' he said. 'But she isn't here any more.'

'Where did she go?'

'I'm afraid I don't know.'

When they had finished with the list the manager took Inspector Müller up to the first floor.

Frau Stinnes received them in her room and once again declared that the doors had been locked. Her window had also been closed, but her husband was in the habit of sleeping with his window open. The cat-burglar had evidently taken advantage of this. It now seemed certain that it was he who had broken in and carried out the robbery.

His task had been made easier by the fact that all the rooms on the first floor of the Adlon had balconies and french windows. This had an important bearing on the situation and on the events that followed. The ground floor of the Adlon had big bay-windows starting a few feet above ground-level and running up to the first floor. The Unter den Linden façade was broken by the main entrance, which had stone pillars with lanterns on either side of it and above them a stone breastwork. On the Pariser Platz side the central window was also flanked by stone pillars. On both fronts these pillars supported the middle section of a balcony that ran round the entire house at the first-floor level.

Inspector Müller went out on to the balcony looking for indications that someone had climbed over the wrought-iron railing. But the thief had left no traces of any kind. It was evident that he had got up by way of one of the pillars flanking the main entrance, which would have brought him directly outside the suite occupied by Herr and Frau Stinnes.

'Have any other thefts been reported?' the detective asked.

'No,' said the manager, startled. 'Why should there be any?'

'It would have been a simple matter for the thief to walk along the balcony looking for another open window.'

The inspector himself did so, going as far as the corner of the Pariser Platz before the manager persuaded him to turn back in order not to disturb the guests. In the event, no other thefts were reported.

The two men returned to the ground floor, and the inspector again studied the visitors' list. He had a remarkable flair for people and names in an hotel, and knew instinctively what to look for.

'Who's in the room above the middle window on the Pariser Platz side?'

'A Swedish industrialist and his wife, from Stockholm.'

The inspector muttered something under his breath and then went outside to look at the Pariser Platz and Unter den Linden façades. But there was not much to be gathered from these, for the building had been badly pitted by the shooting on the Pariser Platz and round the Brandenburger Tor.

There seemed to be no end to the excitements of that morning. Scarcely had the police officers left than the tranquillity of the reception hall was disturbed by sounds of loud commotion at the main entrance. Two soldiers appeared wearing steel helmets and white armbands and carrying rifles. They were clutching a civilian of very dishevelled appearance. The chief reception-clerk hurried towards this group, then suddenly stopped and exclaimed:

'Count Oppersdorf!'

His cry had its effect upon the soldiers, who relaxed their grip, and the civilian took advantage of this to wrench himself free.

'You see,' he said grimly, 'I'm known in this place. I really am Count Oppersdorf!'

An officer now entered the hall, and while the soldiers stood gazing in awe at their elegant surroundings he curtly explained the situation. There had that day been a march of Government troops through Berlin, designed to inspire confidence in the population and to have the reverse effect upon the Spartacists. But the Spartacists had refused to be impressed. There were clashes, and Government soldiers had taken a number of prisoners, of whom Graf Oppersdorf was one. He lived in the Roonstrasse, near the Reichstag, and had come in contact with the troops while on his way to the Adlon, where he had an appointment for lunch.

Since the change of régime in 1918 Count Oppersdorf had taken to wearing a red rosette in his buttonhole, and it was this that had got him into trouble. When he had tried to pass through the ranks at the corner of the Neue Wilhelmstrasse and the Dorotheenstrasse it had been thought that he was deliberately causing a disturbance. He had no identification papers on him, and his name and title had merely aroused mistrust. He had therefore asked to be taken to the Adlon, where he could be identified.

Having explained his side of the matter, the officer said tersely:

'I am Lieutenant Berwitz of the Reichstag Detachment. Are you prepared to identify this man as Count Oppersdorf.'

The reception-clerk said that he was, and he confirmed that the Count had an appointment at the hotel for lunch. In the meantime the Count, still looking rather ruffled, had drawn near to the group, composed of the officer and the receptionists. Ignoring him completely, Lieutenant Berwitz said:

'I must ask one more question. Who invited the Count to lunch?'

The clerk hesitated, glancing towards the Count, who nodded. He then said:

'He was to have lunched with Baroness Dosch and Countess Hetta Treuberg.'

The lieutenant's eyes seemed to flicker as he heard the name of Treuberg. He at once repeated the question that had already been asked by the police officers.

'Is the Countess staying here?'

'No, she has left.'

'Where has she gone?'

'That is not known to us.'

The lieutenant asked to be allowed to see the record of her entry and departure.

At this moment our house-physician, Dr. Küttner, came into the hall. As usual, he walked up to the desk and asked if anyone was ill, uttering his usual lamentation when told that there was no one for him to attend to. On this occasion, however, he was accompanied by a journalist, a certain Dr. von Nagel, the Berlin correspondent of the *Magdeburgische Zeitung*, who was a regular visitor to the Adlon. Nagel listened, smiling, to the familiar dialogue between the doctor and the reception-clerk, but pricked up his ears when, after an exchange of flippancies, the clerk said confidentially:

'You should have been here last night, doctor. You might have met the cat-burglar.'

'Why?' asked the doctor. 'Is he ill? . . . Well, then, I'm not interested. He's Nagel's business, not mine.'

'He robbed Stinnes, did he?' said Nagel. 'That's certainly interesting. What did he get away with?'

He was shown the list of articles, and when he came to the butter-dish he laughed aloud.

'You see, my dear Küttner, how simply the rich live!'

'And keep healthy on it, apparently,' said the doctor. 'Well, you might at least give me a cigarette.'

Tobacco was scarce and expensive in those days, but the exigencies of his calling made it necessary for Nagel to be well supplied. He got out a silver cigarette-case the size of a wallet, very flat and of beautiful workmanship. It had a coat-of-arms engraved on it. He offered it to the doctor, who took the whole case from him with a grin, put one cigarette in his mouth and another in his waistcoat pocket, and then suddenly stared at two lines that were engraved on the inside of the case: he read them aloud:

Borussia,[1] *I belong to thee when living and when dead;*
For life I swear allegiance to thy flag of white and red.

Nagel snatched back the case with a gesture of annoyance, and at the same moment a rasping voice said:

'Excuse me . . .'

Lieutenant Berwitz had been standing unobserved near the reception counter. At the end of the counter was a large, square marble pillar beside which stood a small desk, used by visitors when filling in their registration forms. The lieutenant had unobtrusively taken up his position here to await the arrival of Countess Hetta Treuberg. Of the two ladies who had arranged to meet Graf Oppersdorf for lunch at the hotel only the Baroness Dosch had arrived, and for some minutes past she had been seated in the grillroom with the Baron. The lieutenant, however, appeared to take no interest in her.

'Excuse me. My name is Berwitz. Is that the Halle branch of Borussia?'

Dr. von Nagel made a brief bow and said coldly, 'No—Breslau.' He turned back to Dr. Küttner, but as he did so the police officers re-entered the hall and Inspector Müller said urgently to the head reception-clerk:

'I must have a word with the Swedish industrialist. It's still

---

[1] *Borussia*—old German name for Prussia, from which the English word is derived. 'Borussia' was a students' patriotic league with branches all over Prussia.

possible that the cat-burglar got up by the pillar under his balcony. He may have seen or heard something.'

In any hotel it is a bad thing for the guests to be troubled un-
necessarily. The strict rule at the Adlon was that no guest should
ever be wakened or in any way disturbed except at his own
request. The reception-clerk hesitated, caught in a dilemma between regulations, on the one hand, and his desire to help the
police on the other. Then the presence of Dr. Küttner gave him
an idea.

'Doctor, will you do us a favour? Go up and call on the Swedish
gentleman. A visit from the hotel doctor would be nothing out of
the way, and you may perhaps discover something. If necessary
the inspector can go up later, after you've broken the ice.'

'Very well,' said the doctor, 'although the man's certain to be
in perfect health.'

Herr von Nagel was thus left alone. The lieutenant again spoke
to him, and presently they went and sat together at a table.

When the doctor returned, half an hour later, he was all smiles.

'He gave me some "Johnny Walker",' he said. 'I haven't tasted
whisky like that for years!'

'What did he say?' asked the inspector sharply. 'Did you notice
anything?'

'Nothing special,' said the doctor. 'He wasn't ill, either. I only
strapped up his hand.'

'You did? What was the matter with his hand?'

'Nothing worth mentioning. It was a bit swollen, that's all. He
said he'd had a slight accident.'

The inspector ignored this. He was quivering like a hound on
the scent.

'A swollen hand might mean anything! I shall go up.'

He did so, and presently returned in triumph.

'It's just as I thought. The burglar visited his room as well last
night.'

'What!' exclaimed the doctor. 'He never said a word to me
about it.'

'No. The lady with him is not his wife.'

The hotel-manager, who had come to the reception counter in the interval, hastily intervened to say that the lady had been registered as the Swedish gentleman's wife, and that this was all that concerned the hotel.

'Quite so,' said the detective. 'But it's the reason why he didn't say anything. He didn't want to be involved in a police inquiry. He wasn't robbed, in any case.'

The Swede, it seemed, was something of a boxer. Being aroused in the night, and seeing a shadowy figure in his room, he had leapt out of bed and fallen upon the intruder. He did so much damage that the burglar was forced to make his escape by leaping over the balcony railing down to the pavement below.

Herr von Nagel, having finished his conversation with the lieutenant, had returned to listen to the inspector's story.

'Good God!' he exclaimed. 'That's a long drop! Surely he must have injured himself. Aren't there any traces on the pavement?'

'None at all. I'm having the hospitals called to see if they've taken in a casualty-ward patient with a bruised face and broken bones.'

But the telephone-calls produced no result. Berlin was still in a state of great disorder. Not all the hospitals could be reached by telephone, and those that did reply were so full of casualties from the street fighting that they could not tell one from another. The inspector decided to go himself to the Charité and Elisabeth Hospitals, which were the nearest. Herr von Nagel announced firmly that he proposed to accompany him as a representative of the Press. As they were leaving he made a sign to the lieutenant of the Reichstag Detachment, who added himself unobtrusively to the party.

Some hours later Louis Adlon was called to the telephone. Inspector Müller had rung up to ask whether a lady had entered the hotel at about two o'clock that morning.

Louis made inquiries and found that the Baroness Dosch, who was living in the hotel, had done so. As he reported this to the inspector it occurred to him that this was about the time when the Swede's room had been entered.

'Have you got the cat-burglar?' he asked.

'Yes,' said Müller with satisfaction. 'But I don't want anything said about it at present. However, you may tell Herr and Frau Stinnes that we have recovered all their possessions.'

'Thank God for that!' said Louis Adlon. 'But do you mean to say that Baroness Dosch had something to do with it?'

To this the inspector replied that for the present he could give no further details.

He returned to the hotel at about seven that evening, still accompanied by Herr von Nagel and Lieutenant Berwitz, and asked to be taken up at once to the Stinnes's suite. He had the jewels with him in his case. He also gave the porter instructions to let him know directly the Baroness Dosch came in.

Louis Adlon invited von Nagel and the lieutenant, whose part in this business was still anything but clear, into the bar and ordered a bottle of claret. Von Nagel told the story. They had been extraordinarily lucky. Inspector Müller had found a man in the Charité Hospital who had been brought in during the small hours with a broken leg. His story was that he had been attacked by political opponents and pushed out of a window. It was perfectly plausible in those days, and the Sisters in charge of the casualty ward had accepted him without question, the more so since his papers were in order. These bore the name of Hugo Kassner, of Berlin.

The name was known to the police. It was that of an unemployed music-hall artiste who had already been in trouble with the law, but whose latest activities were not known. Müller had at once searched the room where he lived. He had found a set of black tights, such as acrobats wear, a black mask made out of a stocking, rubber gloves—and the Stinnes jewellery. Confronted by this evidence Kassner had confessed.

He had in fact climbed up one of the pillars flanking the main entrance, being much helped by the darkness of the streets at that time. He had entered the first room of which the window stood open, and after collecting everything he could lay hands on had climbed down again.

'Do you know who it was you robbed?' asked Müller.

'No idea. I hadn't time to look inside the wallet.'

'It was Hugo Stinnes.'

'That swine!' said Kassner.

He had taken his loot round to the Pariser Platz, where he had hidden the suit and overcoat he wore over his tights. Then he had climbed up to the balcony on that side, and thus had fallen foul of the Swede. In his haste to escape he had come near to breaking his neck. For a time he had lain half-stunned, expecting the Swede to come after him, or at least to give the alarm. When nothing happened he had concluded that the Swede must have his own reasons for keeping quiet.

'You get all sorts in the best hotels nowadays,' he said.

This was why he had thought it safe to let himself be taken to the Charité Hospital.

Von Nagel had reached this point in the story when Inspector Müller reappeared and, beaming with pride, displayed the pair of gold cuff-links which Herr Stinnes had given him in recognition of his services.

'But I couldn't help laughing,' he said, 'when Frau Stinnes asked me, quite indignantly, what had happened to the aluminium butter-dish filled with goose-dripping which she had prepared with her own hands.'

Of all the items on the list so meticulously prepared by Herr Stinnes, the butter-dish, number 17, was the only one that had not been found in Kassner's room. The inspector, no less meticulous, had gone back to Kassner and asked him what had become of it. Kassner, who perfectly remembered taking it, was astonished to learn that it was missing. After some hesitation he said:

'Those women must have had it.'

'What women?'

'The ones who picked me up.'

'Some women picked you up, did they? That's not what you

told me before. You'd better come clean, Kassner, or you'll be in even worse trouble.'

Kassner then told the following story. While he was lying on the ground outside the hotel a taxi had come along, a great rarity in those days. Seizing the chance he had raised his arm and beckoned when the headlights fell upon him as it turned into the Pariser Platz. He was seen and the taxi stopped beside him. Two women got out, and this was when he invented the story about having been attacked by political opponents.

'Political opponents?' said one of the ladies. 'Were they Government troops?'

Guessing from the tone of her question which side he had better be on, Kassner at once said that they were and that he was a Spartacist.

'We must help this man,' said the lady. 'We must get him away from here.'

They got him into the taxi. The second of the two ladies then took leave of her friend and went into the Adlon, and the one who had spoken took Kassner to the Charité Hospital.

'And now we must hope to hear the rest of the story from the Baroness Dosch,' said the inspector. 'She was evidently the lady who went into the Adlon.'

'So that's why you rang up,' said Louis Adlon, and sent a page-boy up to the third floor to ask the Baroness if she would mind coming down to the bar.

She came at once. She was a lady of exceptional beauty, very graceful in her movements and always charmingly dressed. She was wearing a smart grey afternoon costume with a bunch of violets pinned to the lapel, another very unusual thing for those days.

Louis Adlon had already told her about the cat-burglar and the Stinnes robbery. She sat down smiling, and the inspector introduced himself and told her Kassner's story.

'Why, of course that must be the man we picked up,' she said at once. 'We had no idea he was a burglar.'

'No one is blaming you in the least, gnädige Frau,' said the inspector. 'But we want your help. An aluminium butter-dish is missing from among the articles that were stolen. Did you by any chance see it?'

The Baroness stared at him round-eyed, as though she thought he was pulling her leg.

'A butter-dish? With real butter inside? I wish I had one!'

'It was the property of Herr Stinnes, and the thief undoubtedly stole it.'

'Good heavens; Is Hugo Stinnes making butter-dishes these days?'

The inspector ignored this.

'You must understand, Baroness, that for us stolen property is stolen property, regardless of whether it is jewellery or merely an aluminium box. Kassner no longer has the box. If you didn't see it then we must question the lady who was with you. Would you mind telling me who she was?'

'Not in the least,' said the Baroness. 'She was the Countess Hetta Treuberg.'

Lieutenant Berwitz, of the Reichstag detachment, had listened to all this in silence, but at the mention of the name of Treuberg again a slight flicker passed over his face. He leaned forward.

Müller asked:

'Where does Countess Hetta Treuberg live?'

'I've no idea,' said the Baroness. 'Until a few days ago she was staying here at the Adlon. But I don't know where she has moved to. She rings me up when she wants to arrange a meeting.'

'And where had you been last night?'

The Baroness replied without hesitation:

'To a "widows' ball" in a dancing-place in the Weberstrasse.'

Her hearers could not conceal their astonishment. A dance-hall in the Weberstrasse was the last place where two ladies belonging to the highest rank of Berlin society might be expected to go unescorted to amuse themselves. It was an obscure east-end street of which most people had not even heard. Seeing that some explanation was called for, the Baroness accounted for her eccentric behaviour by saying that she liked to see how the other half of the world lived and found a particular satisfaction in dancing with the lower orders.

'And this also applies to the Countess Treuberg?'

'Of course. In fact, it was she who first took me to the place. But she doesn't dance as much as I do. Sometimes she suddenly disappears. Naturally I don't ask questions.'

The inspector had no more questions to ask. The Baroness departed smiling, as graceful and composed as when she had come.

'Now,' said the inspector, wrinkling his forehead, 'I shall have to find Countess Treuberg.'

The lieutenant got to his feet.

'I think I know a way of doing that,' he said, and went off without explaining.

When the inspector had also left Louis Adlon turned to Herr von Nagel.

'What's all this between you and the lieutenant? Why did you take him along with you?'

'I'm not very clear about it myself,' said von Nagel. 'He found out that I used to be a member of "Borussia" and so he asked me to help him. The Government troops don't tell all their secrets to the police in these days—they're afraid to trust them too far. The name of Hetta Treuberg evidently means something to the lieutenant. I haven't been able to help him much, but there seemed to be no reason why he shouldn't come with us and see for himself what went on.'

The journalist rose. He stood thinking for a moment and then went to telephone.

The interview with Baroness Dosch, trivial though it seemed at the time, later supplied the key to events of far-reaching importance. Through a chapter of accidents two entirely separate matters had become linked together. For weeks the Government security forces had been trying to discover the meeting-place of the Spartacist Soldiers' Council.[1] They had had word that a new

[1] The German equivalent of the Russian soviets named after Spartacus who led a rising of the slaves in ancient Rome.

revolutionary 'Putsch' was being prepared in Berlin with the help of a prominent delegate from Moscow. Thus far, however, they had not been able to locate the movement's secret headquarters.

Lieutenant Berwitz, who until then had not been directly concerned, was brought into the business, in the first place, by the pure chance that his men had arrested Count Oppersdorf. But it was the mention of Countess Hetta Treuberg that had aroused his interest. She was known to be an active sympathizer with the revolutionaries. But since she had gone underground no one knew where to find her. It was the business of the cat-burglar, and the ensuing investigation, which put him on the scent leading to the Weberstrasse.

The lieutenant promptly got in touch with the authorities, and within a short time of his leaving the hotel the whole of the Alexanderplatz district, in which the Weberstrasse was situated, was surrounded by troops of the Reichstag Detachment. They then raided the curious establishment where the 'widows' balls' were held which the Baroness had visited on the previous evening.

The place was full of men and women whose attitude to the soldiers was anything but friendly. But the raid had come as a complete surprise, and Lieutenant Berwitz with a party of his men was able to force his way through the dance-hall to the rooms beyond it.

Herr von Nagel, who was present, later described the whole affair in detail. These 'widows' balls', or 'diversions for persons of mature age', were not chance affairs. They had been instituted to afford a cover to the Spartacist meetings being held in the back rooms. The delegates came ostensibly to dance. In the same way Countess Treuberg had taken the Baroness with her in order to have an innocent witness to her ostensible reason for visiting the Weberstrasse.

Thus the secret of the Spartacist meeting-place was at last discovered, but the Soviet delegate, whose presence in Berlin had been reported, was not among those picked up at the dance-hall. However, Countess Treuberg was there, and she was caught trying to smuggle a note to someone. It bore the address of a small pension in the Kurfürstenstrasse. Lieutenant Berwitz promptly went there, taking a few men with him and accompanied by von Nagel.

Their arrival at the house caused great consternation. Acting on a hunch, the lieutenant demanded to be shown up to the Countess Treuberg's room, and this was promptly done. It was an ordinary, modest pension bedroom containing nothing but a big wardrobe-trunk to indicate that it was occupied by someone accustomed to better things. But there was also a table littered with typewritten documents and Russian newspapers.

A thin man of medium height, with a black beard and a sharp-pointed nose on which rested a pair of steel-rimmed glasses, was seated at the table. He looked up with tired but very intelligent eyes as the men entered, two of the soldiers, armed with rifles and carrying grenades in their belts, taking up their post at the door.

The lieutenant was somewhat embarrassed. He knew very well that this must be the Russian delegate, but he held no warrant for his arrest.

'I have been ordered to search this house,' he said abruptly.

'On what grounds?' asked the man at the table, speaking in German with a pronounced foreign accent.

'You are under suspicion of being a member of the illegal Spartacist Soldiers' Council. The whole Council has just been arrested in an establishment in the Weberstrasse.'

The man stood up, searching for some papers on the table.

'I must protest formally against this intrusion and against any attempt to lay hands on my person. My name is Karl Radek, I am a Soviet citizen and the correspondent of the Moscow *Pravda*, duly accredited by your Government.'

He had found the document confirming this, and he offered it to the lieutenant. But Lieutenant Berwitz had suddenly noticed something. Standing on the table was the butter-dish belonging to Hugo Stinnes.

He took a deep breath and said:

'Herr Radek, I shall not arrest you on political grounds, but I

I

am in a position to charge you with being in possession of stolen property.'

'What!' exclaimed Radek, utterly taken aback. 'What on earth do you mean? I'm not a thief.'

'Do you claim that this butter-dish is your property?'

'Certainly not. It presumably belongs to the Countess Treuberg. I didn't even know that it was a butter-dish.'

'The police will have to deal with the matter,' said the lieutenant, unscrewing the lid of the container. 'This is undoubtedly the property of Herr Hugo Stinnes, the industrialist. It was stolen from his room at the Hotel Adlon last night, together with his wallet and numerous other objects including documents. Perhaps the documents are also here!'

It was the merest pretext, but it rendered him master of the situation. He nodded to his men to search the room.

Karl Radek was at first so flabbergasted that he could only say, 'Why on earth should I steal a butter-dish from Hugo Stinnes?' He uttered a formal protest as the soldiers gathered together all his papers, but finally he sat back and said resignedly: 'Well, you seem to have won, lieutenant. You've got what I suppose you really came for. But I should like to know what's in that butter-dish. Is it some new "Ersatz" produced by German industry? It certainly isn't butter.'

The lieutenant sniffed.

'It's goose-dripping,' he said, 'mixed, I think, with apple and onion.'

He held it out to Karl Radek, who said:

'It smells wonderful. I wonder—do you think I might have a little?'

'Well, why not?' said the lieutenant, laughing.

And so the involved story, which had started with the entry of a cat-burglar into the Adlon, was finally tidied up. Countess Treuberg had found the butter-dish on the floor of the taxi after leaving the thief at the Charité Hospital, and she had taken it with her to the room where she was hiding Karl Radek.

She got off comparatively lightly, being released from prison soon afterwards and merely ordered by the Government to stay away from Berlin and the Province of Brandenburg for the time being. The Swedish industrialist was less fortunate. The full story appeared in the Berlin newspapers and his wife promptly divorced him.

Karl Radek, as a prominent Russian citizen, a friend of Lenin and leading member of the Russian Communist Party, was not much troubled. He continued to live in Berlin, playing a double role as official Soviet trade delegate and Bolshevik agitator, according to circumstances. In the former capacity he had many dealings with Hugo Stinnes, and it is not impossible that the first exchange between the two men did something to grease the wheels of commerce. When the butter-dish was returned Frau Stinnes at once noticed that some of the contents was missing; and when Stinnes learned who was responsible he ordered a pot of goose-dripping to be specially prepared and sent to Radek.

13

A Personal Interlude

THE Adlon was neutral ground, not only in the struggle between the Republic and the Spartacists, but also in the much wider field of world diplomacy. The Peace Treaty negotiations brought a very large number of statesmen and diplomats to Berlin, many of whom stopped at the hotel or used it for informal meetings. Situated in the very heart of official Berlin, directly on the Wilhelmstrasse with its many Government offices, and within a few minutes of the Reichstag, it was ideal for this purpose—a little Switzerland where the representatives of all nations could meet and talk 'off the record', and where the social threads ran together which play so large a part in high politics.

But politics are not the concern of this book. I shall pass over those troubled post-war years except to record one tragic event which cast a shadow upon the hotel. Lorenz Adlon, the founder, died in the spring of 1921 as a result of an accident that had befallen him eighteen months earlier. There is a touching irony in the fact that the accident was directly related to the downfall of the Kaiser's Germany.

I have already told how, in the sombre days of November, 1918, Prince Max of Baden, the last Chancellor of Imperial Germany, came to stop at the Adlon. As he was going out of the hotel on the morning of the 9th November, two days before the Armistice, he paused to exchange a few words with my father-in-law. Exhausted and depressed by the disastrous situation of the country, the Chancellor let fall a remark which Lorenz Adlon understood to mean that he intended to resign that same day. Horrified by the news, Lorenz stood hesitating for a minute in the hall of the hotel, and then decided to run after the Prince, simply to remind him that even a republic needs a Chancellor.

He hurried out into the street and turned left towards the Brandenburger Tor, going as far as the guard-house. Here, intending to cross over, he looked to his left to see that no cars were approaching the two nearest archways of the Brandenburger Tor.

The Brandenburger Tor possessed five archways, of which the two outer ones on either side were intended for the use of general traffic. But the use of the central archway had always been reserved for the German Emperor. Knowing that the Kaiser was not in Berlin, Lorenz Adler did not trouble to look to the left when he reached this central archway. He had forgotten that Berlin was in the throes of revolution, and that the rules of Imperial etiquette were no longer in force.

A truck loaded with revolutionary soldiers came roaring under the archway as he started to cross. He jumped back, but was none the less hit by it and knocked over.

He recovered, more or less, but later suffered from a thrombosis. Moreover, the shock affected his mind. He never went outside the hotel without looking towards that central archway of the Brandenburger Tor, through which only the Kaiser had been privileged to pass.

As time went on his behaviour came to assume an aspect of ghostly symbolism. Something compelled him to take that short walk every day, out of the Hotel and across the Pariser Platz by way of the Brandenburger Tor. Never would he turn his head as he passed that central archway. And finally, in 1921, the inevitable happened. He was knocked down by a car coming from the Tiergarten on the exact spot where he had had his former accident. He was carried back alive to the hotel, but died shortly afterwards.

A tragic destiny decreed that the death of his only son, Louis Adlon, to whom I was most happily married from 1922 to 1945, should also be the direct result of war and the collapse of Germany. During our years together we shared everything, work and pleasure and travel. The only journey on which it was not granted to me to accompany him was the last of all.

If the story is to be kept in chronological order I must here give some account of myself, although I do so with reluctance. It is not my story, but that of the Adlon, which I have set out to tell. In any case, as my friends know, I am not much given to talking about my personal affairs. I have always been more interested in the life around me than in myself. So I shall confine myself to relating how I made the acquaintance of Louis Adlon and how he introduced me to the world of his incomparable hotel, which became my world.

I am a native of the Rhineland, but as a child I was taken to the United States, where I lived for a long time. I was in the happy position of being able to indulge my tastes, which were, and still are, for foreign languages, geography, folk-lore and folk-music. I had studied these subjects at several American universities when, at the end of 1920, I suddenly made up my mind to visit my relations in Germany.

My family had a country house in Neufahrland, on the Nedlitzsee in the lake district west of Berlin. When I arrived there, in the winter, I found them all in bed with a highly infectious form of influenza. Since it seemed that I should be more likely to add to their burdens if I stayed to assist, I decided to postpone family life for the time being and took up my quarters at the Adlon.

The state of the invalids did not improve during the week between Christmas and New Year, and New Year's Eve found me sitting reading in my hotel bedroom, feeling decidedly less festive than most people in Berlin. Then the Baroness Plettenberg, who was living on the same floor, came in to see me in full evening dress and roundly declared that it was preposterous for anyone to remain alone on this of all nights.

Later, after she had gone downstairs, the telephone began ringing with messages from the Baroness saying that she was with a party of charming people and that she intended to give me no peace until I had the sense to come and join them. So down I went, to be light-heartedly made welcome by a circle of strangers, none of whose names I caught. But there was an unusually good-looking man, with the hair greying over his temples, who seemed to be taking particular notice of me. Not for some time did I learn that he was Louis Adlon.

We said little to one another, but nevertheless on that evening our fate was sealed. We were never again separated. Everything seemed to happen as a matter of course. I did not go back to the States, as I had intended to do. It was some years before I saw America again, and then I did so in company with Louis, after we were married.

The wedding was a quiet one, all the arrangements being made by Louis Adlon's elder sister, who became a sister to me and, after my husband, the dearest and truest of all my friends. She never ceased to spoil me, and I could wish nothing better for any wife than so kind and thoughtful a sister-in-law. I had no mother-in-law, my husband's mother having died when he was a child.

My entry into the splendid house on Unter den Linden was equally informal. I joined at once in the work of the hotel, and was accepted by the staff as the recognized assistant managing-director and 'patronne'. The knowledge of countries and people which I had gained by my studies in America was of great value to me in hotel work.

Louis Adlon was exceptionally busy at this time. Since the death of his father, whom he had deeply loved and greatly honoured, the whole weight of the establishment had lain on his shoulders. Moreover it was the beginning of the inflation period in Germany. He had appalling difficulties to contend with, endless intricate problems to solve, if his business, and indeed all his personal fortune, were to survive that time of financial confusion. These matters so preoccupied him that he had little leisure for private life, or even for private happiness.

Nevertheless my life with that most chivalrous of men was always wonderfully happy. There was never the slightest shadow between us, never to the very end, in 1945. And Louis Adlon met his terrible end in the house in Neufahrland where I had not gone to stay because all my relations were in bed with influenza. Since it was destined to play so important, and finally so terrible, a part in my life, I must say something about this house.

There were in fact two houses, the property of my family, standing close together. They were pleasant, solidly-built farmhouses belonging to a happy period in Prussian history.

Soon after our marriage Louis conceived the idea of converting one of them for use as a guest-house, additional to the hotel. We wanted to be able to invite especially distinguished hotel-guests there in order to increase their liking for Berlin, and to show them something of the beautiful countryside and the lakes which lie so near the capital.

Many were persuaded by this means to stay longer in Berlin than they had originally intended, among them the Maharajah of Patiala, of whom I shall write later. I took many of our privately invited week-end guests on conducted tours of the enchanting Havel region, acting as chauffeur, helmsman or coachman, according to whether we went by car or boat or carriage. I took a particular pleasure in playing hostess on these occasions, for I was very proud of Berlin's wonderful surroundings.

The converted house was for all practical purposes rebuilt. We put in bedrooms, each with its own bathroom, central heating, refrigeration and every other modern comfort. And particular attention was paid to the stables, for Louis was passionately fond of riding. I think we must have had the best stables to be found anywhere in Germany. The other house remained unchanged. Fields were converted into a park, and a boat-house with a big landing-stage was built at the lakeside, with a motor launch and smaller boats of all kinds. In short we made the Neufahrland house into a typical, up-to-date, extremely comfortable country house.

But the night before the work was due to begin I found myself unable to sleep. My heart pounded and I was afflicted by a strange and terrible sense of foreboding such as I had never known before. I had a feeling that I was bringing disaster upon us both. For a long time I struggled with myself, undecided whether to wake Louis and ask him to cancel the arrangements. But he was so much in love with the plan that I could not bring myself to do so.

We drove out there the next day, and I had to turn my head away as I heard the first sounds of the men at work. For days I could not rid myself of the thought that I was acquiescing in something that would bring us both unhappiness. But I could never speak to Louis about it. What could I have said? It was a feeling, an intimation, and nothing more. I had no positive reasons to oppose the plan. And so I let it go on—and Neufahrland became our fate.

When I became the proprietor's wife I naturally took the greatest interest in everything that concerned the hotel, and I studied its working in detail, from the cellar to the roof.

Louis Adlon was in general a man of great reserve. In 1922, that is to say, when we had got to know one another very thoroughly, the arrest took place of the murderer of the postman in the Adlon. Police constantly visited the hotel to question people who might be called as witnesses at the trial. In the event, the trial never took place, because the man committed suicide, as I have already related. But in the meantime the whole staff was talking about his arrest.

Louis did not at first say a word to me. It was only by chance that I heard what had happened, and naturally I was as interested as everyone else. In the end I heard the whole story, but if it had been left to Louis I should never have known a thing about it.

It was a long time before I understood anything of the financial problems with which he had to contend. The hotel, as I have said, originally cost 20,000,000 marks. It was opened in 1907, and war broke out in 1914. There had been very little time, therefore, in which to put the business on its feet and reduce this enormous debt. The war affected it very seriously. Although the rooms were all occupied, the restaurant could make no profit owing to food restrictions, and the restaurant played a very large part in the hotel's economy.

But, as I have also related, Lorenz Adlon had one peculiar fad. He would never buy less than a hundred bottles of any of the carefully selected wines he laid down. At the outbreak of war the stock amounted to a million bottles, not only of wine, but of all brands of brandy, whisky, gin and almost every other spirit and liqueur that the world produces.

This asset, which had been preserved unscathed through the years of disturbance, now brought the hotel enormous profits. The price of wine rose from day to day. Interest on the mortgages was easily paid, and by the end of the inflation period the mortgages themselves had vanished. The holders, that is to say the banks, were only too ready to accept the repayment in marks that Louis Adlon offered, in order that they might reinvest the money in foreign securities before the mortgages became completely worthless.

But against this deliverance had to be set the daily rising costs of maintenance, repair and replacement, to say nothing of wages and salaries. During the war, for example, all the linen had been worn out, and fresh supplies were almost unprocurable. As for wages, at the height of the inflation these had to be paid daily to meet the daily rise in prices.

In short, Louis Adlon had a great deal to perplex him.

14

Page-boys and Other Matters

I PROCEEDED to study the running of the hotel, starting at the reception-desk.

I had imagined, like any other layman, that the reception-clerks had little to do beyond allotting rooms to the arriving guests, answering their inquiries and generally being civil to them. It was with great astonishment that I found in the reception-office a huge and meticulously compiled card-index, of which the following are a few examples:

Count X. Two pillows. Dislikes soft towels, thinks them degenerate.

Frau Meyer, industrialist's wife. No strong-smelling flowers in the room. *Berliner Lokalanzeiger* every morning. Hot-water bottle. Dog (dwarf dachshund) called Morchen, to be taken out by a page in the mornings. Dog has breakfast with mistress, milk and rusks. Remember to inquire after dog's health.

Svenstrom, banker. Smuggles whisky into the hotel and has ice and mineral water sent up to his room. Never gives tips. Has a picnic-basket, and in the evenings eats bread and sausage in his room. Washes the plates himself and dries them on his face-towel. Should never be asked if he wants a taxi.

Schmitz, factory-owner, Solingen. Should be given a room served by an elderly chambermaid.

I found that the reception-clerks were expected to recognize and greet by name any guest, arriving unexpectedly, who had visited the hotel once or twice before; and to know the Christian names of their children, if they brought any with them.

But one of my greatest surprises was the discovery of the importance of the hall-porter.

I had supposed, as most people do, that he was simply an

employee of the hotel, drawing his weekly wage and being tipped by the visitors. Nothing could be farther from the truth. He had paid Lorenz Adlon, and later, Louis, 3,000 marks a month for the privilege of being hall-porter, and his receipts amounted to perhaps 30,000 a month. The private cars in which guests drove about Berlin, or across Germany, were his affair. He booked passages by sea, rail and air. He ordered flowers, settled accounts for the cleaning and pressing of clothes and paid for the purchases made by guests in the town. And naturally he took a commission on all these innumerable transactions, out of which he paid his assistants. The hall-porter at the Adlon, in short, was a decidedly prosperous citizen.

I next turned my attention to the page-boys.

I found a party of good-looking, alert and intelligent youngsters. My first impression, like that of every guest, was that they hung about, more or less casually, in order to be on hand when wanted. Then I realized that their comings and goings, and all their activities, were governed by definite rules; and finally I found the book of rules itself.

It was printed. A copy was given to every boy when he was engaged, with instructions to study it carefully and if possible learn it by heart. I discovered that Lorenz Adlon, who overlooked nothing, had himself compiled it before the opening of the hotel. Since it is an amusing document, that still breathes the spirit of the Kaiser's Germany, I will quote it in full.

DUTIES OF A PAGE-BOY

1. *Personal.* Honesty, punctuality, industry and energy. Absolute cleanliness of body and attire, well-brushed hair, quiet, civil demeanour towards superiors and comrades. Punctiliousness in greeting all known persons, both indoors and out.

2. *Clothing and Wardrobe.* Strict tidiness in the dressing-room and in lockers. Smoking and eating in the dressing-room are forbidden. All uniforms to be handed to the tailor for cleaning and repair before leaving the hotel, and to be collected from him when going on duty. Every page-boy must keep a

clothes-brush and shoe-brushes in his locker, black boot-polish, comb, soap, a handkerchief and two irons. The name of each boy is to be pasted on to his locker. Every boy is to draw white gloves, collars and napkins from the laundry, giving a receipt for them, and to return them as soon as they are soiled. Page-boys serving in the restaurant or at the information desk will also be issued with white waistcoats at the laundry, and these are to be returned to the senior page-boy when going off duty. The latter will return them to the laundry. In wet weather page-boys are not allowed out of doors except wearing capes.

3. *Roll-call.* A roll-call will be held by the senior page-boy of each shift before it goes on duty, and a clerk from the reception office will inspect the pages for neatness and cleanliness. He will allot duties, ensure that all boys are present, and report any deficiencies or irregularities to the senior reception-clerk on duty, if the latter has not himself attended the roll-call. Every boy at roll-call must show prompt obedience to the orders and requirements of the senior page-boy.

Here I must interrupt the list of rules in order to explain something. In German hotels the staff is divided into two broad categories, of which what is known as the 'front-staff' is one. I can well imagine the reader's puzzlement upon encountering this strange term.

It dates from the days of the Empire. The page-boys' book of rules is conceived very largely on military lines, in terms of 'orders' and 'superiors'. The term 'front-staff' applies to any member of the staff who serves at the 'front', that is to say who comes in contact with the guests. The guest is always right, even when he is wrong. The 'front-staff' in an hotel are like soldiers in the front line, except that they face friends rather than enemies. The expression has become customary in Prussian hotels.

To continue with the list:

4. *Service Regulations.*

(*a*) *Hall Service.* Uniform is to be worn, with cap and white gloves. Page-boys to be seated on the pages' bench. Orders to be accepted from the senior page-boy or any member of the front-staff. Before leaving the hall every boy must write his name and number in the duty-book. The next boy on the bench will then answer the next summons and carry out the duty required. Having completed it he will report the fact to the person from whom he received the order. Guests are to be taken upstairs in the lift, messengers by the back stairs. The page-boy is to escort the latter downstairs again. No page-boy may enter a private room without knocking, and he may only enter an empty room accompanied by the room-waiter. Visiting cards, letters and written messages are to be handed to the guest on a silver tray (obtainable at the post-desk). All guests are to be addressed by their titles, if known (Frau Gräfin, Frau Baronin, Durchlaucht, etc.), and all ladies are otherwise to be addressed as 'Gnädige Frau'.

(*b*) *Performance of Hall-duties*. Upon the flashing of the arrival-signal the page next in line for duty will go at once to greet the arriving guest. He will take his hand-baggage from him, overcoat, umbrella, etc., and escort him to the reception-desk. He will obtain the key of the room allotted to him from the post-desk, and will then escort the guest up to the room in the lift. He will open the door and switch on the light if necessary. He will open or close the windows as the guest requires, draw the curtains if it is evening, and ring for the room-waiter, the chambermaid and the floor-messenger. He is to be in all respects helpful to the guest, and to ask him if there is anything he especially requires. All such requests are to be carried out immediately or reported to the senior reception-clerk on duty, if it is not within the page-boy's power to fulfil them. When all these duties have been performed the page-boy will return to his place on the bench in the hall.

(*c*) *Special Commissions on Hall-service*. If a page-boy is asked by a guest to perform some special task he will report this to the senior page-boy, who will give him such further instructions as may be necessary and enter the details in the duty-book. Upon returning from this duty he will report to the senior page-boy, who will settle any outstanding details with the guest.

(*d*) *Front-door attendance*. The page nominated for service at the front door is required to be helpful to all guests entering and leaving. He should turn the door slowly, at a speed appropriate to the movements of the guest. While on door-duty he should not speak to any of his colleagues, but should hold himself rigidly erect and pay close attention to his duties.

(*e*) *Information-service in the Hall*. Costume: full uniform and white waistcoat. Position: in the middle of the hall between the porter's lodge and the reception office. The page-boy's duty is to answer all questions put to him by the guests and, if necessary, to point out the appropriate office of the hotel. He should bear himself rigidly erect in performing his duties.

(*f*) *Restaurant service*. Costume: ordinary uniform, without cap but with white waistcoat and gloves. Each boy, when going on duty, will report to the *maître d'hôtel* who will tell him where he is to stand. The page will himself carry out commissions for guests in so far as they are confined to the downstairs rooms, and will pass on others to the senior page-boy in the hall. He will answer the telephone with the words, 'Restaurant Adlon', and in the case of table reservations or inquiries will call the head waiter, having first asked the inquirer to be so kind as to wait a moment. If a guest in the restaurant is called to the telephone, the page will first ask the head waiter if he knows him. If the guest is pointed out to him, he will very politely tell him that he is wanted on the telephone and if necessary will help him with the use of the apparatus. If, however, the head waiter does not know the guest, the page, acting on his instructions, will call out his name in the restaurant. Every quarter of an hour the page will go to the restaurant cash-desk to collect the bills and take them to the main cash-desk, or to fetch change. At tea-time and in the evening the page will carry the *Lustbarkeitssteuerblock* (pad of entertainment-tax forms) with him, and place a form on the table of all newly arrived guests. When he goes off duty he will hand the pad to the head waiter. In addition he will carry out all instructions given him by the management of the restaurant.

(g) *Telephone service*. The page-boy's first duty in the morning is to clean the two telephones in the head-office, to tidy the desks, sharpen pencils, replace pens if necessary, and watch for light-signals from the general manager. Upon being summoned by him he will enter his office without knocking and carry out any instructions he may give him. He will see to it that the telephone booths are kept clean and tidy, and will summon guests to the telephone upon instructions from the switchboard-operator. This duty is to be performed in the following manner: the page will first inquire at the post-desk whether the guest in question is stopping at the hotel, and, if so, whether he has left any instructions. If the guest has left no message his name is to be called out loudly and clearly in the hall, the reading-room, the bar, the Raphael room, the barber's shop and all lounges and sitting-rooms; and if necessary the restaurant-page is to be instructed to call it out in the restaurant. When the guest appears the page is to conduct him to the telephone, telling him, if possible, who has asked to speak to him. At 3.30 in the afternoon, when the managerial staff has a short rest-period, the page is to draw the curtains in the manager's office.

(h) *Reading-room service*. The page-boy is responsible for the tidiness of the reading-room. He will see to it that there is a sufficient supply of writing-paper and blotting-paper, and that the inkpots are kept clean and properly filled. Costume: ordinary uniform without cap or gloves.

(i) *Floor service*. Pages are to report at 8 o'clock at the post-desk to collect registered or express letters for delivery to guests on their floors. The following procedure is to be adopted. The page will knock at the door and, if the guest answers, will take the mail in to him. If the 'Do not disturb' card is hanging on the door, the page will at once return the mail to the post-desk together with other letters not requiring personal delivery. For non-personal-delivery mail the page will collect a pink form at the post-desk, notifying the guest that there are letters awaiting him. He will attach this to the guest's door-handle. From 8 a.m. until 10 p.m. pages on floor-duty will attend to the pneumatic post-tube. Attention should be paid to the fact that only one cylinder at a time may be sent along the tube, that keys may not be sent in the cylinders, and that letters should not be so folded that they cannot come out of the cylinders. When the light flashes for the chambermaid or house-messenger, the page is at once to notify these and tell them where they are wanted. The page is responsible for the cleanliness and tidiness of the floor-office, and is to empty the waste-paper-basket every morning. All keys handed to him are to be taken immediately to the post-desk. If he is called out of the floor-office he will leave written word of the time when he left it and where he has gone. Whether on or off duty, he is always to be on the alert for suspicious persons or happenings, and is to report these in detail to the reception-office. In the event of the outbreak of fire he will operate the bells marked 'fire alarm' and report in detail to the telephone switchboard. Finally he must attend all guests entering or leaving the lift. Costume: ordinary uniform, without cap or gloves.

Those page-boys! Those children! A charming story, which illustrates their capacity for self-education, was told me long afterwards.

An older page, whom we may call Max, was supervising a younger one, Moritz. Moritz was summoned by the post-desk to take a telegram up to a certain Herr X, a company-director. Just as he was about to go up, with the telegram on a silver salver, he was called back and given three more telegrams, also for Herr X. So that made four. When he returned from this errand he was questioned by his youthful colleague. Their conversation was overheard, and the following is a faithful reconstruction:

MAX: What did you do with the four telegrams?

MORITZ: I gave them to Herr X, of course.

MAX: What did you say?

MORITZ: Why, I just said, 'Herr X, here are four telegrams for you.'

K

MAX: And what did he say?

MORITZ: He just thanked me.

MAX: How much did he give you?

MORITZ: Fifty pfennigs.

MAX: Well, I can tell you one thing—you're a disgrace to the hotel!

MORITZ (greatly put out): Why, what did I do wrong?

MAX: You did everything wrong. You know what old X is like, and what a lot he thinks of himself. He's frightfully proud of his new car, and it's worth a mark, any day, just to tell him what a smasher it is. Well, the other day I had to take a sheaf of telegrams up to him, like you did. And I'll tell you how I did it. To start with I just put one on the tray and stuffed the rest in my pocket, and I went into his room all smiling and said, 'Telegram for you, Herr X.'

So that was fifty pfennigs. Then I went along the corridor and waited a bit and then went back, all smiles, same as last time— 'Another telegram for you, Herr X.' That cost him another fifty.

The third time I thought I'd better vary it a bit, so I went in looking respectful and said, 'Sorry to keep disturbing you, Herr X, but here's another telegram just this minute arrived.' So he says to me, 'You know, Max, it's a terrible life people like me lead. Nothing but telegrams and phone calls—hard at it from morning till night.' Well, I didn't say anything to that. I just sort of looked admiringly at him, which is a trick you have to learn. And that time he gave me a whole mark, making two altogther.

Well, I still had one more telegram, and I wondered what line to take this time. You have to be careful, you see. You don't want to overdo it. For instance, one time I said to a newspaper correspondent, 'It must be wonderful to live your sort of life, sir—all that excitment and responsibility.' And all he said was, 'Don't be a silly little twerp!'

Still, I reckoned that'd do for old X, all right, knowing how he likes to feel important. But in the end I didn't need to say it. I waited quite a long time and then I went in puffing as though I was out of breath with running upstairs, and he says, 'My poor lad, I'm really sorry to give you all this trouble. It must be pretty hard work, being a page, isn't it?'

So I said, 'Oh, yes, sir, it's very hard work being a page at the Adlon. But we don't mind a bit, sir, on account of the interesting people we meet.'

'Know what he coughed up for that? Three marks! He did, honest—three marks! So you see, my lad, you've got to pull yourself together or you'll be spoiling the market for everyone.'

The story made a great impression on Moritz, who said after thought:

'Yes, I see what you mean. But there's one thing. You must have been away the dickens of a long time. What did the senior page say when you got back?'

'There you go!' said Max. 'You see, you don't know anything yet. The senior didn't say a word. He just held out his hand and I put a mark in it!'

15

Kitchen Affairs

HAVING studied the activities of the hall-porter, the reception-clerks and the page-boys I turned to the part of the hotel which interested me, as a woman, more than any other—the kitchen. I must now describe that remarkable domain.

To start with what is most important: in a big glass case in the middle of the kitchen sits the chef.

In a hotel the word 'chef' always means the head cook, whose rank is indicated by the fact that he wears the highest white cap. The specialist cooks—fish-cook, sauce-cook, 'cold-cook', pastry-cook and so on—wear stiff white caps somewhat lower than his and are graded according to their status.

With the chef in his glass case sits his secretary. That he should need a secretary may astonish the layman, but it will surprise no one who knows what his office entails. This lady's busiest time is round about mid-morning, when the chef in an international hotel has to make his arrangements for the following day. Above all, he has to buy, and buying is no simple matter. In any big hotel banquets, dinner-parties, after-theatre suppers, and private dances with a cold buffet, are of almost daily occurrence, besides many unheralded events. All contingencies must be provided for in advance. The chef's motto is, 'Be prepared'. He must have everything on hand, from the rarest delicacies to plain soused herrings. The buying of these materials, their use, distribution and pricing, must all be so contrived as to ensure that, after allowing for the most careful preparation, they will still bring the hotel a profit.

Let us say, for example, that a carcass of venison is bought. The saddle will do excellently for a banquet, a *ragoût* of venison can be served in the grill-room and a *paté* at the cold table. It takes years of study and much experience to estimate exactly how much of any given material should be bought in order to ensure that there are no 'left-overs' of which no use can be made, and which simply add to the overhead costs of the kitchen. Tomorrow's menus, both for midday and for the evening, must be dictated and typed. The secretary must see to it that the orders go out, and above all she must keep the larder-list up to date.

A big kitchen naturally has a big larder. Countless varieties of preserves must be kept in stock, in greatly varying quantities, to say nothing of such things as flour, rice and potatoes. It is the secretary's business to check all the lists. There is, of course, a larder-steward, but he merely sees to the arranging and stowing, while the secretary attends to the records. The paper-work of these three people, chef, secretary and larder-steward, is the deciding factor in the profit-and-loss account of the kitchen. I know that many big hotels have failed owing to weakness at this point. Shrewd, skilful buying is everything.

But on the other hand the hotel can also lose money if the chef allows himself to become too preoccupied with this side of his activities. Vital though the work in the glass case is, it is still time taken from his principal task, which is to supervise the cooking. He should be going round the stoves, watching, tasting, giving instructions and sometimes himself applying the final touches. There are dishes whose preparation he has to oversee from the beginning, if they are to be completely successful. He must be everywhere at once and always on hand.

And it is not merely the more exotic forms of cooking that should concern him. Truffled capons, fish in caviar sauce, all the many complicated and exquisite dishes naturally call for extreme care in their preparation, but he must not on their account neglect the simple, everyday dishes which constitute so large a part of the kitchen's work. Homely, familiar dishes can be dull or delightful, according to the amount of flair and imagination that has been used in preparing them.

In addition to all this, the chef has to look after his staff. It was a matter to which, from the very beginning, Lorenz Adlon attached the highest importance. Staff-welfare played a very large part in the running of the Adlon, and from the proprietor down the hotel was pervaded by a strong family feeling.

There is an unwritten law according to which the chef, like his assistant-chefs and indeed all members of an hotel staff, must take his meals in the hotel. He is, however, not obliged to eat at the same table as his assistants, but can have his meals separately if he prefers. In this matter the great chefs always draw a parallel between their own position and that of the captain of a warship, whom etiquette requires to eat alone, as a rule, in order that there may not be too much intimacy between his subordinate officers and himself. It is wiser not to smile when this parallel is evoked. The chefs don't like it.

Care was taken at the Adlon to ensure that staff meals were always good and sufficient. They had also to be well varied, and the chef had to pay particular attention to this, for business as well as for the obvious social reasons. The kitchen-apprentice should not need to be constantly purloining and eating oddments of food. He should be so well fed as to prevent this kind of wastage.

Good relations between the chef and the head waiter is also a matter of the highest importance. The latter, in his own sphere, is a functionary of equal status. His pay is far less than that of the chef, but the tips he receives bring him in a princely income. Or perhaps it would be more true to say that they used to do so. But guests, as a rule, only give princely tips when they are served in a princely manner. Hotel guests before 1914 not only knew how to eat, they understood the art of eating. They scarcely glanced at the menu, but left it to the head waiter to advise them. He would tell them, for instance, of out-of-season delicacies, strawberries at Christmas, asparagus-tips, truffles, or the arrival of newly shot woodcock, or whatever it might be. But he had also to draw their attention to the *plats du jour*, so that everything could be served fresh and there should be no serving of left-over dishes. And he had to make a practice of taking into account the guests' particular and sometimes extraordinary tastes, which were carefully noted in a book kept for the purpose, so that they should not escape his memory. After referring to it he would have a brief conference with his colleague, the chef. The guest must always be satisfied.

A waiter who left the visitor to suppose that there was nothing more available than the items listed on the menu did not belong in a luxury hotel in the old days. On the other hand, he could not afford to spend a long time in conversation with the diner, but had to be quick in apprehending his mood and pleasure.

A book could be written on the changes of taste which have occurred in the past few decades, and indeed I am half-inclined to write it. Although I am not a cook, I think I must have tasted all the kinds of food there are, good and bad alike, in every corner of the world, but naturally with particular interest in the Adlon.

A comparison of pre-1914 menus with those of today affords an insight into the whole course of world history. There is the change in sauces, for instance.

A French cookery book dating from before the 1914 war contains the following general prescription:

To the making of a good sauce three things are essential:

1. The *fond* (I will explain this in a minute);
2. Unsweetened cream;
3. Cognac.

Let me take the last item first. If as a rule good relations prevail between the chef and the head waiter (because these are essential) there is, on the other hand, nearly always a running fight between the chef and the head wine-waiter. The chef, who spends his days in a warm place, must be allowed a certain warmth of temper. But this is something that those whose days are spent in a much cooler atmosphere do not always understand. When the chef calls for brandy for the sauce, or for some particular wine for use in preparing a dish, the wine-waiter is certain to ask:

'Is it for cooking?'

If it is, then it is customary for the wine-waiter to put some salt in the wine or brandy. He is afraid that otherwise the kitchen staff may drink it!

I have already spoken of the importance of sauces. The reader will therefore understand that the sauce-chef is the most important functionary in the kitchen, after the chef himself. He is the chef's deputy. No one becomes a sauce-chef without having occupied all the other posts in the kitchen. He must have the finest palate of them all, for with the majority of dishes it is upon the sauce that the whole flavour depends. Very little may be needed, but what there is must be perfect. It must have exactly the right flavour, and not merely taste of something indefinite.

The most elementary of the sauce-cook's tasks is the preparation of the *fond*, or basis, which figures as the first item in the French recipe. It must be taken directly from the meat or game or fish for which the sauce is intended. Never, for example, should the *fond* from venison and hare be mixed, or the result will be one of those nondescript, round-the-week sauces that have brought German cookery into such bad repute. The sauce-cook prepares his *fond*, and having done so he can keep it for some time, so as to have it handy.

The good sauce-chef can be recognized by his tidiness. He should have everything ready to his hand, spices, peeled onions, cooked tomato-sauce, fresh parsley, marjoram, thyme, chives, garlic and lemons. He never uses ready-ground pepper, but always a pepper-mill, because the difference is enormous. Only freshly-ground pepper has the right scent and flavour. Above all, the sauce-cook must have a steady hand. He must know precisely how much salt and pepper he needs, and must be able to add exactly the right amount with a flick of the wrist.

Good vegetable-cooks and good pastry- and sweet-cooks are very rare. This is because they are the hardest worked men in the kitchen. They are always busy, because no meal, and in Germany very few dishes, are served without potatoes and vegetables. They also need to be very expert in buying and in estimating the quantities they need. One has only to think of the difference between a salad that has come fresh out of the earth and one that has lain all day in the greengrocer's shop. The vegetable-cook is also the man who makes the *bouillon*, which of course serves as a basis for many other soups.

In this matter of soup there was a tale told by the older members of the Adlon staff.

When Lorenz Adlon was beginning his career in Berlin there appeared on the market tins of what was called 'shark soup'. If I remember rightly it was the product of a Canadian manufacturer, and the advertisements proclaimed that it was a great Chinese delicacy.

Lorenz Adlon bought some, being always ready to try anything new, and when one day a delegation of leading Chinese personalities arrived in Berlin he caused this shark soup to be served to them. He had tasted it himself and was at a loss to understand how anyone could drink the stuff, which seemed to possess nothing but a vague, watery flavour of oriental spices. The fin itself, from which it was supposed to be made, was equally tasteless.

When the Chinese gentlemen saw this item on the menu they appeared somewhat astonished. However they ate it with their accustomed politeness, making no comment. The youngest member of the delegation, a young man belonging to a distinguished Chinese family, came again to the Adlon a few days later, and Lorenz Adlon took the opportunity of asking him how he had liked the soup.

The young man grinned, invited him to sit down, and said in his limited German:

'Soup great misunderstanding.'

'Good God!' said Lorenz Adlon. 'Why?'

The young man then told a long tale from which it appeared that the Chinese predilection for shark-fin soup really arose out of that age-old superstition that is at the root of all cannibalism. The fishermen of China believed, or had once believed, that the fins of a shark which is known to have eaten a man possess an especial virtue. Since such sharks were not easily come by, these fins naturally commanded a high price; and the price rose according to the wealth and importance of the man the shark was believed to have eaten. In the end the consumption of the fins became merely a matter of custom, but they kept their price; and since the trade was profitable some western concern had evidently thought it worth while to join in. The young man concluded:

'Shark-fin superstition, not good taste.'

I give the story for what it is worth.

I have mentioned the cooking of vegetables. This is something that can be learnt. But no one can learn the cooking of grills. A good *rotisseur* is born, not made.

The *rotisseur* must, in fact, be brought from England, for it is in that country that the roasting and grilling of meat over an open fire has been brought to the highest pitch of perfection. The secret lies in the fact that no kind of furnace, electrical or any other, can compare with a wood fire. The reason is that the fat drips from roasting meat. If it falls on to hot metal or any equivalent substance it vaporizes, and the meat, particularly in the case of mutton, is impregnated with the very penetrating fumes of the burning fat, which give it a bad flavour. But the fat is instantly consumed in a wood fire, and so the flavour of the meat is unimpaired.

The whole apparatus of the *rotisseur* is complicated. All kinds of meat can be roasted in all kinds of ways, and it needs an especially acute instinct to determine when it has been cooked to exactly the right extent.

There are two other important cooks concerning whom a word must be said—the cook who is responsible for the cold table, *hors d'œuvres* and so on, and the pastry-cook, who prepares the sweets and cakes.

There is a general rule which applies to both, although it must, of course, be kept within the bounds of good taste. All cold dishes, and all sweets, *petit fours*, ices and pastries, must be pleasantly coloured—appetizing to the eye as well as to the palate. The cold tables in England, Sweden, Denmark, Russia and Finland are incomparable.

The pastry-cook has lost something of his prestige in recent years, owing to the ladies' habit of eschewing sweets for the sake of their figures. Nevertheless the proper ending to a good meal should still be something sweet or something cold. I hold to it that this settles the stomach and tranquillizes the spirit.

Very soon after my arrival at the Adlon the fantastic rise of prices began, eventually reaching such astronomical figures that it was scarcely possible to count the rows of noughts. New bank-notes for ever larger sums were incessantly issued, and the prices on the menu had to be no less incessantly raised. The bank-note which sufficed for a dinner one evening was scarcely enough to pay for a cup of coffee next day.

The effect of these conditions on people with fixed incomes, retired civil servants, army pensioners and so on, was of course appalling. They were also highly bewildering to people in more fortunate circumstances.

In 1923, at the height of the inflation, a former regular visitor to the hotel, the writer, Fedor von Zobeltitz, came back to Germany from America. He went into the Adlon Bar and ordered a glass of beer, asking the price. The waiter replied briefly, 'Three-fifty.' Von Zobeltitz asked what this meant, not being abreast of the situation, and the waiter told him that it stood for the sum of three million five hundred thousand marks.

That was what the inflation was like. A tram-fare cost three hundred thousand marks, and the municipal authorities reckoned gas- and water-rates in a curious fashion: they made the price retrospective, basing the rate on the price-level of the last day of the month. Other institutions adopted other measures. The State-subsidized theatres fixed different prices for Germans and foreigners. A stall at the Schauspielhaus cost a German three milliard seven hundred million marks. But he had to produce identity papers before he could get one, because the American visitor paid eighteen milliard seven hundred million marks for the same seat.

Prices went even higher than this—into billions, figures with a row of twelve noughts! The cashiers of large concerns were finally given a so-called 'key-figure', based on the price of the dollar in marks, and this figure was used in calculating the day's commodity prices.

A day came when the authorities and the banks simply cancelled sums entered in their books which no longer possessed any value. First the thousands went, then the ten thousands and presently the millions. I well remember the glad day when Louis Adlon handed me a letter informing me that the sum of 9,500,000 marks had been struck off my post office account.

Strange things happened in the Adlon at that time. One day a young gentleman from Frankfurt arrived at the hotel. He asked for a first-floor suite and described himself in the register as a bank director. No one paid any attention to the discrepancy between the high-sounding title and the young man's evident youth. Members of the Adlon staff were not supposed to be surprised by anything. In any case, there were so many changed appearances, new careers, new titles, the whole social fabric was so shaken, that the old standards no longer applied.

So the young man got his suite and was lavish in his spending; but it was observed that he paid for everything in notes of small denomination, and this gave rise to the first suspicions.

'There's something not quite right about our bank director,' said the cashier to Louis Adlon.

He was a man who had been with us for many years, and his remark was based on a long experience of the hotel business. Broadly speaking, guests at the Adlon could be divided into three categories.

First there were the regular guests who came to us again and again and were known to us personally. They very often did not pay at once but had the bill sent on to them.

Then there were the guests who paid by cheque. Although they were often very rich, they never carried money in their pockets, except small change for tips and so forth. Most of these were also known to us, or at least they had good references.

The third and largest category, as in all hotels, was that of the guests who paid cash. In a hotel such as the Adlon they ordinarily used large notes, whether they paid in marks or in foreign currency.

There was in fact a fourth category—that of the guests who did not pay at all, but whose bills were returned to them receipted by Louis Adlon. I shall have more to say about this later.

In view of what the cashier had said, Louis Adlon communicated with the police, and it was not long before the doors closed on the young man from Frankfurt—the doors, that is to say, of the establishment on the Alexanderplatz. He was no director but a Frankfurt bank clerk who had made off with the bank's entire reserve of dollar currency. He had been living a wonderful life at the Adlon until his use of small notes betrayed him. Most of the dollars were found to be still in his possession. After reading the account of his robbery in the papers he had been afraid to change them. It was over-cautiousness, rather than recklessness, that proved his undoing.

But I have told this story because of the light it throws upon the inflation period. The young man employed an astute advocate who based his defence upon the argument that the theft had caused the bank no loss whatever. At that time the banks had to make a daily return of foreign currency to the authorities, and were credited with the equivalent in marks at the current rate. The 10,000 dollars the young man stole were worth 580,000,000 marks on the day he stole them; but by the time he was arrested the value of those remaining was about 2,000,000,000 marks. Even allowing for the few millions he had squandered, so the defence argued, the bank had made a large profit, which it would not have done if the dollars had been entered at the original rate.

It need hardly be said that this ingenious plea did not help the young man. He went to prison, and by the time he was discharged the introduction of the rentenmark had brought about a more stable economy.

16

Emil Jannings and the 'Earthquake'

ON THE last night of 1923, that is to say, shortly after the ending of the inflationary period, the Adlon revived the traditional New Year's Eve supper-dance. Although the menu was not to be compared with those of before the war, the revival was welcomed everywhere as a sign that better times were on the way. Many former habitués of the hotel were induced to return to celebrate in those historic rooms which, despite everything, could still wear the aspect of a friendly private gathering.

'Tonight it's going to be a proper party again,' said one of the pages, delighted at the prospect of solid tips. 'Not just millions shoved into your hand because people don't know what else to do with them, but real money—marks and pfennigs!'

The many changes that had taken place naturally left their mark on the New Year festivities of post-revolutionary Berlin. To understand their significance one must know something of what New Year's Eve means to Berliners. For them the occasion is something like the equivalent of the Rhineland carnivals. The leading hotels and restaurants always prepared special suppers, the menus being published, so that the public could decide, according to the bill of fare and the price, where they would go to celebrate the passing of the Old Year. The establishments, and the streets wherein they are situated—the Friedrichstrasse, the Leipziger Strasse, the Kurfürstendamm—were, and still are, scenes of tumultuous revelry, reaching its climax with the tolling of the church bells at midnight, and, before the war, the firing of guns.

Before the war New Year's Eve was followed on New Year's Morning by the 'Great Awakening' of the Berlin garrison. All Berlin came to Unter den Linden to witness the New Year celebrations of the Royal Family. The Hohenzollerns were not late sleepers. The 'Great Awakening' actually began at eight o'clock,

142

when most of the previous night's celebrants were sleeping off
their hang-overs, or treating them in the traditional manner with
pickled herrings or Pilsener beer.

It was started by the band of the 2nd Dragoon Guards playing
a chorale from the gallery encircling the cupola of the palace; and
following this spiritual greeting to the New Year came the worldly
greeting in the inner courtyard, accompanied by the band of the
4th Regiment of Guards playing 'Rejoice in Life'. Immediately
afterwards the Royal Family attended divine service in the chapel,
and this was also attended by most people having entry at Court.

Thus from the early morning onwards Unter den Linden presented a magnificent spectacle. The people of Berlin streamed up
and down the avenue, flooding over the roadway from the Brandenburger Tor to the armoury building, while others watched from
the windows of the Adlon. Later in the morning came the procession down the central lane of the avenue, between the two rows
of trees, the carriages of the *corps diplomatique* with their occupants in gold-embroidered ceremonial dress, and the brilliant
military uniforms of the German princes and generals.

After the church service came the New Year's reception in the
White Hall of the palace, and then the Kaiser went with his sons
to perform the age-old ceremony of giving out the password in
the armoury building. It was on one such occasion that the photograph was taken of Kaiser Wilhelm II marching with his six sons
in a row beside him. A postcard was made of it which became
world-famous in the years before the 1914 war. The password was
announced by the Kaiser himself, always the same one, embody-
ing the old Prussian tradition:

'Königsberg—Berlin.'

In the evening there was a gala performance at the Opera,
generally attended by the Royal couple, while the boxes were
filled with their guests and other members of the Court. Many of
these later went on to a final New Year's party at the Adlon, where
Lorenz Adlon was always present to receive them personally.

All that lay in the past, but the Berlin tradition of celebrating
New Year's Eve was far from being forgotten. On the contrary,

after the hardships and austerities of the war, the post-war up-
heavals and the inflation, the desire to celebrate was greater than
ever; and the mass of confetti, paper-balls and streamers which
littered the rooms and had to be cleared away the next morning,
bore witness to the gaiety of the proceedings at the Adlon during
that last night of 1923, the hotel's first official New Year's Eve
ball for so many years.

It was on this night that Alfred Braun, the popular Berlin
broadcaster, gave his first New Year's commentary from the
Adlon. He was less concerned with the menu with its fixed and
stable prices, remarkable though this phenomenon seemed after
the financial nightmare Germany had lived through, than with
the dance-band, the name of which was being publicly announced
for the first time, and which was destined to become a very important addition to the amenities of the Adlon. Even Fritz Kreis-
ler praised it and especially its leader.

The band was that of Marek Weber. Louis Adlon engaged it
when I suggested to him that the Paris habit of the five o'clock
tea-dance was one which might well be made popular in Berlin.
There was, of course, dancing in the evening as well, but the tea-
dances, designed for members of the best society, rapidly became
a particular attraction of the Adlon. Other hotels imitated them,
but none could rival them.

I also suggested to my husband that we should adopt another
Paris custom and engage male professional dance-partners—
'gigolos' as they were so sadly called—for the tea-dances. There
were eventually three of these, and their presence was in itself a
reflection of the change in the times, for they were young men of
good appearance, excellent education and impeccable manners.
The Adlon thus rendered socially acceptable a custom that had
hitherto been associated only with inferior establishments, and in
doing so added to its own attractions. The young men, it need
hardly be said, were all expert in the newest dances. A weight was
lifted from the hearts of non-dancing husbands; and ladies no
longer in their first youth, who still longed to dance, need no
longer be wallflowers.

Arising out of this another thought occurred to me which turned out to be even more important both for the Adlon and for the social habits of Berlin. There should be two orchestras playing alternately, either uninterrupted dance-music or, if they were called for, occasional concert-pieces.

Louis Adlon agreed to this, too; but although the idea had come quickly enough, it was not so easily realized. The two bands had to provide a contrast in styles, with a hint of competition between them that would catch the interest of the public.

We were obliged to wait some time before we found what we wanted. We travelled about, taking careful note of any dance-band that might suit us. Finally we went on a trip to Egypt, and at the Heliopolis Palace, in Cairo, we discovered a tango orchestra containing a number of Italian instrumentalists and directed by Giovanni Muzzi. After listening to it several times we decided that this was what we had been looking for. Louis was no less enthusiastic than I, for besides being a wonderful rider he was an extremely good dancer.

'We'll take them back with us!' he said.

We made Giovanni Muzzi an offer on the spot. He at once arranged to be released from his contract in Cairo, and a few days later the entire orchestra set sail for Germany at the expense of the Adlon. Its appearance in Berlin caused a sensation.

From then on we always had two dance-bands playing alternately. When Marek Weber, who was Polish, left us, we engaged the band of Dajos Bela, a Hungarian. His pianist was Franz Grothe, who soon made a name for himself as a composer of song hits, many of which were heard for the first time at the Adlon. The two bands, those of Dajos Bela and Giovanni Muzzi, rapidly achieved an international reputation.

Thus the social occasions at the Adlon acquired an added flavour of cosmopolitanism, and they came to have a place of their own in the gay Berlin life of that time.

I will end this chapter with an account of a small personal experience which occurred at about this time, and which, I venture

L

to say, bears witness to my judgment in human affairs and instinctive knowledge of people, a knowledge that has served me well all my life.

One evening Louis Adlon and I went to the Schauspielhaus (the State Theatre), in the Gendarmenmarkt, to see a comedy entitled 'Duel on the Lido'. I will be frank and confess that we went only because a guest at the hotel had returned two tickets at the last minute. However, the piece had a brilliant cast, which included Lucie Mannheim, Friedrich Forster, Fritz Kortner and Albert Patry.

Albert Patry played the part of an old-fashioned, highly respectable general whose daughter was everything that was sophisticated, modern and decadent—a young lady, in short, of the kind that was called a 'vamp' in those days. She wore a monocle, smoked cigarettes and was altogether most seductive and dangerous. She did not, however, have a great many lines to speak, but had to convey the character by her expression and by the use she made of her beautiful and expressive hands and no less expressive legs.

Owing to the fact that we arrived late, so that I only had time for a quick glance at the programme, I did not discover the name of the young actress who played this part. But I saw at once that here was someone who was destined to have a great career on the stage. She had shown remarkable skill in portraying breeding and sensibility as well as the general 'queerness' of the time.

After the performance, when I was making my customary tour through the restaurant and public rooms of the hotel, I noticed a small, lively party in a remote corner of the bar. One of them was a girl whose face seemed very familiar, and I asked Otto Fix, our barman, who they were.

'They're actors from the Schauspielhaus celebrating their first night.'

'From the Schauspielhaus! Why, that's where we've just come from!'

'The girl lives just down the road, in Felsing's house.'

Then I realized why I had known her face. Her name was

Maria Magdalena von Losch. She lived with her mother, an army officer's widow, at 19 Unter den Linden. Both mother and daughter were known to the hotel, but I had not heard that the daughter had gone on the stage.

'She's the young actress who pleased me so much tonight,' I said. 'She'll go a long way.'

In the years that followed she was destined to pay many visits to the Adlon. She was very energetic, very purposeful, and she always knew exactly what she wanted. She also knew exactly what she could and should eat, having regard to her figure. She was always calling for special dishes, and no matter how difficult they might be to procure she always got exactly what she ordered. But by that time she was no longer Maria Magdalena von Losch. She had run her two Christian names together and borrowed her father's Christian name for a surname. The result was—Marlene Dietrich.

It happened, some years later, that the Adlon played a part in her rise to fame. In 1929 Emil Jannings returned to Germany from America and resumed his visits to the hotel, where he very often came to drink Pilsener beer in company with Josef von Sternberg and Erich Pommer. He had been engaged to play the star part in the film of the short story by Heinrich Mann, 'Professor Unrat', which became world-famous under the title, 'The Blue Angel'. He was very much absorbed in the part, and seemed to be positively living the life of that seedy schoolmaster.

'He reminds me of a figure from my own schooldays,' he told Louis Adlon.

Jannings was extremely fond of Pilsener beer. When he entered the bar the waiter was in the habit of bringing him a glass without waiting for the order, and as a rule he would drink half of it at a gulp.

But one afternoon while he was preparing the role of Professor Unrat he came in looking depressed and quite unlike his usual self. The glass of Pilsener was brought to him as usual, but on this occasion he merely sipped it and at once exclaimed:

'What sort of beer's this? It's not real Pilsener.'

'It's just the same as usual, Herr Jannings,' said the waiter, hurrying back to him.

'It tastes of the cask,' barked Jannings, growing angrier every instant.

The waiter silently removed the beer and went to fetch another glass.

As everyone knows, the drawing of Pilsener takes a little time because the *Haube*, as it is called—the head of froth—must be tall, firm and flowery. Perhaps the barman took especial pains, so that he may have been rather longer about it than usual. Suddenly Jannings banged with the flat of his hand on the table and shouted:

'Where the devil's my beer? This place is a pigsty today!'

The waiter brought the fresh glass. Instead of tasting it, however, Jannings got a coin out of his pocket and said sarcastically:

'Now we'll see if it's the real thing or not.'

Connoisseurs are fond of testing the genuineness of Pilsener by laying a copper coin on the froth, which should be so stiff that it will support its weight without letting it sink to the bottom of the glass. Jannings applied this test, and of course the beer passed it—the coin remained on the surface of the froth. But instead of appeasing him this seemed only to increase his anger. He seemed to be looking for any excuse to relieve his feelings. Clearly there was something very wrong with Herr Jannings that afternoon.

At this moment Louis Adlon entered the bar, having just come in from riding. He saw Jannings, himself a keen horseman, eyeing his riding-breeches, which he had not yet changed. So he went over to him and started to chat to him about horses and kindred matters, which finally had the effect of soothing him down. When Jannings eventually seized his Pilsener and gulped down half of it, as usual, Louis thought that the time had come to try to discover the cause of the trouble.

'How's the new film going, Herr Jannings?'

The actor's face grew dark again. He grunted and said:

'It's the very devil. My first talkie, and I'm in despair over it!'

'But why? No one could have a better voice for talking-films than you.'

This remark seemed to surprise Jannings. He emptied his glass, called for another, and looking sternly at my husband said in a formal, precise way:

'That's not the point, Herr Adlon. So far as I am concerned we could start shooting immediately. But the most important thing is still lacking.'

'The most important thing?'

Herr Jannings sipped his fresh glass of beer, this time without testing it, and said:

'The woman.'

'But good heavens, there are plenty of actresses in Berlin!'

'You've no need to tell me that,' said Jannings. 'We've auditioned twenty in the last week or so. And do you know what I have discovered?'

'What?'

Jannings leaned across the table with his glass in his hand and a twinkle in his eye.

'It's no good unless we can find a young woman who can make even a hardened old-timer like me sit up and take notice.'

He finished his beer, glanced with a faint grin at Louis, winked and set down his glass with a thud.

'In other words, what we want is an erotic earthquake!'

And with this he left the hotel.

At the time Marlene Dietrich was playing in a Berlin revue. We had been to it and had been greatly impressed by the immense growth of her talent. By unobtrusive means we contrived to direct Jannings' attention to the piece and to her. He went to see it, went again, and then insisted that Erich Pommer and Josef von Sternberg should accompany him. It was Marlene Dietrich's voice above all, harsh yet tender, which convinced him that she was the 'erotic earthquake' for which he was looking.

And so the partnership was brought about which led to one of the most sensational of all films, and which, with the song 'Falling in Love Again', made Marlene Dietrich world-famous. It is pleasant to think that the Adlon had a hand in it.

17

The Maharaja of Patiala

So MANY worlds met and mingled in the Adlon. That of the Maharajah of Patiala, for instance, who brought with him a world of his own.

One day after the Maharajah had been stopping some time at the hotel he came into the hall and said:

'The grand old man was angry.'

He had just returned from a private visit to President Hindenburg, of whom he was a great admirer.

'The grand old man was very angry,' he repeated. 'He threatened the chauffeur with his stick!'

The chauffeur who had driven the Maharajah to the presidential palace was Carl Mirow, our own private chauffeur, who for a time had driven the field-marshal during the war. President Hindenburg therefore knew him well, but this was something that the Maharajah did not know. I saw Mirow standing in the background, gazing towards me with an expression of extreme embarrassment. I made a sign to him and he vanished into the head office.

We then sat down with the Maharajah in a quiet corner of the lounge and asked him to tell us what had happened between the President and the chauffeur. As we knew, from the day of his arrival in Berlin the Maharajah had sought an audience with the President. It would be hard to imagine a greater contrast than that existing between the two men—the elegant, charming Indian prince and the massive, rugged Prussian field-marshal.

The Maharajah was still very much affected by the impression the President had made on him. He talked for a time of his face, 'like a ravaged landscape', and his voice, 'that rolled down upon me like distant thunder'. But he had been most struck by his soldierly bearing and his extreme, old-world courtesy—'He made me feel that he was particularly glad to meet me . . .'

Finally he came back to the extraordinary episode in which the President had seemed to be threatening our chauffeur.

But before going on with the story I must say something about Carl Mirow, who, besides being the head of the hotel car-service, was our personal chauffeur and our good and loyal friend. He was, and still is, one of the oldest motorists in Germany, with a licence dated 1900 and bearing the designation, No. 1, List 3. As I write these lines he is just celebrating his three-millionth kilo-metre! The Mercedes company has given him a gold pin for every million, and when he completed his second million they gave him a gold engraved wrist-watch as well. Not long ago he received a gold medal from the German Automobile Club for fifty years of accident-free driving. He still lives in Berlin, and until very recently was driving the chairman of the Berlin Central Bank. Before he came to us he had been chauffeur not only to Field-Marshal Hindenburg but to a great many other distinguished people.

When Hindenburg became President he sent for Mirow and asked him to return to him as his chauffeur. But after a brief in-ward struggle Mirow decided in favour of the situation at the Adlon, with its not inconsiderable material advantages. The pay of the President's chauffeur, honourable though the post was, was governed by the scale laid down for State employees of his grade.

All this, however, was unknown to the Maharajah. The greatly desired interview with the legendary 'grand old man' of Germany had passed off to the satisfaction of both parties. The President, slightly bowed over his ebony stick, had personally escorted his visitor back to the car, and then the untoward incident had occurred. While the Maharajah was seating himself Hindenburg had seen who the chauffeur was. He had shaken his stick with mock severity over his head, saying:

'I've still got a bone to pick with you, Mirow, for not coming back to me!'

Mirow sat stiffly in the driver's seat, not knowing what to say except, 'Zu Befehl, Herr Generalfeldmarschall!' while he took his hands off the wheel and rested them on his thighs in correct, soldierly fashion.

The Maharajah had witnessed the incident with the utmost bewilderment, not understanding a word of it. As the car started along the Wilhelmstrasse he asked his interpreter to question Mirow, who was now plunged in embarrassment. How could he hope to explain to the Maharajah, who knew nothing of wages or tips, that he had rejected a post of honour in the service of the President for the sake of his job at the Adlon?

During the painful three-minute drive back to the hotel he sought to escape from his predicament by pretending not to understand the question, but this only had the effect of irritating the Maharajah. He had been not only mystified but greatly put out by the incident, as his agitated voice proclaimed while he was telling us the story. And, failing any other explanation, he had invented one of his own, based upon his understanding of the 'Hindenburg legend'. He had come to the conclusion that the President's wrath had been occasioned by the fact that Mirow's bearing had not conformed to that laid down by the rigid Prussian military code. He had, he said, seen the chauffeur start when the President spoke to him, and then pull himself together and sit stiffly upright.

'The old man was really very cross indeed,' he said again; and it was clear that the Maharajah of Patiala did not like the idea of being driven by a chauffeur of whom the great President Hindenburg disapproved.

Thus there was a ticklish situation. Knowing that Hindenburg was very fond of Mirow, I ran into the office to hear his side of the story, and burst into laughter when he told me what had really happened. But, like him, I did not feel that the Maharajah could be told the true story of why he had refused the President's offer, even though it reflected credit upon the hotel. Something else had to be found. I had already told the Maharajah that Mirow had been Field-Marshal Hindenburg's driver during the war. I went back to him and said:

'Your Highness, it seems that the whole thing was nothing but a joke between old war-comrades. The President often invites Mirow to go and see him, and they sit and chat about old times. But recently Mirow has been particularly busy. The President was reproaching him, in the friendliest fashion, for having neglected him.'

Well, it was a story containing more truth than falsehood, for they were indeed old friends. Its effect upon the Maharajah was enormous. From then on Mirow was the apple of his eye. He was obliged to accompany him everywhere, and the Maharajah constantly referred to him as 'the Field-Marshal's driver', to such an extent that this became a joke in the hotel. It was on Mirow's advice that he bought three Mercedes cars during his visit to Germany—the most luxurious Mercedes had ever built.

The Maharajah brought a very great deal of money into the country. He bought and bought, as did his numerous retinue.

He engaged a whole orchestra, a photographer with his entire family, and he bought a great many large canvases from Fischer, the Court painter in the Unter den Linden arcade. To convey some idea of his fantastic wealth I will tell a story which became a legend in the Adlon.

It need hardly be said that the subject of tips loomed large in the thoughts and conversation of the staff. In all German hotels the ten-per-cent service charge which is added to the bill goes into the pool, the contents of which are divided among the staff according to a system of points reflecting the relative status of each member. In an hotel of the Adlon's class, however, it is not this ten per cent that they talk about, but the private tips bestowed directly on individuals for special services. In this matter habits vary very greatly. Experienced hotel-nomads tend to tip immediately on arriving, believing that by doing so they get better service. It was certainly not the case at the Adlon, where every guest was personally and individually served regardless of his open-handedness. There are other guests who consider it wrong to give any tips at all. They pack their trunks in secret and leave at short notice, sometimes at night. Yet others press a coin into every hand that has assisted them. But upon his departure the Maharajah of Patiala gave the staff manager the sum of no less than 40,000 reichsmarks to be divided among the staff. The chauffeur, Mirow, received a gold wrist-watch, a cigarette-case and no doubt a substantial sum in cash, about which he tactfully said nothing.

The Maharajah and his Court brought many strange things with them, but there was one in particular which makes an entertaining story.

They were very particular about what they ate. The dishes served to the Maharajah and his attendants were composed mainly of chicken and rice, and prepared by the cook he had brought with him from Patiala.

This was a man of great dignity, much given to rolling his eyes in a solemn manner. To safeguard against the risk that any 'impurity' might contaminate his cooking a separate place was cleared for him in the kitchen, and, of course, special utensils were placed at his disposal.

This singular man, who always wore a turban, allowed no one to help him when he was engaged in preparing a dish. The most he would permit was that the hotel scullery staff should do the washing-up, and he never left the kitchen until this was finished. He then himself stored away the dishes and utensils in a special cupboard, murmuring incantations as he did so. He murmured in similar fashion while engaged in the act of cooking, which he preferred to do over an open fire. It was understood that he was repeating religious incantations designed to ensure that the dishes should have the proper nutritive or purgative virtues. The dishes thus prepared for the Maharajah and his household were also eaten by the Maharajah's servants.

The cook was deeply mistrustful of all European customs, and indeed of all Europeans. He insisted upon buying live poultry, which he selected himself, being taken to the Alexanderplatz market for the purpose. The birds he selected were housed in a special fowl-run in one of the hotel gardens, its door secured by a large padlock. The cook kept the key to this on a green cord hung round his neck, and the cocks crowed in the mornings to the amusement of drowsy guests who thought themselves in the country.

The cocks and hens were slaughtered under the cook's own mistrustful gaze, and so from time to time the stock had to be renewed. His appearance at the Alexanderplatz, with his beard and turban, always aroused the liveliest interest among the broad-beamed ladies of the market. 'Here comes Mohammed!' The word went round directly the turban came in sight, and the nickname was adopted by the Adlon staff and received by its bearer with a good-humoured gleam of white teeth.

He was accustomed to examine the birds he bought in a highly professional manner, but on one occasion a hen escaped from his grasp and fluttered away, cackling, to land in a crate of eggs. Greatly concerned, Mohammed asked the hotel servant who accompanied him, and who acted as his interpreter, to inquire whether any of the eggs were broken. The stall-woman grinned and said, 'Only a bit bent!' and the reply, when finally he had understood it, gave him immense pleasure.

In the course of my tours of inspection of the house and kitchens I often visited the fowl-run. On one occasion I found there two ladies belonging to the Maharajah's household. They were veiled, and one of them was chirruping to the fowls and scattering corn with a child-like hand adorned with rings and deep red finger-nails. She looked more like a young girl than a woman, and it appeared that this feeding of the fowls was one of her duties as a member of the Maharajah's household, conferred upon her because she was the youngest, and regularly performed, always veiled and in the company of another woman.

One of our youngest page-boys, his name was Fritz, had the job of fetching the corn and placing it in readiness, in a white linen bag, outside the Maharajah's apartments. There seemed to be no harm in this. It certainly never occurred to me that those two children, the girl from the Maharajah's household and the youthful page-boy, were destined one day to set the whole hotel in an uproar.

The Maharajah and his household occupied the entire first floor of the hotel, the so-called 'ducal apartments'. These looked partly on to Unter den Linden and partly over the Pariser Platz towards the Brandenburger Tor and our beloved Tiergarten.

The ladies and members of the entourage always took their meals in their rooms. The Maharajah alone dined with us in the restaurant, at our invitation; and in return he sometimes invited us to a meal upstairs in his suite. A few Indian ladies were sometimes present, but they were always very quiet and reserved. They sat there, each more lovely than the last, like a circle of bright-feathered, fragile birds, but with far less twittering than would have gone on had they been a party of European women. They were to be seen but very seldom to be heard. I find this a charming custom. The atmosphere of tranquil harmony did great service to the wonderful food, and especially to the exquisite rice dishes which Mohammed was so skilful in preparing.

After the Maharajah had been staying some weeks at the hotel we invited him to spend a few days with us at our country house in Neufahrland. The party was composed of about twenty people, including the Maharajah, the Maharaneee, their eldest son and a number of ladies and gentlemen of the household. It goes without saying that Mohammed and the rice-cook who assisted him were also brought along, and a private corner of our big kitchen was allotted them. The rest of the Maharajah's large party remained at the Adlon.

The Maharajah, a man of most elegant and distinguished appearance, extremely handsome and impressive in his bearing, wore European clothes and the turban of his country, but this was never adorned with any jewellery such as he would have worn in his native land when he was in full Indian costume. He never wore jewels in Europe except to mark some particular ceremonial occasion.

The Maharanee and the other ladies wore wonderful, brightly-coloured saris. Their shoes were exquisite examples of oriental workmanship, adorned with silver buckles and pearls, and, needless to say, they wore silk stockings. They all had costly jewellery, and beautiful brooches gleamed upon them wherever brooches were called for.

While the gentlemen talked and occasionally played tennis, the ladies sat quietly together. It was not the custom for Indian ladies of their rank, and they all came of princely families, to take any part in the general conversation. I had leisure to study them and can only say that they were indescribably lovely creatures, with big, soft eyes and exquisite, refined faces. They had an air of delicate fragility such as one never sees in European women.

I wanted to talk to them, but it was out of the question. We exchanged friendly smiles, and that was as far as it went. I could only gaze and wonder, lost in admiration.

The Maharanee, the mother of the eldest son and heir, was treated by everyone with especial consideration. As the wife who had borne the Maharajah's first son she was throughout her life the first lady of the Court. The others were not only all exceptionally beautiful, they were all young. When they grew older and began to lose their looks they would be left behind in the Royal Harem in the palace in India. They lived entirely cut off from the world but in circumstances of the utmost luxury, and I was told that they were perfectly contented and happy.

In general it is not an easy matter for a European to talk informally with an Indian prince, the less so when he is the Maharajah of Patiala, one of the richest and most exalted of the world's princes, and a member of the religious sect of the Sikhs. There are so many subjects which may not be touched on—family matters, for instance, and women and love. To mention any of these would be the greatest *faux pas*, and the Maharajah would at once bring the conversation politely to an end. However, there was still plenty of scope for general discussion, for the Maharajah and his gentlemen-in-attendance were all highly educated men, the equals in knowledge of any European. Indeed, they knew far more about Europe than we did about their country.

We went for excursions on the lake in our big motor-launch, of which I took the wheel. This caused the Indian ladies great astonishment; but I have always taken particular pleasure in driving a car or steering a boat.

The Maharajah's first visit to our country house was followed by others in the course of which our relations became increasingly informal. And one day he invited us to take tea in his suite at the Adlon. When the meal was over the gentlemen withdrew to another room, leaving me alone with the ladies. There now occurred a slight but very pleasant rapprochement between us. I begged them to abandon something of their reserve and to tell me what they thought of their visit to Europe, and I also asked them to tell me if there was any special thing they would like during their stay at the hotel.

The youngest of the ladies, the same small, elfin creature whom I had seen by the fowl-run, whispered something to the Maharanee which caused that lady to burst out laughing and repeat to the other ladies, in Punjabi, what she had said. She then told me that the elf, as she called her, was dying to have some toys.

'All our women adore toys,' said the Maharanee.

I had not known until then of the attraction that toys possess for the people of Eastern countries. Children are seldom given them because of their enormous price. So it can happen that a doll with real hair, which says 'Mamma', may become the treasured possession of an elderly woman; and mechanical toys of all kinds possess for them a sort of enchantment such as children of the West may find in the reading of fairy tales.

Then the other women began timidly to express their secret wishes. One had a particularly feminine ambition. She was longing to visit a hat shop.

'But,' I said, 'you can't wear a European hat in Patiala!'

She laughed, and the others all laughed with her.

'No, but everyone would be so excited if I could take some home with me.'

We greatly enjoyed ourselves discussing the ladies' many and varied aspirations, but they did not seem to me easy of fulfilment. It was not customary for the ladies of the Maharajah's household to go out shopping, and indeed their rigorous protocol forbade them to show themselves in public at any time, except in his company.

I sat thinking over the problem while they plied me unceasingly with oriental sweets—dates in honey, candied fruits and nuts, an endless variety of sugary delights which it would have been impolite to refuse, but which threatened to have a disastrous effect on my figure. Of course I could easily have gone out and ordered all the things they wanted, but I knew that what they really longed for was to go to the shops and choose for themselves. We put our heads together and I promised to find a way.

Presently the Maharajah returned to the room with my husband and the gentlemen of his entourage. The ladies, including the Maharanee, at once rose and made a deep obeisance. And by now I had made my plan and was confident that, despite all the rules and formalities of the strict Indian Court, I would be able to rejoice the ladies' hearts by taking them shopping at Wertheim's.

By the use of careful diplomacy such as women understand, and such as must be constantly practised by anyone at the head of an establishment like the Adlon, I contrived to make the request a personal favour which it would have been awkward for the Maharajah to refuse, and which he most graciously granted. The matter was agreed, but of course on the understanding that one of the gentlemen of his suite would escort us.

So the next day we went shopping, going on foot down Unter den Linden. The Berliners had long grown accustomed to the sight of exotic figures in their streets, but the group of Indian ladies in their bright saris, their faces hidden by veils, naturally attracted many interested glances.

It was a good deal worse than this at Wertheim's—the large department stores. I had rung up the shop to arrange for a member of the staff to show us round, and he was awaiting us at a side entrance where we hoped to attract less attention. Nevertheless the toy-department, where we first went, was speedily thronged with shoppers gazing in fascination at the Indian ladies' rapture as they contemplated the bright counters displaying the products of the Nuremberg toy-manufacturers.

They bought with seeming recklessness, but their good taste was always apparent. Dolls and mechanical animals interested them most, but they did not overlook boxes of bricks for the children at home. And the little 'elf' got her heart's desire—an electric train! I shall never forget her look of happiness.

Altogether their purchases amounted to a vanload. At the ladies' request I ordered everything to be packed and sent round to the hotel immediately, so that they might lose no time in enjoying them. By the time we got back to the hotel the van had just arrived, and the ladies hurried excitedly up to their rooms. I called to some of the page-boys to help with the unloading of the van and take the parcels upstairs. The boy, Fritz, was one of them.

'Be particularly careful with the electric train,' I said to him.

This shopping excursion occurred towards the end of the Maharajah's visit. A few days later came the day of his departure, and only someone who actually saw the extent and lavishness of his household can realize what this entailed.

The private and separate events occurring in a great hotel should, so far as is possible, go unperceived by the other guests. The wheels should continue to turn smoothly, whatever happens. But that complications and crises can spring up out of nowhere goes without saying, and of these the nightmare moments attending the Maharajah's departure furnish an unforgettable example.

At the last moment the Maharajah expressed the wish to visit a new chemical factory recently opened by the famous Leuna works at Merseburg. As it happened, Louis Adlon was on terms of particular friendship with Dr. Carl Duisberg, the head of the 'I.G.-Farben' concern, of which the directors commonly stayed at the Adlon when they came to Berlin. He was therefore in a position to forward the request to the proper quarter, without the need for bureaucratic formalities, and an invitation to the Maharajah to visit Merseburg was promptly forthcoming.

The Maharajah at once accepted, and this led to an alteration in his travel arrangements which caused us a severe headache. Trunks had to be packed at once and loaded on to vans, a difficult and laborious task in itself, when they contained the effects of a vast oriental household of ladies, equerries and servants. While I was doing what I could to maintain order in the confusion, amid the hurried coming and going of Indian and hotel servants, I heard a sound of bitter weeping coming from one of the ladies' apartments in the Maharajah's suite.

The page-boy, Fritz, happened to be handy, and I sent him through the muddle of trunks, valises and gaping wardrobes to find out what the trouble was.

He came back and said:

'It's the youngest lady who's crying. They're putting her train in one of the packing-cases, but she wants to take it with her in the car.'

The ravishing little creature—I could not bear to think of her unhappy.

'Pack up the train yourself, Fritz,' I said, 'and put it in the car when no one is looking.'

Fritz's eyes twinkled with delighted naughtiness. It was a job after his own heart. But I would never have given the order if I had known what it was to lead to.

I went downstairs preoccupied with a thousand details. Mirow was to drive the Maharajah to Cannes, and we should have to find someone to take his place. We were lending one of our managers to act as travel-agent to the party for four weeks, and he would have to be sent off in advance. Two police officials were peering about in the lounge, having been appointed to the task of safeguarding the Maharajah and his family. And then a reporter from the publishing house of Ullstein came up to me and would not let me go.

He had heard that the Maharajah's ladies had been buying toys at Wertheim's, and he was most anxious to know what kind of toys they were.

'It will interest every mother in Germany,' he kept saying.

M

'I've no time for mothers at the moment,' I said, but he would not be shaken off.

'Were they mostly dolls, or toy soldiers?'

'No toy soldiers,' I said, and in my impatience I added: 'One of them bought an electric train.'

At this his eyes opened very wide.

'An electric train? What in the world does the wife of an Indian prince want with an electric train? Have they got electric light at the palace? I hope it won't blow the fuses!'

The silly remark annoyed me, and I was just about to give him a sharp answer when something occurred to rob me of my breath.

The lights went out!

It was early evening. There was a brief interlude of cloistral calm, and then confusion broke loose. Since the light-signals no longer worked the voices of room-guests could be heard upstairs, calling for attendance. A cry for help came from the lift, which was stuck between two floors, and one of the cooks came out of the kitchen scolding loudly on his way to the central light installation. The diners in the restaurant stayed quietly in their places, but the waiters rushed agitatedly about, bumping into one another. There were sounds of falling crockery. The hall-porter had at once fastened the revolving door, only to find that he had locked someone in.

As I sank in exhaustion on to a chair someone came hurriedly up to me.

'We're the police. Will you please take us to the Maharajah of Patiala. We're supposed to be looking after him.'

'The Maharajah isn't in the hotel,' I said. 'You'll find all the members of his household on the first floor, if you care to go upstairs.'

They went off, lighting their way with electric torches. And then, just as emergency lamps were being fetched, the lights went on again as mysteriously as they had gone out.

I was most curious to know what had caused the disturbance. Louis Adlon and the manager came from the control room. They had found everything in order, and the chief electrician was quite unable to explain the failure. He was now checking the wiring. I turned round and again encountered the reporter from Ullstein's, who was smiling somewhat sardonically, it seemed to me.

'Have they found the cause of the trouble, gnädige Frau?' he asked. At this moment the lights went out again.

There was further confusion, and I heard the head page-boy asking:

'Where's Fritz got to?'

'He went up to the first floor,' someone said.

Suddenly the manager came up to me.

'Frau Adlon, the Maharanee wants to see you. The youngest of the ladies has disappeared!'

I was terrified. What were the police doing? No one had seen them. Probably they were crawling under the beds, looking for the saboteur who had caused the failure of the lights. I seized a lantern and went up to the first floor, where I found the Maharanee seated in despair on a trunk.

'What can have happened to the child?' she said with tears in her eyes. 'If the Maharajah hears of this she will never be allowed in his presence again. Something must be done. Do you think it possible that someone has kidnapped her?'

Undoubtedly something had to be done. The Maharajah was due back in half an hour. I hurried downstairs again, calling for my husband.

And then, as though the name of Louis Adlon possessed some magic, the lights went on again, this time for good. Within a few minutes everything was back to normal. The lift was working, the light-signals were flickering, the revolving door was spinning like a windmill. Soon afterwards the page-boy, Fritz, hurried past me, carrying a large parcel in his arms. Behind him strolled the Ullstein reporter, and then a chambermaid came from upstairs and whispered to me:

'She's back!'

'Who is?'

Of all the idiotic questions! But the girl simply answered:

'The little princess.'

'Where was she?'

'I don't know. She came back to their suite, and she was laughing. The Maharanee asked her what she was laughing at, but she wouldn't say.'

Suddenly I thought of the parcel Fritz had been carrying; but as I swung round I found myself again confronted by the Ullstein reporter. He smiled at me and said:

'You'd hardly believe it, gnädige Frau, but I know all.'

'You know all? And aren't you going to tell me?'

He glanced at the clock and then became exceedingly serious.

'Frau Adlon,' he said slowly, 'the Maharajah is due back very shortly. I want an interview with him directly he arrives. I want to know what they showed him at Leuna, and whether his visit is likely to lead to any kind of commercial contract. If you will arrange this for me I will tell you the true story of what happened here this evening, and I will promise not to tell anyone else. If not, the story will be printed in tomorrow's paper.'

It was shameless blackmail, but what was I to do? I had no means of knowing whether the story was harmful or not, but I did know that no hint of scandal must be allowed to touch any member of the Maharajah's household. So I promised to try and arrange the interview. I was only just in time, for a moment later the porter pushed the revolving door and the Maharajah entered. I went up to him and made the request. He looked hard at the reporter and finally nodded—

'Five minutes.'

In fact, the interview lasted half an hour, and the reporter spent another half-hour telephoning before finally we sat down together in the lounge.

He then told me how the second failure of the lights had caused him suddenly to think of what I had just said to him about an electric train, and to wonder whether it could be this, operated by someone who did not understand it, which was causing the trouble. He had crept upstairs and presently had heard the sound of voices in agitated discussion coming from behind the half-open door of a big linen-room at the end of the first-floor corridor.

Looking round the door he had found the little princess, still veiled, seated on the floor amid the railway lines, demanding to know why her train had stopped. The set had been plugged into a light-point, and operating the control-box, evidently not very skilfully, was Fritz, the page-boy.

The two children—what else can one call them?—seemed to be quite unconscious of the havoc they were causing. It was the journalist who had broken up this happy party and sent the girl scampering back to her room while Fritz packed up the train and took it hurriedly downstairs.

So that was it, and I heaved a great sigh of relief to think that it had been no worse. Then a waiter came up to us and said that the police were anxious to interview a suspicious character who had been seen lurking in the hotel, both upstairs and downstairs.

'That must be you,' I said to the Ullstein man. 'You'd better go and talk to them.'

He obligingly did so; and presently returned mopping his brow and calling for a large whisky.

'I've had the worst ten minutes of my life,' he said. 'They suspected me of planning to abduct the girl!'

18

'Car-and-Jewels' Contest

ANOTHER episode which is worth recalling took place at the time of the Maharajah of Patiala's visit. I was talking to the Maharajah in the reception-hall when I perceived that he was glancing over my shoulder. I had my back to the main entrance. Looking round I saw a remarkably good-looking and elegant blonde, so like Marlene Dietrich that for a moment I thought it was she. In fact, however, it was the actress, Manny W., whose beauty had made her a leading figure in stage and sporting circles. It was not surprising that she had attracted the Maharajah's notice.

She walked composedly through the lounge, with the air of one accustomed to admiration, and went on into the restaurant; and it struck me that the performance had been carried out with one eye on the Maharajah. Our restaurant manager, who knew her, said to me later:

'She's a particular friend of an Austrian industrialist, a Herr Egermann, who stops here quite often. She had tea with him here yesterday. But he flew to Vienna this morning.'

So Herr Egermann was in Vienna.

Manny W. was young and extremely attractive, with a particular talent for keeping several men on a string at once. It was in England, where she had passed a season under distinguished auspices, that she had gained the nickname of 'Manny Double-You'. She was an only child, the daughter of respectable middle-class parents who had had quite different plans for her future. She adored clothes and jewellery, and it was fruitless to try to interest her in anything else. After starting as a dress model she had gone on the stage, winning some fame with her looks.

Many entertaining stories were told about Manny, some of them invented, no doubt, but which none the less throw light on

166

her character. It was said, for instance, that long before the outset of her career, when she had reached the age at which it becomes necessary to instruct the young in the facts of life, her mother had undertaken this delicate task. She had explained the matter fully and carefully, and Manny had listened with close attention. Then, after thought, she had wrinkled her forehead and said:

'Yes. I see. It's very interesting. But what does one wear for it?'

So that was Manny, and with great interest I watched her attempts to enslave the Maharajah, knowing perfectly well that his strict religious principles, if nothing else, debarred him absolutely from taking any serious interest in a European woman. I also heard more about the Austrian, Herr Egermann, who was said to be deeply in love and highly jealous. If the rumour was true that he had set Manny up in a dress-shop on the Olivaer Platz, he evidently had some title to jealousy.

And then another exotic guest came to stay at the Adlon, also inordinately rich, and not restricted in his feminine interests by caste or any other principles. He was a merchant from the Middle East, very well known at that time, who had first made his money out of carpets but who now dealt in diamonds, and also, it was said in informed circles, in arms. He had a very long name, but was always known as 'Mister Mahmed'.

His visit to Berlin and the Adlon, so rumour had it, was not wholly fortuitous. He was particularly anxious to make the acquaintance of the Maharajah, no doubt with an eye to business. But the Maharajah took great care to avoid him.

Being thus frustrated in his main object, Mister Mahmed looked round for such consolations as the life of Berlin might afford, of which there was no shortage. It was inevitable that he should bump into Manny W., herself suffering from a similar disappointment and, moreover, deprived of the company of Herr Egermann. Within a little while they were seen everywhere together.

At that time Motoring Beauty Contests were a popular vogue in Berlin. Cars were exhibited in conjunction with displays of beauty queens, flowers, furs, dogs, jewels and other adornments. I myself had recently taken part in one of these contests with my dogs. I possessed twenty-eight pure-bred Royal Pekinese, most beautiful little dogs of which I was very proud. With these and my white Mercedes I had won a first prize, and as a result I had been invited to act as one of the judges in the latest contest, of cars and jewels, in which Manny W. was taking part at the instance of Mister Mahmed.

It thus turned out that I had a particularly close view of a little comedy that was played to a large extent in the public eye. I was seated in the front row of the stalls when the curtain rose and the three protagonists, Manny W., Herr Egermann and Mister Mahmed, appeared on the stage.

Herr Egermann had by this time returned from Vienna, and not being blind at once perceived what was going on. He and Mister Mahmed were close neighbours at the Adlon, but fortunately everything remained smooth on the surface. The rivals carefully ignored one another when they met in the lift or the hall.

This called for great self-control on the part of Herr Egermann, whose jealousy was without bounds. His attempts to catch Manny W. at her dress-shop and have it out with her were all in vain. How was he to win her back? Mister Mahmed, the diamond-dealer, possessed all the allurements of the exotic East, in addition to enormous wealth and countless diamonds. What woman could fail to be moved by such attractions? Herr Egermann was a wealthy man himself, but how was he to measure his fortune against that of a man whose dealings were wrapped in mystery?

Mister Mahmed had left no stone unturned. He had bought a superb Cadillac, and when Manny W. drove this past the judges she was decorated with a dazzling display of diamonds, pearls and rubies.

These, however, were not Mister Mahmed's property. He had acquired them on loan from the firm of Markgraf & Co., on Unter den Linden. Taking into account his fabulous wealth, extravagance and amorous state, Herr Oppenheimer, the head of the firm, regarded the arrangement as an excellent stroke of business.

When Manny won the prize Mister Mahmed would naturally buy the jewels for her as a reward, this being customary in such cases. It was certainly what Herr Oppenheimer expected, and so did the beautiful Manny. So, indeed, did everyone.

For my own part I was somewhat astonished when I heard where the jewels had come from. Did not Mister Mahmed possess enough of his own? As a dealer in precious stones, why had he had to go to another dealer? It seemed the more strange if he intended to present her with the jewels in any case.

However, these questions, like the chances of Herr Egermann, paled into insignificance beneath the brilliance of the display as Manny drove by in her Cadillac. There could be no possible dissent among the judges. Manny was unanimously voted the winner of the Car-and-Jewels contest, and, all things considered, everyone felt that there was good reason to congratulate her.

That evening Mister Mahmed took Manny to the opera. Louis Adlon and I were also there, occupying our usual place in the front row of the stalls, and they were in the same row, only a few seats away from us. The piece was 'Tosca', with Frieda Leider in the title role, while the part of Cavaradossi was sung by an Italian guest-artiste who was stopping at the Adlon.

After we had taken our seats I looked about me as usual to see who was there. As a rule the seat immediately behind us was occupied by the theatre-doctor, whom we knew. I was rather surprised to find that on this night it was occupied by Herr Oppenheimer, of Markgraf & Co. How did he come to be in this particular seat? Was he keeping an eye on his jewels, which Manny W. was again wearing? Or were they already sold to Mister Mahmed, and had he come to take leave of them? I had not thought him to be a man of so much sentiment.

The third act of 'Tosca' is comparatively short, and when Cavaradossi has sung his famous aria the end is not far off. While the applause that always follows the aria was dying down, Mister Mahmed and Manny got up and left. Being in the front row, they could do so without disturbing anyone; but then I noticed that Herr Oppenheimer was also leaving.

At the end of the performance we walked back to the hotel along the 'Linden', and looking into the restaurant I had a further surprise. Seated together at one of the reserved tables, Number 5, to be exact, were Herr Oppenheimer and Manny's abandoned lover, Herr Egermann!

The waiter in charge of table Number 5 was known as 'Abd el Krim'. All our waiters had nicknames, bestowed upon them by their colleagues, which for the most part stuck to them throughout their careers. Abd el Krim, who looked after tables 5 and 7, was called after the Moroccan rebel leader because of the cut of his beard. He was, incidentally, the only waiter at the Adlon who was allowed to wear a beard. The rest were all clean-shaven.

It was from Abd el Krim that I heard the details of a story that became known to nearly all the guests who were present.

Herr Egermann and Herr Oppenheimer were talking about 'Tosca', so loudly, in the case of Herr Egermann, that they could be overheard at the neighbouring tables.

'Cavaradossi's aria,' said Herr Egermann, and laughed, although there was a certain tensity in his manner. 'Isn't it something about glittering stones?' He then looked hard at Herr Oppenheimer, as though awaiting some particular answer.

Herr Oppenheimer, however, returned his gaze calmly. He drew a breath and recited the words from memory:

> *The stars glittered,*
> *The earth misted . . .*
> *She came like a goddess*
> *And sank on my breast.*
> *Oh, sweet kisses, intoxicating caresses . . .*

Herr Egermann listened with his head resting on his hand. The violinist, Georges Boulanger, who that evening was playing at the Adlon for the first time, heard what Herr Oppenheimer was reciting. In the manner of *tsigane* violinists he had wandered away from the piano and was hovering near them. He stopped playing and hummed the aria, and Herr Egermann joined in. Georges Boulanger was wearing a handsome solitaire diamond on his little finger. As he started to play again, still standing by their table, he held his bow so that the diamond caught Herr Egermann's eye. As though it reminded him of something that he must not allow himself to forget, he leaned towards Herr Oppenheimer and said:

'You didn't get the words right. It should be: "The stars glittered, as brilliant as diamonds . . ." '

Herr Oppenheimer merely shook his head without saying anything.

'Waiter,' called Herr Egermann, 'would it be possible to find out in the hotel the exact wording of Cavaradossi's aria from the third act of "Tosca"?'

'Certainly,' said Abd el Krim.

He was away scarcely ten minutes. He came back with the words written on a sheet of paper, and Herr Egermann read aloud:

> *The stars glittered,*
> *The earth was misted.*
> *The garden gate creaked,*
> *Hurried footsteps approached.*
> *She came like a goddess*
> *And sank on my breast.*
> *Oh, sweet kisses, intoxicating caresses! . . .*

'Well, anyway,' said Herr Egermann, 'you left out two lines. I hope you aren't always so forgetful.' He was again gazing with a nervous intensity at Herr Oppenheimer.

'Where did you get these words?' Herr Oppenheimer asked Abd el Krim.

'From a young lady who is studying music in Berlin,' Abd el Krim answered. 'She's stopping at the hotel. I happened to find her in the telephone exchange.'

At this Herr Egermann jumped up and went out of the restaurant, to return a few minutes later with a young girl of singular good looks. She had reddish-brown hair, and her high cheekbones, wide, sensual mouth and slightly slanting eyes suggested that she was of Slavic origin.

She came and sat for a few minutes with the two gentlemen, while Abd el Krim fetched a vase of red roses and put it on the table. Herr Egermann was talking in a low voice, evidently asking some favour, and suddenly the girl stood up and went towards the orchestra. She exchanged a few words and a smile with the pianist, and then took his place at the grand piano. She played a few chords, and suddenly her clear, soprano voice rang through the restaurant.

> *To beauty alone I gave my life,*
> *To art and love wholly devoted;*
> *My hands were open to the poor,*
> *My gifts given in true faith . . .*

It was Tosca's aria from the second act. The singer continued:

> *My jewels I desired to give to the Church,*
> *That strayed souls, by holy song*
> *Might be brought back to Heaven.*
> *Why, almighty God,*
> *Do you try me so harshly?*

When the singer had finished she seemed to be quite overcome by the song and her own feelings. She dabbed her eyes with a handkerchief, got up and ran quickly out of the restaurant. Herr Egermann sprang to his feet while the guests clapped and encored. But the girl, she could not have been much more than twenty, was not to be persuaded, and he returned alone. He repeated a line that she had sung:

'My jewels I desired to give to the Church . . .'

Once again he gazed at Herr Oppenheimer in that strangely questioning manner. But the jeweller seemed to be resolved to keep the conversation on non-committal lines, and finally Herr Egermann grew weary of the jewels or stars of Tosca. He sat staring absently in front of him, paying no attention to the performance of Georges Boulanger, who, with the gipsy's fine nose for money, continued to hover about them. The solitaire diamond on his finger continued to glitter.

Suddenly Herr Egermann looked up and once again sprang to his feet. Standing in the doorway of the restaurant was Manny W.! She was alone. She still wore the dress she had worn at the Opera, with all the jewels; but Mister Mahmed was not with her.

As though nothing had happened she allowed Herr Egermann to lead her to their table. Herr Oppenheimer rose to greet her, and their handclasp was longer than is customary and there was an exchange of glances between them. Herr Egermann's state of nervous anxiety, his absence of mind, had now entirely vanished. His face glowing with happiness he beckoned to Abd el Krim and ordered a bottle of the 1911 Veuve Cliquot-Ponsardin rosé, one of the most expensive wines on our list. And when it was poured out he raised his glass and said, stressing the words with voice and gesture:

'Servitore, Herr Oppenheimer! Servitore!'

It was a most surprising and unexpectedly happy ending to a situation that had seemed fraught with dramatic possibilities. But as to what lay behind it all, that is another story.

19

The Music Student from Prague

WITH the departure of the Maharajah of Patiala, a few days later, the life of the hotel became somewhat calmer. Mister Mahmed also unobtrusively took leave of us on the same day, and I do not think this was entirely accidental. I think he still hoped to interest the Maharajah in some sort of commercial transaction, although whether in the sphere of carpets, jewels or arms I cannot say.

In the upheaval attending the removal of the huge Indian household the story of the beauty contest and Manny W's jewels was for the time being forgotten. But I was drastically reminded of it one morning when I chanced to overhear the tail-end of a conversation between the hotel-manager and Louis Adlon.

'Shall I inform the police?' the manager asked.

'Wait a little. It may turn out to be a false alarm,' my husband said, and then hurried out of the office because he was wanted on the telephone.

'What has happened?' I asked.

The manager replied that one of the guests had reported the theft of a pearl necklace from her room.

'From her room!' I exclaimed, very much concerned. 'But how was that possible? Who is she, anyway?'

'We don't yet know how it happened,' said the manager. 'The guest is Miss Manny W.'

This was a real shock to me.

'How do you know it's really theft?' I demanded. 'And what's more, how does Miss Manny W. come to be staying at the hotel without our having been told?'

The manager made an apologetic gesture.

'I'm very sorry. I've only just had a chance to look through the latest visitors' list.'

'Nowadays we don't seem to hear anything of what goes on in this place,' I said sharply. 'We shall end up like Wilhelm II, getting nothing but newspapers with pieces cut out of them!'

I was really angry, not only because it was Manny W. but because it was a case of an unescorted female. We only accepted single women as room-guests at the hotel if they were well known to us or came with a special introduction. As a rule their visits were arranged in advance either by some member of their family or, in the case of business-women, by the secretariat of some firm which was known to us.

A case in point was that of the young music student to whom I referred in the previous chapter. She had been sent to us by her uncle, a lawyer in Prague, who paid her expenses in advance and had asked the management to keep an eye on her becausse she was a newcomer to Berlin. I shall have more to say about her later, and so I may here mention that she was seldom seen in the hotel. She went out at nine in the morning, took her meals at a students' hostel, and went straight up to her room when she returned in the evening. Her readiness to sing on that one occasion in the restaurant was something quite out of the ordinary.

'I should like to know,' I said, 'how Miss Manny W. came to be admitted.'

'She was vouched for by Herr Egermann,' the manager said. 'He's a guest of long standing.'

Well, that was different. The important thing now was to clear up this matter of theft as quickly as possible. Knowing that the pearl necklace was part of the collection of jewels borrowed by Mister Mahmed for the beauty contest, I took the first opportunity of asking Herr Oppenheimer what it was worth, with an eye to a possible claim for damages or insurance.

Herr Oppenheimer smiled when I told him about the theft, and said enigmatically:

'Herr Egermann should be very grateful to me.'

I had no idea what he meant.

'Do you mean he should be pleased because the necklace came from Mister Mahmed?'

'Mister Mahmed doesn't come into it. The jewels were bought by Herr Egermann as a present for Manny W.'

This was news to me.

'In a sense it was my doing,' said Herr Oppenheimer. 'I had some reason to suspect that Mister Mahmed wouldn't stay long in Berlin after the Maharajah of Patiala had left, and I did not think it very likely that he would want to spend a large sum of money on jewels for the sake of an affair that would probably be short-lived.'

'And so you gave Herr Egermann a hint?'

'Well, selling jewels is my business. I just asked him if he would be interested in buying them, if it turned out to be a means of improving his own prospects. And when I found that Mister Mahmed was not anxious to exercise his option I dropped a word into Manny W's ear and then hurried to find Herr Egermann. The rest you know.'

'All the same,' I said, 'I don't understand why Herr Egermann should be grateful to you now that the necklace has been stolen.'

'He should at least be more grateful than the thief, when he discovers that he has got nothing but an imitation that Manny has been wearing on my advice. The real necklace is in the bank.'

I might have guessed. It was a time when the making of artificial jewellery had reached such a stage of perfection that many ladies who would consider themselves naked without jewels had taken to wearing imitations. So where Manny W. was concerned there was nothing much to worry about. But for the Adlon it was another matter. The theft was still a theft. The guests naturally do not hear of these things, but for any hotel it is a matter of life and death that they should be promptly cleared up. Until this has been done there can be no peace of mind for anyone.

We were no nearer to solving the mystery of the stolen necklace when another theft occurred in the hotel. A wallet was stolen from the bedroom of an American guest, on the first floor. He was quite

Sources of Supply

Sumptuous Stairs

His Excellency's Party

The Buried Hatchet

LOUIS AND HEDDA ADLON WITH AN EXOTIC GUEST

The Proud Proprietors

LOUIS AND HEDDA ADLON

A Prince of 'Bohemia'

ANTON KUH (CHAP. 20)

positive that he had left it lying on a small table in front of the Empire mirror in his room when he went to bed. In the morning it was no longer there. It had contained the sum of 585 dollars.

The list of guests on the same floor was studied, but there was no one on it who could possibly be suspected. Then the name and origin of every guest in the hotel was subjected to a careful scrutiny, but there was nothing for police or house-detectives to work on. All were either well known to us or had come with unimpeachable credentials.

This applied to an English lady—we will call her Mrs. Morris, although this was not her name—who had been staying at the hotel for some little time. Particular attention was paid to her because she had arrived a few days before the first theft. But there was nothing at all against her. Her papers were all in order, she appeared to be well off, and she had come with an introduction from an English man of business who always stopped at the Adlon when he was in Berlin. She lived very quietly, and spent her days visiting the museums where she made sketches—among others, of the Pergamon Altar. These were later displayed at the Pergamon Museum and aroused considerable interest.

She had become friendly with our restaurant-manager, with whom she was in the habit of chatting at her table after dinner. He had the highest respect for her, but was very much taken aback by a remark she made to him in the course of one of these conversations. She had dined particularly well that evening, and after drinking a bottle of champagne by herself had ordered another, at which she invited him to join her. She had talked for some time about her drawings, and then had abruptly asked:

'What are the safety arrangements like in this hotel?'

The manager started, wondering what she meant by the question. Had she heard something about the thefts? As it happened, a third had just become known to us, although the victim, a manufacturer from Mannheim, who had lost his wallet and a gold watch, had not reported it for several days. He had, moreover, said that he did not wish the police to be informed. This in itself was remarkable, and so was Mrs. Morris's question. Fortunately

N

the conversation was in English, which made it possible for the restaurant-manager to take his time in answering and to pretend not to have understood her.

'I can assure you, you have no need to worry,' he said. 'There are fire-extinguishers everywhere.'

Mrs. Morris hesitated for an instant and then said:

'I wasn't thinking of the danger of fire. But supposing, for instance, someone were attacked and robbed in their room, would it be overheard? Would a shot be heard from outside?'

This made the manager sit up. Was it conceivable that Mrs. Morris was the thief? Or if she had heard about the thefts, how had the information reached her? No member of the staff would say anything about them to the guests.

He finally returned a non-committal answer, assuring her again that she had nothing to fear, and that anything of the kind was impossible at the Adlon, where all the guests were personally known to the management. This seemed to satisfy her, and she presently left the restaurant to go up to her room. But it seemed to the restaurant-manager, as he thought it over, that there had been something altogether strange in her manner that evening.

He at once reported the incident, and that night the safety precautions were increased. Two member of the staff and two female house-detectives patrolled the floors. They went off duty at seven in the morning without having seen anything unusual; but at eight o'clock a young American woman on the first floor began flashing furiously. She had awakened to find a necklace, three valuable rings, a gold evening-bag and a note-case missing from her room.

The question then arose, should Mrs. Morris's room be searched? The matter was discussed at length, but it seemed that the objections to so drastic a procedure far outweighed the possible gain, considering how slight was the suspicion attaching to her. In the meantime the lady was presumably still in bed. Her shoes were outside her room, and a dress for the cleaners hung between the double doors. A tentative knock by the chambermaid brought no response.

The morning passed in a state of general agitation. It was all concealed from the guests, of course; but anyone familiar with the hotel business will know what we were feeling.

At this time a number of foreign cavalry-officers were visiting Berlin, the guests of one of the Reichswehr cavalry regiments, and they had been invited to a ball at the Adlon that evening.

Many of them came to the tea-dance that afternoon, so that the lounge was unusually crowded. Half a dozen different nationalities were grouped round the tables, and the elegant young men, as they led their ladies on to the dance-floor, made a gay and lively spectacle.

All this came within the domain of the restaurant-manager. He was himself the son of a Prussian general and an ex-officer, so that he was well-fitted for his position socially as well as professionally. He said later that this was a day he would never forget.

There was first a slight stir occasioned by the arrival of two gentlemen in light overcoats and felt hats who came to the desk and asked to speak to Herr Adlon. Assuming from their appearance that they had something to do with the cavalry-ball that evening, the clerk took them to the restaurant-manager. But they then produced documents which showed them to be British police officers from Scotland Yard. They had come straight from the Tempelhof aerodrome, having flown from London in quest of a titled English lady whom they were anxious to interview in connection with the death of two of her relatives.

This lady had last been heard of in Holland, but word had reached Scotland Yard that she had removed to Berlin. The visitors' book was produced and the detectives noted down the particulars of all the British subjects staying at the hotel. The lady did not, however, appear to be one of them. They then politely withdrew, to report their arrival to their German colleagues in the Alexanderplatz and then proceed to study the visitors' lists of other hotels.

Harmless though this visit seemed, it had done nothing to soothe our nerves. In the meantime the music for the tea-dance had started, the orchestra being led by Georges Boulanger. Boulanger had come to the Adlon as a result of the great success he had achieved in Berlin, but I did not altogether see eye to eye with him. He was a gipsy from the lower Danube basin who could not shed some of the habits of his origin. He would hover over feminine guests, playing softly in their ear, while his eyes glowed with smouldering passion. This made a great impression on some elderly ladies, who were often persuaded to buy the diamond ring he wore on his little finger, as a souvenir or 'love-token' or whatever it might be. The ring was genuine enough, but the price was far more than it was worth. Boulanger would then run round to a jeweller with whom he had an arrangement and buy another. It was a profitable side-line. In justice it must be said that his family life was impeccable, and he devoted his earnings to the education of his only daughter, whom he adored.

The sound of his music was reaching us faintly in the head office when suddenly the door opened and one of the chambermaids burst in, in such a state of agitation that she could scarcely speak.

'For God's sake, what is it now?' exclaimed the hotel-manager. 'Don't say there's been another theft!'

Our thoughts were naturally of theft, but this time it turned out to be even worse.

The girl had just been to the room of Mrs. Morris to take back the dress she had put out for cleaning in the morning. Nothing had been seen of Mrs. Morris all day. A strange and terrifying sound was coming from inside the room, a sound of groaning. The chambermaid had tapped on the locked door, but getting no answer, other than groans, had hurried downstairs to report the matter. She had seen nothing of Mrs. Morris all day, but the shoes were gone from outside her room; and since she must have taken them in herself, the girl had assumed that she simply did not want to be disturbed.

The manager at once rang up the room, but got no reply. He then applied to Louis Adlon for permission to open the door with a pass-key, and Louis decided to go up with him.

They found Mrs. Morris lying, fully clad, on the settee in her room. Her head and shoulders were wrapped in an expensive leopard-skin coat which she was in the habit of wearing, and blood was dripping from beneath it on to the settee. A revolver lay on the floor beside her. The blood came from a wound in her head. She had shot herself through the leopard-skin coat, and this had deflected the bullet, so that the poor woman was still alive, half-conscious and groaning.

The house-doctor was, of course, at once summoned; but since this was a clear case of attempted suicide the police had to be notified. An emergency call was put through to the Alexander-platz. The fact that the lady was English was stressed, and it was suggested that the two Scotland Yard men should be informed. As it happened, they were actually in the police-building. They came round at once, accompanied by German police officers, and were able to identify 'Mrs. Morris' as the woman they were looking for. She died soon afterwards, but not before she had been able to say enough to confirm their suspicions that she had poisoned her two elderly and wealthy relatives.

She was a lady with a position in London society, whose crime bore evidence of having been carefully planned. But although, by the use of a false identity and forged papers, she had contrived to deceive the hotel and momentarily to put the London police off the scent, she must have come to realize that this state of affairs could not last. Her flight in itself was a damning circumstance. She was bound to be traced. So her strangeness of manner the night before could now be accounted for. The restaurant-manager, who had been the last person to talk to her, was interviewed by the police. Clearly the strange question she had asked him had had nothing to do with the hotel thefts. Already resolved upon suicide, she had been afraid that the sound of a shot might bring assistance before she was dead. It was presumably in order to muffle the sound that she had buried the muzzle of the revolver in the soft folds of the leopard-skin coat.

And on that last night she had talked about her drawings of the Pergamon Altar. She had hurried to finish them before taking her life. There was something touching, after all, in the story of 'Mrs. Morris'.

The person most affected by that grim happening was the restaurant-manager, who had known the lady better than anyone else in the hotel and genuinely liked her. But this poor man's troubles were far from over. He had a minor crisis to deal with a little later, when he sat in the head office sipping a whisky and soda while he recovered from his interview with the police.

It was the six-o'clock pause. The tea-dance had ended and the orchestra was silent. Suddenly Georges Boulanger tottered into the room and dramatically announced that he was ill and probably dying, and would certainly not be able to play that night.

He dropped into an armchair and lay there groaning and mopping his forehead while I gazed at him in consternation. He was wanted for the cavalry ball, and as it happened we had no violinist of sufficient standing available to replace him. I was in the act of reaching for the telephone, to summon the doctor, when the restaurant-manager forestalled me. He got his wallet out of his pocket and said calmly:

'How much?'

Boulanger opened one eye.

'Two hundred.'

The restaurant-manager handed over the money without a word, and Boulanger sat up, grinning faintly. He was not the man, he said, to fail in an emergency. Although at death's door, he would heroically sacrifice himself for the good of the hotel. Upon this exit-line he withdrew.

I was outraged, not being accustomed to Boulanger's methods.

'Pure blackmail!' I exclaimed. 'Does he always do that?'

'Only when he thinks he can get away with it,' said the restaurant-manager. 'To give him his due, he always plays in the end. Technically, of course, it's simply an advance on his salary. We work things out in one way or another. We're quite friendly. I think it really does make him feel ill when he finds he's run through his money. He's a gipsy, after all. It's a thing he wouldn't want us to forget. He also doesn't overlook the fact that he's a great attraction.'

There was nothing to do but laugh.

In fact, Boulanger played that night as well as ever, and the cavalry ball was a complete success. But the mystery of the thefts was still unsolved.

The restaurant-manager, who had been in charge of the ball, was a very tired man when, between three and four in the morning, he was at last able to go upstairs to bed.

His room was on the second floor, on a corridor leading to the Wilhelmstrasse extension. He went sleepily through the silent house, of which the passages at this hour were only dimly lighted. As he approached his bedroom he heard the sound, from somewhere near at hand, of a door softly closing. This was followed by other sounds the furtive nature of which aroused his curiosity. He stood waiting at the corner of the corridor.

The figure of a woman clad in a fur coat came down the stairs from the floor above. In the faint light he could not see who it was. He went silently up to her and said:

'Have you lost your way, madam? Can I help you?'

She swung round convulsively to face him, and he saw to his astonishment that it was the girl from Prague, the little music student who had sung in the restaurant a few nights before. She murmured something about having mistaken the floor, and then hurried on along the corridor.

The restaurant-manager gazed after her, at first merely surprised that she should be up at that hour, apparently fully dressed. Then it occurred to him that she must surely be occupying one of the smaller and less expensive rooms on the top floor, and not one of the luxury suites below. So why had she been on her way downstairs? The thing suddenly appeared to him so suspicious that he ran after her and said firmly:

'Gnädige Fräulein, I must ask you to accompany me to the office. I do not altogether understand how you come to be on this floor.'

As he said this his hand was reaching out to the bell-push operating the light-signal, of which there was one at either end of every corridor. But now the girl made a rapid movement and interposed herself between him and the bell-push. It was an awkward situation for the restaurant-manager, who had already taken a risk when he asked her to go with him to the office. If he tried to get at the bell-push by force, and some other guest appeared, the girl could easily claim that he had tried to assault her.

Nevertheless he did try, and then a remarkable thing happened. The girl pushed him back, smiling a little, and deliberately drew apart the folds of her fur coat. He saw that beneath it she was wearing shoes and stockings—and nothing else.

She stood there offering him her naked body and still smiling in a manner which made it clear that it was not the first time she had used this expedient to get herself out of trouble. He could no longer doubt that this was the thief for whom everyone had been searching. He thrust her aside and vigorously pressed the bell. The girl drew the coat tightly about her and leaned against the wall, not saying a word; and he stayed with her until help arrived.

The woman house-detective who searched her found a gold bracelet and other small but valuable articles of jewellery loose in the pocket of her coat. It was all the confirmation that was needed.

The police were at once notified, and when they searched her room they found jewels sewn into garments and hidden in the false bottom of a leather suitcase. They also found empty wallets; but the contents of the wallets—notes, identity papers, visiting-cards, or whatever they might be—were nowhere to be found. The girl refused to say what had become of them.

She had recovered her cool aloofness of manner. She answered no questions and disdainfully watched the proceedings of the police; but in the presence of the restaurant-manager she drew her coat more tightly about her and turned her head away. She had a moment of weakness as she was being taken out of the hotel. She sank on to the page-boys' bench by the lift and sat there for a

short time in silence while her hand stroked the red velvet upholstery. Then she got slowly to her feet and was led out by way of
the Wilhelmstrasse entrance.

And the next morning the hotel-manager exclaimed:

'But scarcely any of this fits!'

He was comparing the list of articles found in the girl's room
with the list of things reported stolen in the hotel. The first list
was very much the longer of the two, and this seemed to exas-
perate him. The police had a fine haul of stolen goods and they
had the thief—but where were the owners?

The mystery surrounding the music student from Prague was
the subject of very lively discussion among the hotel staff. As the
police pursued their investigations new facts emerged and new
tales were told, but our people for the most part refused to believe
that this pretty, modestly-behaved girl could really be the thief
who had been setting the hotel by the ears for so long. The men
in particular inclined to the view that it had been only a first lapse,
to be accounted for by the fact that she was desperately hard-up,
and so had resorted to desperate measures in order to be able to
continue her music studies. The younger men and the page-boys
were great readers of cheap thrillers. They saw her as the innocent victim of a gang of criminals using hideous threats to exploit
her beauty.

The women were more critical, but even they were inclined to
romanticize her as a girl of good family forced by straitened circumstances to adopt this deplorable, but none the less ingenious,
method of earning a living.

The truth surpassed all expectation. The girl turned out to be a
member of a powerful international criminal organization that
specialized in hotel thefts. She had actually studied music, at the
gang's expense, in preparation for the part she was to play.
Nothing could have been more fortunate, from her point of view,
than the argument between Herr Oppenheimer and Herr Egermann which had ended in her singing the 'Tosca' aria in the
restaurant—so shyly and charmingly!—so that she was able to
establish herself in the eyes of everyone, not only as an innocent

and modest young girl but as the music student she professed to be.

She had also been schooled in languages and in the manners proper to a young lady stopping at the best hotels. The head-quarters of the gang were in Prague, and it was there that they expertly built up her various identities, supplying her with the documents and introductions necessary for her to secure the entrée to such hotels as the Adlon. She had had successful and undetected seasons at hotels on the Riviera and at Claridges in Paris, and was known to have passed under three different *noms de guerre*; but her real name, if it became known to the police, was never divulged.

A number of members of the Adlon staff were summoned to appear as witnesses at her trial, and the proceedings were also followed by a number of leading police officers, both German and foreign. The student—she clung obstinately to this designation of herself—could not be brought to utter any name which might incriminate the people behind her, and this added greatly to the difficulties of the investigation. Moreover a good many of her victims preferred to remain anonymous or refused to bring charges, and these, it seemed, were all men.

The gang's operations were based on a thorough knowledge of the behaviour of hotel guests, which is often extremely careless. People leave objects, sometimes of great value, lying about on tables and go off to sleep without bothering to lock their doors.

Clad in nothing but shoes and stockings under the fur coat, with its useful pockets, the girl would flit silently along the corridors in the small hours, always with her hair dishevelled, as though she had just got out of bed and were looking for a lavatory. It was a part of her business, of course, to learn as much as she could about the occupants of the different rooms. She would stand listening at a door—or in the space between the doors where double doors existed, as they did at the Adlon—and if all was quiet, and the door unlocked, would slip softly in, ready to withdraw instantly, with a murmured apology, if any voice spoke.

But there were occasions when she had no need to withdraw.

There were single gentlemen by no means indisposed to welcome the alluring visitor, with her flustered tale of having strayed into the wrong room, who turned out to be naked under her coat. And when in the morning they found their wallet gone, and the gold watch and cigarette-case as well, they might have good reasons for saying nothing about the matter, or at least for not desiring a police inquiry—as in the case of the factory-owner from Mannheim.

The contents of the wallets could be sent by registered post to Prague, but this would have been too risky in the case of the jewels and other valuables. These had to be kept hidden until the gang's messenger came to collect them. To judge by the number of articles recovered when the girl was caught, his visit must have been about due.

And so Manny W's necklace was restored to her flawless neck. I myself gave it back to Herr Egermann, who took the opportunity of reading me a little lecture on the merits of imitation jewellery. Theft or loss were the merest trifles, he said, when the real thing was safe in the strong-box.

'Whose strong-box?' I asked.

'Why, the owner's, of course,' said the prudent Herr Egermann.

20

The Great Anton Kuh

I HAVE already described how we divided hotel guests into three categories, according to their manner of paying their bills; and I mentioned that there was a fourth category, those who did not pay at all but whose bills were passed to them receipted by Louis Adlon.

One such guest, and one for whom we had a great affection, was the writer, Anton Kuh. A Viennese by birth, he had settled in Berlin, and he lived for years at the Adlon, in a room on the first floor. He wrote a great many newspaper and magazine articles, published books and delivered lectures; but since, despite these activities, he never had any money, money and finance were the things he most liked to talk about.

He came to us at the Adlon in consequence of a remarkable bet.

It was in 1930. The American novelist, Sinclair Lewis, was awarded the Nobel Prize that year, and on his return journey from Stockholm he stopped at the Adlon with the lady who was then his wife, the well-known journalist and broadcaster, Dorothy Thompson. He had been brought to us by Ernst Rowohlt, his German publisher, who was an old habitué of the hotel.

Sinclair Lewis and Rowohlt were seated one day in the bar when Kuh entered the hotel, asking to see Lewis. As he entered the bar Herr Rowohlt cried:

'Kuh, you're just the man we want. There's something you can do for us.'

'How much?' asked Kuh, his pockets empty as usual.

Rowohlt burst out laughing.

'Don't say you're ready to pay back your advance!'

Kuh spoke and wrote meticulous German, but he could, when

he chose, break into the rich, broad dialect of Vienna. He did so now as he replied:

'A writer who accepts an advance is a man in debt. I have been told so personally by publishers. Well, what do you really want?'

A huge pile of letters lay on the table between Rowohlt and Lewis, and on the floor beside them was a washing-basket bearing the name Adlon.

'You can help us with this job,' said Rowohlt, throwing another letter into the basket. 'It's more than I can manage.'

The letters were begging-letters that had been addressed to Sinclair Lewis since the papers had announced that the Nobel Prizewinner was in Berlin, stopping at the Adlon. Lewis himself could not read them because they were nearly all in German. He had asked Rowohlt to help him deal with them.

The two men had been hard at work, Lewis opening the envelopes while Rowohlt glanced over their contents and then tossed them into the basket. Kuh was now added to this conveyor-belt. He sat in the middle, taking the envelopes from Sinclair Lewis after he had slit them, extracting and unfolding the letters and passing them on to Rowohlt to read. Except for this the routine continued unchanged. The letters, as before, all went into the washing-basket.

Sinclair Lewis was drinking whisky and Rowohlt was drinking gin. When the waiter came to ask Kuh what he would have, he said in his broadest Viennese:

'Bring me some champagne.'

Our Adlon waiters were not easily put out of countenance. Without moving a muscle the waiter replied in a Viennese that was even broader:

'Certainly, Herr Graf. Would the Herr Graf prefer Cliquot, Mumm, Heidsiek or Roederer?' (The word 'Roederer', pronounced in a long, soft sing-song, with much rolling of the r's, became 'Roe-derr-air'.)

Anton Kuh was the one to be disconcerted. He gazed at the waiter in astonishment and could find nothing better to say than:

'Have you really got all those?'

The waiter then delivered himself of another sentence, in a language derived from the very stews of Vienna, so broad that even Kuh could scarcely understand it; and Kuh, defeated, ordered Mumm—extra dry.

The business of the letters went on all the afternoon and finally developed into a lively drinking-party, joined by other arrivals who came and went. It was late at night before Rowohlt and Sinclair Lewis finally broke it up, and then only Anton Kuh was left. When he had emptied the last bottle the waiter asked him if he wished to order anything else.

'No, thank you,' said Kuh. 'I'll wait for old Rowohlt to come back.'

'If you'll forgive my mentioning it,' said the waiter, 'you may have to wait a long time. Herr Rowohlt has gone home to bed.'

'Do you mean to say he's walked out on me? Well, in that case,' said Kuh, 'I would like to have a word with Herr Adlon.'

Louis Adlon was fetched. Kuh introduced himself and said:

'Herr Adlon, I should like to have a bet with you.'

'Yes?' said Louis.

Although he had not met Anton Kuh before, he knew him by reputation, and he was tolerably sure that he had no money on him. Louis had a fondness for eccentrics and the sort of people who become known as 'characters'. He liked to have them in the hotel, where they brought life and colour, as he said. He guessed at once what the trouble was, and was perfectly ready to allow Kuh all the credit he needed. But he did not say so, being curious to see how he would handle the situation.

'A bet,' Kuh repeated. 'I will bet you, Herr Adlon, that I will have a pair of shoes made for me by the best shoemaker in Berlin without paying a penny for them.'

'Well, that's more than I can do,' said Louis. 'How do you propose to go about it?'

'That's my affair,' said Kuh. 'But that's not all. You will have an exactly similar pair, and you'll pay for both!'

Louis burst out laughing.

'Not on your life! You don't catch me paying for your shoes. I'll take the bet. What is the stake to be?'

'The amount of my bill tonight,' said Kuh with dignity.

The remarkable thing about this bet is that Kuh won it; but I must disappoint the reader by confessing that I cannot, after so many years, recall exactly how he did so. It was, I know, by means of an elaborate stratagem which entailed the ordering of two similar pairs of shoes from two separate shoemakers and then sending them back for alteration—the right shoe of one pair, if I remember correctly, and the left shoe of the other. There was a good deal of mystification of this sort, and, of course, both pairs had to be delivered to the Adlon. But as to how the fastidious Louis came to be deceived, and still more how Anton Kuh contrived to get him to pay for both pairs—this I no longer remember, if I ever really understood it. I suspect the connivance of the hall-porter, who was accustomed to look after such matters on Louis's behalf, as he did for the hotel guests. I think it also possible that Louis was so attracted by Kuh, and so amused by his impudence, that he did not, perhaps, look very closely.

At least it is certain that this was the beginning of the friendship between the two men. Soon afterwards Kuh came to live at the hotel, and Louis even went so far as to let him have a room on the first floor.

The Adlon was always renowned not only for its elegance but for its orderliness. This was the case everywhere except in the room where Anton Kuh lived and wrote. Here chaos prevailed, a grisly litter of empty bottles, cigarette-ends, books, papers, garments scattered haphazard, with Kuh in the middle of it, working away with a monocle in his eye. Chambermaids and valets who came to try and tidy him up were promptly shooed out again.

He promised them all 'princely' tips. In fact, his earnings were very large, but the money was always spent before he got it. His hotel-bill reached such proportions that he preferred to avoid encounters with Louis Adlon, and crept in and out by the Wilhelmstrasse entrance. One night, however, returning late, he found this door locked. He was forced to use the main door, on Unter den Linden, and the first person he saw was Louis, who was also up late. There was no escape. Louis had already seen him and greeted him in the friendliest manner. The way in which Kuh rose to this occasion has become famous. Drawing himself up to his full height, and fixing his monocle firmly in his eye, he said:

'I'm particularly glad to see you, Herr Adlon. I've been meaning for some days to ask you if you would be good enough to lend me eight hundred marks.'

'What!' exclaimed Louis, flabbergasted. 'Eight hundred? But——'

'To pay my bill,' said Anton Kuh. 'I'm sick and tired of being dunned by this hotel of yours.'

He stalked on up the stairs, but paused at the half-landing to add:

'I should be obliged if you would have the money ready for me in the morning. Goodnight.'

From then on Kuh's monthly bill was always receipted when it reached him. He paid his way by joining intimate parties of hotel guests at Louis's request (he was a noted *raconteur*) and giving readings of his latest works.

And the 'sick of being dunned' story appeared a few days later in a Berlin newspaper. Kuh had carefully written it down, making the point quite clear but putting the words into the mouth of a well-known Berlin banker. He was paid a hundred marks for the story, and he spent it on a wonderful spray of orchids which he handed to me, monocle gleaming.

What was known as the 'Prominenten-Ecke', or V.I.P's corner, was, of course, not the part of the hotel inhabited by Kuh. It comprised the rooms numbered 101–114, directly over the Norddeutscher-Lloyd offices, and among its famous occupants was Charlie Chaplin, whose arrival at the Adlon gave rise to an incident so in keeping with his screen character that I have been surprised not to see it reproduced in any of his films.

Page Parade
RUDOLF VALENTINO'S ARRIVAL AT THE ADLON

The Whispering Fountain

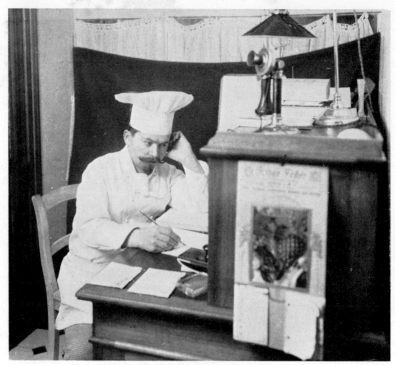

At the Planning Centre

Pomp for the Bride

The news of his coming had been spread abroad, and the pavement on Unter den Linden was covered by a dense mass of people through which he had to fight his way from the car to the hotel doors, shaking hands, signing albums, returning smiles and greetings and struggling frantically not to be trodden underfoot. His navigation light, as he was washed to and fro on the bosom of this human tide, was the pale-blue peaked cap of the Adlon porter, who finally managed to rescue him and thrust him to safety through the revolving door.

But then, when it seemed that all was well, he suddenly stopped in the middle of the reception hall and gazed at himself in comical bewilderment. His trousers were coming down! Souvenir-hunting admirers had robbed him of every button. He could do nothing but clutch them and make hastily for the lift, using that shuffling gait that all the world knows.

The visitors' book for those years—alas, it has vanished—contained many American names that were household words—Aston, Rockefeller, Vanderbilt, Ford, Doris Duke, Barbara Hutton (then the wife of a Count Haugwitz-Reventlow), and countless others, more than I can recall. But there were not only Americans, and there is one name in particular which cannot be overlooked—that of Alexandra Kollontai.

At the time I am speaking of this very remarkable woman was Soviet Ambassador in Stockholm; but she paid frequent weekend visits to Berlin, where she was on terms of close friendship with the Prussian Secretary of State, Herr Weismann.

Alexandra Kollontai was always a lover of the unusual and a doer of the unexpected. She was the daugher of a Czarist general and had been the wife of a Czarist officer; but he joined the revolutionary movement at an early stage, and was eventually forced to take refuge abroad. From America she wrote Lenin a stream of letters, urging him to action, and she went to join him in Petrograd in 1917. She was one of the prime movers behind the mutiny in the fleet which led to the overthrow of the Kerensky Government, living for a time on board a cruiser in Kronstadt harbour

O

until she fell in love with a sailor and went off with him, to marry him in the Crimea.

Her career with the Bolsheviks was unparalleled. She occupied one high office after another, at first in company with her second husband, the sailor, who, rising no less rapidly, presently reached the rank of admiral. But while Madame Kollontai drew closer to Stalin her husband went another way, and was eventually shot as a Trotskyite. After this she preferred to serve her country abroad. First in Mexico, then in Oslo and Stockholm, she lived a life of intensive diplomatic activity and extreme luxury. Her methods and her passions soon became known, as did her book on free love.

During her visits to Berlin she always stayed at the Adlon, and this, together with the clothes she wore, the costly gowns, furs and jewels, incurred the disapproval of the Berlin Communist Party. An article appeared in the party newspaper, the *Rote Fahne*, urging Moscow to recall Comrade Kollontai to Moscow, in order that she might be cured of her bourgeois habits.

For some reason Anton Kuh took particular exception to Madame Kollontai. He was a writer with a love of contrasts and extravagance, but with a very real sympathy for the poor and oppressed. This, no doubt, was the reason for the very successful practical joke he played on the lady.

Kuh spent much of his time with the singer, Richard Tauber, and Erich von Stroheim, the actor and film-director, who just then were also stopping at the Adlon. A warm friendship existed between him and Tauber, but with von Stroheim he had frequent disputes because he did not approve of his manner of depicting Austrian characters.

'I make my own world,' von Stroheim was accustomed to say.

'But your people aren't really Austrians,' was Kuh's retort. 'You pick on certain aspects, but you miss the whole.'

'You don't understand naturalism, my dear fellow,' was von Stroheim's reply.

And then Alexandra Kollontai appeared on one of her weekend visits, and Kuh's lively mind went to work on the comedy which set all Berlin talking.

Without telling anyone what he intended to do, he took pains to discover everything he could about her arrangements. Then he dropped a hint to certain of his friends of the Press. Finally he told Tauber and von Stroheim, under pledge of the strictest secrecy, that a social-political gathering of the very highest importance was to take place that night. He had been invited to attend and could take them with him if they cared to come. Both men accepted.

'Then come to my room at seven,' said Kuh. 'White tie, white carnation in the button-hole, and monocle.'

The monocles! Different though they were in other respects the three men had this in common, that they all wore monocles. Stroheim's was the largest, Tauber tormented himself with a rather small one, and Kuh's had a silver fillet and hung from a black ribbon. He was much given to letting it fall from his eye during conversation and quickly catching it again, and the gesture never failed in its effect.

Punctually at seven Tauber and Stroheim arrived at Anton Kuh's room, wearing full evening dress. They knocked and entered in response to his summons, and then stood speechless with astonishment. Kuh was seated at his typewriter, wearing nothing whatever but his monocle fixed firmly in his eye, with its black ribbon round his neck!

Erich von Stroheim stared at him and finally said:

'Kuh, what the devil are you doing?'

'I'm working,' said Kuh, without looking up.

'But for God's sake, aren't you going to get dressed? It's seven. You said the party was at eight.'

Kuh tapped away at his machine without answering.

'What are you writing, anyway?' von Stroheim asked.

Kuh at length turned his head. He looked coldly at von Stroheim and answered:

'A biography.'

'Whose biography? Why do you have to sit there naked?'

Kuh rose in his nakedness and came towards them.

'I'm writing Adam's biography—just a matter of naturalism, my dear fellow.'

He then let the monocle fall from his eye while he smiled blandly at von Stroheim, whose exasperation was extreme. Tauber relieved the tension by asking with a laugh:

'If this is the biography of Adam, where's Eve?'

'I haven't got to her yet,' said Kuh. 'She comes in Chapter Two.'

He pressed the light-button and a waiter appeared, as he had arranged, bringing champagne and glasses. Presently Tauber said:

'But what about this party? Time's getting on, if you're going to dress for it.'

'Go down and wait for me in the lounge,' said Kuh. 'If I should be a bit late, join up with the others—you'll have no trouble in recognizing them. I'll follow you.' He added solemnly: 'The reception is to be held at the Russian Embassy, but that is strictly confidential!'

So Tauber and von Stroheim went downstairs and waited in the lounge. Kuh did not come. But presently Alexandra Kollontai swept through the lounge in evening dress and fur coat, with jewels glittering in her hair. Awaiting her in a black evening cloak, with his silk hat in his hand, was her friend and protector, Secretary of State Weismann. A group of ladies and gentlemen were also standing in readiness.

'That must be them,' Tauber said, nudging von Stroheim. 'They're going now.'

'But where's Kuh?' muttered von Stroheim uncertainly.

'He'll come later, I suppose. We'd better go.'

Tauber moved forward and von Stroheim could only go with him. They followed the elegant party out of the hotel.

The breadth of pavement between the door of the Adlon and the roadway where the cars stood waiting was about twenty yards. As Madame Kollontai walked across it with her escort a beggar approached her. It was winter and bitterly cold. The man wore no overcoat, his clothes were ragged, his shoes gaping. Silently he reached out a shivering hand.

Madame Kollontai needed both her hands at that moment to gather her costly garments about her, preparatory to entering the car. With a lordly movement of her head she waved the man away. But he refused to be put off. He followed the party to the car and again thrust out his hand, uttering oaths and prayers, until finally he was thrust aside by the police officers in discreet attendance. Madame Kollontai and Herr Weismann got into the car.

Suddenly the beggar wrenched himself free from the police, ran to the car and shouted in a voice that could be heard fifty yards away:

'Wait till we get Communism! Things will be different then!'

The driver let in his clutch and the car sped rapidly away. Tauber and von Stroheim had been watching the episode with the utmost interest. And now the beggar turned to them. With a stately gesture he produced from his tattered garments a monocle on a black silk ribbon and put it in his eye.

'Kuh!'

'In person,' said Anton Kuh. 'Go back into the hotel and I'll join you there.'

They did so, and Kuh, who really was shivering with cold, sprinted round to the Wilhelmstrasse entrance in order to gain admission to the building.

This story rapidly became known throughout Berlin, but at the request of the Foreign Office the newspapers refrained from printing it for fear of diplomatic repercussions. Only a few people knew who was responsible. It was generally believed that the man had been an authentic beggar who had no idea that he was addressing a representative of the Soviet Union.

Kuh himself said afterwards that having watched Alexandra for some time, and knowing that this was the way she was in the habit of treating beggars, he had been quite confident of the success of his little comedy. He rejoined his friends shortly afterwards, clad in evening dress as they were. The three passed a pleasant

evening together, but Kuh rose to leave the others at an unexpectedly early hour.

'Now what are you up to?' demanded von Stroheim. 'We're
only here because of that joke of yours. You can't suddenly desert
us like this.'

Kuh screwed the monocle into his eye.

'I'm sorry,' he said. 'I have an important piece of naturalism
to attend to. The biography of Adam—Chapter Two.'

21

The Nazis

IN THE autumn of 1931, the French Prime Minister, Pierre Laval, and the Foreign Minister, Aristide Briand, paid an official visit to Berlin. Peace-lovers in both countries had high hopes of this occasion; but there was also a threat of unfriendly demonstrations upon the arrival of the two statesmen on a Sunday morning in September.

The party to welcome them at the Friedrichstrasse station included the new French ambassador, M. François-Poncet. There were indeterminate cries from the crowd as they drove away, but a very large number of police had been drafted to keep order, and no one was able to break through the cordon.

The Adlon was also surrounded by a cordon of police. We watched these preparations from the hotel and thought them altogether excessive and over-cautious in view of the entirely peaceful atmosphere of Unter den Linden. Louis Adlon personally received our French guests at the door and showed them up to their rooms in the 'V.I.P. corner'.

I have never been interested in politics, and I know nothing of what was discussed during this visit, but I believe it was principally matters of trade and finance. The talks took place in the Reich Chancellery, in the very room, as the French visitors noted with pleasure, where the Congress of Berlin had been held fifty years previously under the presidency of Prince Bismarck.

The newspapers told a pleasant tale about Hindenburg's official reception of the French delegates. The President was then 84, whereas Briand was only 69; but it was Hindenburg who made the livelier impression. Briand had been overtaxed by the negotiations and was looking very exhausted. With his customary consideration Hindenburg therefore cut the proceedings as short as possible. He accompanied his visitors to the door of his study, and, letting Briand go first, murmured to François-Poncet:

'It must have been very strenuous for the old gentleman.'

But Briand, who was by no means hard of hearing, caught the remark. Although he knew that it had been uttered in genuine sympathy, his spirit of mockery flashed out and he said:

'The fact is, your Excellency, there are days at my Ministry when I have my nose to the grindstone from morning till night. But then again there are days when I haven't a thing to do, and I find that even more exhausting. So you will understand why at present I am a little overwrought.'

He spoke in French, and it is possible that Hindenburg did not immediately understand him. He bowed the visitors out with all his customary ceremoniousness. But when later Briand's retort was translated to him he was greatly amused, and he often repeated it.

On Monday, the 30th January 1933, President Hindenburg appointed Adolf Hitler to be Chancellor of the Reich.

The news spread like wildfire through Berlin, and even before it was officially announced in the midday broadcast the telephones at the Adlon had begun to ring incessantly. Room reservations were being called for from all over Germany, above all rooms with windows overlooking Unter den Linden. A mass torchlight procession was to take place that night, forming on the Charlottenburger Chaussee to march under the Brandenburger Tor, past the hotel and down the Wilhelmstrasse. In consequence every available corner of the Adlon was in demand.

The hotel had had to ask for police protection, which was provided. Our doors were shut from six o'clock onwards. By that time every nook and cranny was occupied by guests whom it was quite beyond our power to accommodate, but they were customers of long standing who had the right to make use of the hotel whenever they wished to do so.

The list of Ministers in the new Cabinet contained many names which were known from earlier days, and so to many of our guests

the Cabinet appeared acceptable despite the fact that it included
a number of ornaments of the Third Reich, who, it was assumed,
would remain merely ornaments. Above all it was sponsored by
von Papen, who was generally considered to be more powerful
than Hitler because he had President Hindenburg behind him
and was Goering's superior in the State of Prussia.

Among the huge crowd of guests watching the procession from
the Adlon windows was the flying ace, Ernst Udet. Udet had not
yet returned to the Wehrmacht, but it was known that he was to
play an important part in the creation of a new Luftwaffe, so his
corner of the Adlon was particularly crowded. But regardless of
the enthusiasm of many of the guests, Udet talked scornfully of
the 'Hurra-Kanaille', the screeching mob.

When the appointment of Hermann Goering was announced,
Udet went to see our Frau Schmidt, whom he had known for
many years. Frau Schmidt was responsible for entering up the
small red notebook in which important data relating to our guests
were recorded, and it was she who sent out the telegrams of con-
gratulation on the occasions of birthdays, wedding anniversaries,
appointments and promotions. She drafted them herself, and as a
rule Louis Adlon only asked what had been said after seeing the
letter of acknowledgment. So on this evening Ernst Udet went to
Frau Schmidt and asked:

'Do you think I should send Goering a telegram? We served in
the same unit during the war.'

'What were your respective ranks?' asked the experienced Frau
Schmidt.

'I was his commanding officer.'

'Well, then,' said Frau Schmidt, 'I should just telegraph "Hals
und Beinbruch".' It was the familiar, wryly-humorous toast of
student clubs and Service messes, untranslatable, but which
roughly signifies, 'Here's to sudden death!'

Udet laughed.

'Do you really think so?'

'Why not?' said Frau Schmidt, shrugging her shoulders.

And so that was the message which Hermann Goering received

from his war-time comrade, Ernst Udet, when the Nazis came into
power.

The torchlight procession began at eight o'clock. Densely
packed columns streamed out of the darkness of the Tiergarten
and passed beneath the gaze of the Goddess of Victory on the
Brandenburger Tor. Bands marched between the columns, their
big drums beating the rhythm while they played military and old
Prussian marches. But as each band crossed the Pariser Platz,
where the French Embassy was situated, they stopped whatever
they had been playing and with a preliminary roll of drums broke
into the tune of the challenging war-song, 'Siegreich wollen wir
Frankreich schlagen'—'We mean to defeat France.'

Many of the spectators on the crowded pavements were carried
away with enthusiasm and burst into frenzied cheers at the playing of this song, but the members of the Embassy, watching from
behind drawn curtains, listened with heavy hearts.

The London *Times* correspondent in Berlin, a former British
naval officer named Norman Ebutt, told the following story in the
Adlon later that night:

As the procession moved down the Wilhelmstrasse, Hitler, with
some of his closest associates, was standing at a window in the
Reichs Chancellery. The head of the Berlin police, Herr von
Levetzow, also a former naval officer, told Hitler of the way the
bands were behaving on the Pariser Platz. It had somehow become known that the members of the French Embassy were listening from behind their drawn curtains. There were considerable
differences of opinion as to the desirability of the bands' behaviour, but amid the general enthusiasm nothing was done about
it. According to the *Times* correspondent, however, Goering asked
Hitler what he would have done in the circumstances if he had
been the French Prime Minister. He answered without an instant's
hesitation:

'I should have marched.'

The seemingly endless procession went on until midnight, the
torches, like an unbroken stream of fire, winding their way

through the heart of the capital. Did anyone think, on that night, of that other stream of fire that was destined twelve years later to pour down from the heavens, to put the torches out? . . .

And like a danger-signal to us all, the light of another fire glowed a few weeks later from behind the Brandenburger Tor. This was on the night of the 27th February, when the Reichstag building was burnt down.

On that day the directors of I.G.-Farben, the huge chemical combine, had held a conference. I have said already that Herr Duisberg, the founder of the combine, was an intimate friend of Lorenz Adlon and one of the oldest guests of the hotel. But since the combine had come into existence, in 1925, nearly all the leading figures in the German chemical industry had been in the habit of stopping at the Adlon, the more so since the combine had taken over an office building exactly opposite the hotel, on Unter den Linden. It was here that the conference was held, its subject being the development of synthetic materials. There was a scheme for setting up a Synthetics Research Establishment under the direction of a very distinguished chemist, Dr. Georg Kranzlein. Herr Duisberg and Dr. Kranzlein were both stopping at the Adlon, and they were sitting together in the Goethe garden after dinner when the hall-porter announced:

'The Reichstag's on fire!'

Naturally all the guests ran out into the street. From the Pariser Platz corner of the Adlon the glass dome of the Reichstag could be seen. It was bright red, as though illumined from within with Bengal lights. Duisberg and Kranzlein stood together watching the fire, and suddenly Duisberg gripped Kranzlein by the arm and said with an expression of extreme foreboding:

'This fire is a sign that one day all Germany will be communist!'

The remark was naturally not repeated by anyone belonging to the I.G. combine; but the words were overheard by a member of the hotel staff, and thus they travelled from mouth to mouth. The I.G. people did their best to make light of them, saying that Herr

Duisberg had returned in a highly pessimistic frame of mind from a world tour he had made a few years previously.

During this tour he had stayed for some time with Chiang-Kai-Shek in China; and it was with Chiang-Kai Shek that a prominent Berliner took refuge, following the night of the Reichstag fire—the former Deputy Chief of Police, Dr. Bernhard Weiss.

The fate of this man was extremely tragic. He was a fanatical opponent of Communism, and at the end of the First World War he had been appointed head of the political branch of the Berlin police with the express task of keeping a watch over the communist movement and its leaders. In this capacity he had signed the police notice offering a reward for the apprehension of the communist leader, Max Holz.

But political developments had made it increasingly necessary for his department to deal not only with the Communists, but also with the National Socialists—and these had now become masters of the country. Weiss did the wisest thing he could do in the circumstances: he left Germany. An anonymous warning reached him on the very night of the Reichstag fire. He left his home and came to the Adlon, where Louis Adlon at once put a suite on the first floor at his disposal, for him to occupy as long as he liked.

In the event, however, he did not need to stay long. His plan was to escape into Holland, and all the necessary formalities were attended to by the Adlon. By seven in the morning everything had been arranged and a car was in readiness. Bernhard Weiss crept out by the Wilhelmstrasse entrance, taking leave of the hotel with the words:

'This is something I shall never forget.'

22

The Changing Times

FOR Berliners as a whole the dawn of a new epoch was manifest in innumerable political happenings, but for us at the Adlon it cast its shadow in other and peculiarly perceptible ways. At that time, for example, we opened an outdoor café extension of the restaurant—a *terrasse*, as the French call it—along the Pariser Platz side of the building. It was arranged in the customary Berlin manner, with a trellis of flowers and greenery through which the guests could see the street without themselves being seen. Every table was protected by a brightly coloured sunshade.

As everyone connected with the catering business knows, there is a superstition attaching to the opening of any new establishment or resort. It is generally believed that the tone of the place, the kind of public it may be expected to attract, will be indicated by the first customer who enters it. This first customer appeared at ten o'clock in the morning of the day the outdoor extension was opened. He was a respectable-looking man, aged about fifty-five, in a shabby suit. It was not easy to say what his calling might be, but nothing could be more certain than that he did not belong in the Adlon.

He himself seemed to feel this, for he hesitated for some moments before entering, while the waiter on duty uttered a hurried prayer to all the patron saints of gastronomy that he might change his mind and decide to go elsewhere. But, no; he entered, and seating himself at the best table ordered a glass of Pilsener.

The waiter went rather glumly to execute the order, only to find on his return that even worse had happened. The first guest of the *terrasse* had made himself at home by taking off his shoes and putting his feet up on another chair; and the feet were nakedly visible through the holes in his socks.

Superstition turned out to be right. The kind of guests who frequented this part of the hotel were not such as were to be found inside, and so Louis Adlon was not really sorry when he received a communication from the Berlin Municipality. The new Chief Magistrate, concerned to preserve the traditional Prussian appearance of the town, requested him to close the extension, since it was not appropriate to the Pariser Platz, which was protected as a public monument.

Political circumstances and the proximity of the Chancellery drew the Adlon even nearer than before to the centre of public events. Louis Adlon could do nothing to prevent it when presently the 'foreign policy office' of the Party began to rent parts of his premises for the purpose of lecture and discussion groups: any refusal on his part would have been the equivalent of suicide. And so on these evenings we were subjected to an invasion of uniforms. But the thing we noted with interest was that the number of people invited to these gatherings, or who chose to attend them, grew smaller month by month, and that there were fewer of the former leading personalities among them.

A constant guest at the hotel, until he was sent to Vienna, was the Vice-Chancellor, Franz von Papan. He was accustomed to sit at a favourite table at the left end of the terrace; and here an accident occurred one day which won him much sympathy. A waiter, a very tall, heavily built man, was passing his table with a tray loaded with glasses of beer while behind him came another waiter pushing a service-trolley. The first waiter stopped abruptly for some reason, and the trolley, going at full speed, caught him behind the knees. He tottered, the tray tilted, and the contents of all its glasses flooded over von Papen's back. Von Papen ducked forward over the table, drawing in his head, then turned up his collar and looking cautiously round asked with a smile:

'Is there anything more to come?'

No, nothing more was to come to Franz von Papen at the Adlon; but soon after this came the 30th June 1934, and what was to become known to history as 'the night of the long knives'.

At about eleven o'clock on the morning of this day the Swiss newspaper correspondent, Dr. Oeri, appeared at the Adlon with the news:

'The whole Tiergarten quarter is surrounded by troops armed with machine-guns. Revolution has broken out!'

A stream of news and rumour followed, and the foreign press correspondents stopping at the hotel were summoned to the Propaganda Ministry. I was told that there were troop concentrations in the Budapesterstrasse and the Königsgrätzer Strasse, to protect the Government headquarters against the 'revolution'.

The Königsgrätzer Strasse, as all Berliners know, developed peacefully under this name for half a century, but was then, so to speak, parcelled out. One half was first called Ebertstrasse and the other half Stresemannstrasse; but these names had recently been removed. The two halves were now Hermann-Goering-Strasse and Saarlandstrasse. Lively military proceedings were to be observed in both halves.

The muzzles of machine-guns looked down from the walls of the Chancellery garden, and gendarmes with steel helmets, the straps buckled beneath their chins, were bivouacked outside Goering's palace on the Leipziger Platz. The people of Berlin, however, did not seem to be altogether convinced of this revolution. They strolled serenely through the streets, went about their business, and made the sort of jokes that on these occasions seem to spring out of the very pavements of the town.

The day had an especial significance for us at the Adlon because the King of Siam was staying at the hotel, and the Government was holding a State Banquet in his honour in the Schloss Bellevue, which was to be prepared in the Adlon kitchens. The separate courses were to be sent from the hotel to the Schloss Bellevue in a hotel-van especially designed for this purpose. The driver of this van was an S.A. man—a member, that is to say, of the 'Brown Shirts', the National-Socialist private army controlled by Ernst Röhm—and it happened unfortunately that on this day he was wearing his brown uniform shirt under his civilian suit. He drove off expecting no harm, but the van had not gone farther than the

Brandenburger Tor before it was stopped by a patrol of the S.S., Hitler's private bodyguard. Throughout the day the S.S. had been disarming all members of the S.A. The men of the patrol accosted our harmless driver in a threatening manner.

'Where are you going?'

The driver was a Berliner with the Berliner's sense of humour. He replied briefly, 'To the King of Siam', and grinned at them.

This merely enraged the S.S. men. Thinking that they were being made fools of they yanked the driver out of his seat and forced him with blows and threats to open the van. The sight of the lavish and costly foods prepared at the Adlon aroused even deeper suspicions. The patrol-leader asked:

'Is all this muck intended for another of the S.A. boss's orgies?'

The driver answered dourly:

'No, it's for the King of Siam.'

None of the S.S. men knew anything about the King of Siam or his visit to Berlin. Finally two of them climbed on to the van with the driver and escorted the van to the Schloss Bellevue.

The van was stopped several times more on the way, and the same thing happened with every journey it made. The banquet was in consequence an intermittent affair, with endless waits between the courses. It was not only our restaurant-manager who sweated blood, with the food waiting on the streets while it was being examined by members of the S.S.: the guests probably suffered even more from having to fill the interminable pauses with suitable conversation. Since no reference to the day's[1] events could be made, no reason for the delays could be given!

But it was the blood-bath itself that eventually rescued our restaurant-manager from his plight. A stream of messengers came to the Schloss Bellevue, bringing ever more horrifying news, and one guest after another withdrew in terror from the table of the

---

[1] On this day, and the previous night, Hitler broke the power of the S.A. Röhm and a large number of other leaders were 'executed' at his order. Many private scores were settled. Hitler made the strange admission in the Reichstag that the number of dead was 'more than seventy-seven'. It is now known that it ran into hundreds and possibly thousands.—Trs. note.

King of Siam. When finally Goering left the building in great
haste the banquet was abandoned.

It was this year that marked the beginning of the architectural
changes to the face of Berlin which above all plunged the so-
called 'old west' of the city into mourning. The Brandenburger
Tor and the Pariser Platz, as I have said, were protected as historic monuments, and our hotel also benefited by this protection.
But the building of the connecting line between the Anhalter and
the Stettiner stations, the 'North-South-S-Line', brought the
metropolitan railway very close to the Adlon. The Unter den
Linden station was built between the Neustädtische Kirchstrasse
and the Wilhelmstrasse, and the excavations led to the heaping up
of dismal sandhills along the central lane of the avenue. Then
the first of the old blocks of houses vanished to make way for the
tunnel, and finally all the trees between the Neustädtische Kirchstrasse and the Pariser Platz were felled—a melancholy sight
indeed!

Unter den Linden had contained many other kinds of trees besides the lime-trees—Lindenbäume—which gave it its name.
Among the 250 which came down at the first felling were several
dozen magnificent maples as well as some big plane-trees. Later
on, just before the Olympic Games, more trees were sacrificed to
rebuilding at the western end of the avenue, and so a part of the
roadway directly in front of the Adlon was robbed of its adorn-
ment. The Mayor of Berlin, Dr. Lippert, protested in vain against
this deforestation. He had received countless letters from Berliners
who loved those trees, and he packed them in a big trunk and sent
them to the Chancellery with his own protest. But all he got was
a blunt rejection. The old avenue of Unter den Linden became a
new street for the purpose of military parades, with its central lane
narrowed in order that columns might march twelve abreast along
the carriage-ways.

> *So long as the old trees bloom on Unter den Linden*
> *Nothing can defeat us—Berlin will stay Berlin....*

P

Such was the refrain of the Berlin marching song by Walter Kollo, and as the trees came down superstitious forebodings spread among the people.

'No more lime-trees on Unter den Linden ... presently there will be no more Berlin ...'

The prophecy was whispered round, and the new masters of the land made haste to plant new trees, for another omen appeared which caused them great embarrassment. The tunnel for the S-Bahn, the metropolitan railway, had been constructed with considerable difficulty. In the Königsgrätzer Strasse, now the Herman-Goering-Strasse, directly in front of the house occupied by Dr. Goebbels, a terrible accident took place. A fully-loaded tram crashed through the weakened road-surface into the newly excavated pit beneath.

'We shall all go crashing down in front of Dr. Goebbels' house in the Hermann-Goering-Strasse,' the whisper ran—and to avert further accidents, and further omens, the work of excavation was thereafter conducted with greater care. The houses at No. 1 Pariser Platz and No. 22 Hermann-Goering-Strasse, which stood over the S-Bahn tunnel, were supported with an iron bridge.

We at the Adlon watched with great excitement as new lime-trees were planted along our beautiful avenue. They were American lime-trees, four years old, which had come from the nurseries at Elmshorn in Holstein. They were about sixteen feet high, their roots protected by baskets of osier, in which they were planted. The young saplings were staked and enclosed by protective railings and gratings, and finally they were most carefully sprayed.

All Berlin waited to see if they would grow. Despite the trouble that had been taken with them, the saplings, set about twenty-five feet apart, had a most dreary effect, the more so since new street-lamps, designed in the mid-nineteenth century Biedermeier style, had been installed. These were taller than the trees, and in consequence various nicknames were bestowed on the once-proud avenue, which became known, among other things, as 'Under the Lanterns' instead of Unter den Linden.

·   ·   ·   ·

The Berlin Olympic games, which opened on the 1st August 1936, were an impressive and dramatic spectacle for both contestants and spectators. Of the athletic performances I need say nothing. Not only the records that were set up, but also the social and artistic functions and adornments that provided a background for the Games aroused the astonishment and admiration of the many world-famous persons who attended them.

Once again royalty and nobility thronged to Berlin. The King of Bulgaria, the Crown Prince and Princess of Italy, the Heir to the throne of Sweden, the Crown Prince of Greece, the sons of Mussolini, the Duke of Hamilton, Lord and Lady Londonderry and many other notables from all over the world were present at the opening ceremony.

Most of them stopped at the Adlon, and it was at this time that I again met Prince Philip of Hesse and his wife, Princess Mafalda, the second daughter of the King of Italy. I have often thought of the Princess's large, dark, ardent eyes, and of the appalling fate that awaited her eight years later.

Princess Mafalda of Savoy had married the elegant and charming Prince Philip in 1923. They had four children, and had lived quietly in Kassel or in Rome, withdrawn from public affairs, until the birth of the Nazi-Fascist alliance, the 'Axis', compelled them to play a part in high politics.

The reserved attitude of the King of Italy had from the first been displeasing to Hitler and the Nazi Government. What could be more appropriate than to make use of the King's son-in-law as an ambassador to bring about more friendly relations. So Philip was appointed Governor (Oberpräsident) of the Province of Hesse. He took up his residence in the town of which his father had once been Elector, and became an unofficial envoy and negotiator between Germany and Italy. Whenever Hitler produced a new political sensation Philip of Hesse would be sent to Rome. When guests appeared at the Adlon with the news that 'Philip of Hesse set out for Rome this morning, looking pale but determined', we knew it meant that something dramatic was going to happen.

The Prince's frequent comings and goings invested him at the time with an aura of mystery and glamour which bore little relation to reality, and which his wife endured with an evident lack of enthusiasm. The pale, slender, romantic-eyed princess had a passion for harp-playing and lived only for her family and children. She hated the use that was being made of her husband and herself, and her greatest longing was to be able to move to Rome before the outbreak of war.

But it was in her native land that tragedy overtook her. She had always been regarded with suspicion. In September 1943, when her parents and her brother, Umberto, left Rome and went over to the Allies, she remained there with her children and was arrested and brought to Berlin. Philip of Hesse was also arrested. The husband and wife were never again allowed to meet or be united with their family. Mafalda of Hesse-Savoy was sent to Buchenwald and died in August 1944 after an air-raid.

I have often wondered whether she had some foreboding of this end when she stood beside her husband at receptions at the Adlon. She looked gravely and with detachment upon the feverish doings of those days, and not even the most brilliant of functions could distract her.

Tall white flagpoles had been set up along Unter den Linden, and outside the hotel fluttered the flags of all nations. Between the rows of flags shone the powerful light of the new 'Biedermeier' street-lamps, and along the central lane, which had been strewn with red sand so that it looked like a tennis-court, strolled the great host of visitors to Berlin. During those August days tens of thousands of foreigners visited the historic buildings of the capital —young, fashionable Frenchwomen with high, fragile heels to their elegant shoes, sporting American women with Goodyear soles, British visitors in search of antiques and historical souvenirs; and, mingling with these civilians, officers in every known uniform —such was the general, lively impression that has remained in my mind.

·　　·　　·　　·

In January 1937 the newspapers published banner headlines across their front pages, quoting Hitler's latest speech—'The period of surprises is at an end.'

The words were intended to allay the fears of a worried world, but people in informed circles wagged their heads and remarked: 'If he's saying it so loudly it's pretty certain that the real surprises are about to begin.'

In September that year Mussolini came to attend the grandiose Army manœuvres in Mecklenburg and also to visit Berlin.

His train drew in at the Spandau-West station, and from here to the Wilhelmstrasse the streets were thickly lined with spectators. The route of the cortège lay along the Charlottenburger Chaussee, through the Brandenburger Tor, across the Pariser Platz, past the Adlon and so into the Wilhelmstrasse.

To do Mussolini especial honour it had been decided that he should not be housed at the Schloss Bellevue, as was customary in the case of State visits, but should stop at the old presidential palace, that is to say in the house where Hindenburg had lived as President. This was only a few doors away from the Adlon. Turning into the Wilhelmstrasse you passed Braun's shop, the British Embassy, the Adlon trade-entrance, which has been so often referred to in this memoir, the Ministry of Food and the Foreign Office, and then came the President's palace.

Owing to this proximity the task of installing and waiting upon Mussolini in the palace was entrusted to the Adlon. It was a ticklish assignment, because we knew that Hitler attached very particular importance to this visit and would fuss over the details even more than he generally did. On no account, so we were repeatedly reminded by his adjutant, must Mussolini have the slightest cause for complaint. Everything must be perfect.

Members of the Adlon staff, therefore, got the palace in readiness for Mussolini's visit, and when all the preparations were complete Hitler himself came to make sure that nothing had been overlooked.

Everything was in order, or so it seemed.

What was not in order was something that neither Hitler nor our manager knew about. When President Ebert had lived in the old house a new hot-water furnace had been installed, but for reasons of economy the existing plumbing had been used. The system was antiquated and anyone turning on a tap had to wait at least five minutes before hot water flowed into the baths and wash-basins. No one seems to have known, or remembered this, and in consequence an unhappy contretemps occurred.

During his visit Mussolini made a speech to the Berlin public in the Olympic Stadium at Maifeld—a Berlin suburb. The route to Maifeld was by way of the Brandenburger Tor and the Pariser Platz. A fantastic scheme of decoration had been erected, with flaming torches, bundles of fasces, enormous eagles, and masts flying innumerable Italian and German flags. Huge flags covered the fronts of the houses on both sides of Unter den Linden, the Adlon among them.

The Pariser Platz resounded with the tune of the Fascist hymn as Mussolini and Hitler drove together to the Stadium, where, speaking in German with a harsh accent and much rolling of the 'r's', Mussolini vowed eternal fidelity to the German Reich. The crowd applauded, but in the middle of his discourse a violent thunderstorm broke out and torrential rain streamed down on speaker and audience alike.

Mussolini was soaked to the skin, but the return journey had nevertheless to be made in an open car in order that the two leaders might show themselves to the people. Hitler draped his coat about his guest's shoulders, and when they separated on the steps of the presidential palace he said solicitously:

'You must have a hot bath at once, Duce. Have a cup of camomile tea and then go straight to bed and sweat for two hours!'

That was in the afternoon. In the evening Mussolini went to the Chancellery to attend a banquet in his honour. Hitler asked:

'Duce, did you take my advice?'

'I wanted to,' said Mussolini, 'but the hot water didn't run.'

Hitler's expression became stony.

'So what did you do?' he asked in a stifled voice.

'I went round to the Adlon.'

That closed the subject; but not, alas, for Hitler. He was a man who did not readily forget such things. While the visit was still on officials of the Secret Police appeared at the Adlon to question the manager responsible for the arrangements at the palace. They had come to investigate the possibility of sabotage. They were not long in satisfying themselves, however, that the fault was not deliberate or the result of any serious negligence, but was simply due to the fact that our people had had no experience of the palace plumbing.

When this was reported to Hitler he refused to believe it. No sooner had Mussolini departed than he himself visited the palace. Our manager was summoned, and in his presence Hitler turned the tap in Mussolini's bathroom and waited, watch in hand, for the hot water to run. It took exactly five minutes. Even Hitler had to admit it. Silent and tight-lipped he went away again.

The plumbing in the presidential palace was never renewed; neither was any other distinguished visitor installed there.

The Queen of Persia, Tadj Moulouk, the first wife of the late Shah, Reza Pahlevi, and the mother of the present Shah, Mohammed Reza Pahlevi, was resident in Berlin from October 1935 to January 1938. She came for treatment by the celebrated Professor Dr. Sauerbruch, of the Charité Hospital, but incidentally she discharged a delicate mission on behalf of her husband.

Among the supporters of the former Persian ruling dynasty, which had been driven from the throne by Reza Khan, was the head of the Bakhtiari family, Prince Esfandiari. From fear of Reza Khan, Prince Esfandiari had left his home in Ispahan, the 'carpet town', and come to Europe, where he spent his time principally in Germany as an importer of carpets. It was in Germany that he met his wife, a blonde Berlin girl named Eva Carl. A daughter was born to them in 1932—Soraya, now the ex-Queen of Persia or Iran. The Queen's task was to persuade Prince Esfandiari to return to Persia.

The Adlon was in consequence visited by Prince Esfandiari and his wife with the five-year-old Soraya. The negotiations with the Queen were successfully concluded, and they returned to Ispahan before she herself left Germany.

Another task which the Queen performed during her stay in Berlin was connected with the furnishing of the royal palace in Teheran, where the Peacock Throne now stands, the present dwelling of the Shah. Nearly all the lavish equipment of the palace was bought at that time in Germany. Eight railway trucks filled with costly porcelain, rare woods, lighting equipment and special hand-made fittings of all kinds went to Teheran. The central heating for the building, as well as the cold-storage plant for the kitchen, was all ordered and assembled in Berlin, and the person who supervised these purchases was our chauffeur, Mirow, in whom the Queen had unbounded confidence. So extensive was her shopping that four unemployed friends of Mirow were kept busy for a month, packing the things and getting them ready for transport.

Queen Tadj Moulouk stopped at the Adlon with her daughter, Ashraf, the twin sister of the present Shah. Although the princess was only eighteen, she had been married for three years, having been forced by her father into a political marriage with a member of a powerful Persian family when she was fifteen. Her visit to Berlin was the first spell of freedom she had ever known, and I think she enjoyed every minute of it.

She was on friendly, informal terms with all the members of the hotel staff, to whom she went for information about things to see and do in Berlin, and her pretty, almond eyes would shine with delight when someone made a suggestion that pleased her. As a rule she went riding in the Tiergarten in the mornings. She had a wonderful seat on a horse, and indeed rode better than most men. She also sometimes went to the University, where she followed a course of lectures in social science.

On one occasion she went out and bought no fewer than two dozen hats at a shop on Unter den Linden; but she did not take any back to Persia with her. When she and her mother left the

Adlon, in January 1938, the princess made a present of all her hats to the women members of the staff. She left them in a bunch, and there was a good deal of dispute among the beneficiaries under this legacy, much argument and bartering before our ladies were able to settle the vexed question of which of them should have which hat.

The Queen aroused some interest by not returning to Persia by way of the Balkans. Instead she took the route through Soviet Russia to Baku, where a Persian naval vessel bore her across the Caspian to the Persian port of Inseri. Shortly before leaving she made me a present of an exquisite silken rug from Ispahan.

23

The Deepening Shadows

THE political crises of 1938 brought about a degree of change in the patronage of the Adlon, since many distinguished foreigners kept away from Berlin, for fear of being caught there in the event of the sudden outbreak of war. But this in no way diminished the popularity of the hotel with those foreign visitors who did come. The hall-porter, whose income was a sort of measuring-rod by which both the quantity and quality of patronage might be roughly reckoned, earned just as much that year as in previous years.

The post of hall-porter in a big hotel is, as I have already said, much sought after, and it is by no means easy to find the right person to fill it. Essentially it is a matter of confidence, and that is why hotels are generally disposed to bestow it on an old and trusted member of the staff. To have reached the position of hall-porter of an international hotel is to have achieved the ultimate reward of a long period of honourable service.

It goes without saying that the first qualification for the post is a knowledge of men and women. The hall-porter must be able to sum up the visitor at a glance, and I hope I may be believed when I say that his evaluation will not be based merely upon the elegance of their luggage. It will depend far more upon imponderables. And it is to the hall-porter that the guests turn for information, and for help and guidance in their personal perplexities, from a feeling that the secrets of their daily lives are safer in his hands than if they were entrusted to the manager or the chief reception-clerk. Indeed, broadly speaking there are only two functionaries in an hotel with whom the guests are, as it were, on Christian-name terms—the bar-tender and the hall-porter. It is not for nothing that Mark Twain referred to hotel-porters in general as 'the guardian angels of the foreigner'.

The protection of the hotel against undesirable visitors is in itself a task calling for great tact and adroitness, and one concerning which many stories could be told. On one occasion our hall-porter found himself confronted by a man dressed as Napoleon III —the French Army uniform, the low-slung sword, the imperial beard. Thus arrayed he had marched to the hotel along the central lane of Unter den Linden, accompanied by a crowd of yelling small boys and other interested sightseers. The hall-porter saw him coming and hurried out, and the bogus Napoleon, haughtily approaching, demanded to be received by the hotel with all the ceremony appropriate to his rank. He spoke German without a trace of foreign accent.

The hall-porter decided that this was a matter that called for humour in its handling. Standing stiffly to attention he formally greeted the Emperor and assured him that the hotel would do its utmost to receive him in a fitting manner. But he said it in French.

This took the wind completely out of the Emperor's sails. Not having understood a word, and not wishing to give himself away, he executed a military salute, turned and marched off in the direction of the Tiergarten.

Another Berlin 'original' was rather more difficult to deal with. He was accustomed to go about in full Bavarian attire, the leather shorts, the little cap with a feather, and red and yellow cross-gartering round his calves. Moreover he had a bath-thermometer slung round his neck and carried a large, green botanist's case over his shoulder and a butterfly-net in his right hand. He was well known in the town, for he often showed himself on the Friedrichstrasse or Unter den Linden, and sometimes appeared outside the university, where he delivered al fresco lectures to the students.

By some unexplained means he contrived to get into the Adlon. He appeared suddenly in the hall, seated himself in the nearest chair, crossed his legs and refused to leave. To all requests to do so he replied firmly:

'Hotels are open to everyone.'

It seemed impossible to get rid of him without the use of force, but on the other hand the matter was not so serious as to warrant an appeal to the police. The hall-porter finally found the solution. Producing a twenty-mark note he tore it in halves and gave the man one half, saying:

'You'll get the other outside.'

The effect was instantaneous. The untoward visitor sprang to his feet, cordially thanked the porter, and went out. Having received the other half of the note he produced a whistle from his pocket, summoned a taxi, and drove away.

A dignified exit, it must be said.

The hall-porter had a more ticklish part to play in another very interesting case.

During the years 1937 and 1938, Dr. Goebbels, the Minister of Propaganda, took a very particular interest in the famous dancer, La Jana. The protection of so powerful a man was naturally a matter of great consequence to her. To profit by it was tempting, and to refuse it, on the other hand, was dangerous. But this view was not shared by a certain well-known concert singer who had been La Jana's friend for some years.

La Jana was accustomed to make use of a room at the Adlon when she had finished dancing. The singer was furiously jealous, and the lady went in terror of any open expression of his jealousy. He could not, of course, prevent Dr. Goebbels from offering his protection to La Jana; but what he did hope to do was to prevent her accepting it.

At the same time he had to avoid any open scandal. So whenever La Jana was at the Adlon he posted himself at the main entrance to keep a watch on her movements, pacing incessantly up and down. The hall-porter, needless to say, knew exactly who he was and what it was all about. It was the rule at the Adlon that in all private affairs the strictest discretion was to be observed, and that anything in the nature of a public scandal was at all costs to be avoided. So La Jana was always warned when her jealous lover was patrolling the main door, and she would slip out by the Wilhelmstrasse entrance, which served so many useful purposes.

The complicated situation was brought unexpectedly to an end when Dr. Goebbels learned of the remarkable impression which the Czech film-actress, Lida Barowa, had made on Hitler. There was something about her, it seemed, which reminded Hitler of his mother, and he called for repeated private performances of her films. Directly Dr. Goebbels heard of this he transferred his favour wholly and unreservedly to the girl from Prague. So La Jana's affairs were relieved of the tension which, deservedly or otherwise, had disturbed them for so long, and she was again able to use the front door of the Adlon.

The major events of 1938 took place outside Berlin and bore the names of Berchtesgaden, Godesburg and Munich. But there were repercussions which came within the sphere of the Adlon.

In August 1938, a representative group of French air-force officers, led by General Vuillemin, paid an official visit to Berlin and stopped at our hotel. They made an extremely good impression, and the Luftwaffe officers appointed to act as their hosts said of them that they were the élite of the French Army. They spent some days in Berlin and were shown a number of factories and flying grounds. This was evidently in accordance with high policy, for the Luftwaffe colonel who acted as General Vuillemin's escort made no bones about saying:

'The French are to be shown everything so that they can see for themselves that within a few days of the outbreak of war they won't have a machine or an airfield left.'

The outbreak of war . . . the fearful words had been spoken, and we could no longer doubt that, as the foreign correspondents said, war stood on our doorstep. Within two years the colonel's threat had been made good.

More ominous still was the visit paid to Berlin in March 1939 by Dr. Hacha, the President of Czechoslovakia, and his Foreign Minister, Dr. Chvalkovsky. Both gentlemen stayed at the Adlon, and the elderly Dr. Hacha remains an unforgettable figure in my memory. He had the gentle, courteous manner of the old Austria, and I have often wondered what effect this had on Hitler, himself an Austrian.

They arrived at very short notice on the evening of the 14th March 1939. I remember that day very well: it snowed, and the melting snow lay over the streets of the town. The gentlemen from Czechoslovakia sat for some hours in the Adlon, scarcely speaking, while they waited to be summoned to the Chancellery.

The small, bowed figure of Dr. Hacha was in marked contrast to that of the tall, elegant Dr. Chvalkovsky. Besides Chvalkovsky sat his daughter, a big, sturdy girl who took after her mother, the daughter of a Dutch diplomat. She had found a box of chocolates, a present from Hitler, awaiting her at the hotel, but she sat with it unopened on her lap while her fingers tapped nervously on the cellophane wrapping.

Not until one o'clock in the morning did the summons to the Chancellery arrive, and the ailing, delicate Dr. Hacha had to be almost carried to the door while he gazed about him with unseeing, despairing eyes in a face flushed with agitation.

The conference with Hitler lasted until daybreak, and all this time Anita Chvalkovsky sat motionless in the lounge of the Adlon, paying no attention either to the hotel staff or to the foreign newspaper correspondents who hovered about, hoping to get a few words from her.

It was perhaps five in the morning when the gentlemen returned, and a glance at Dr. Hacha was enough to show how the interview had gone. He seemed to be in a state of utter collapse, his eyes almost disappearing beneath his heavy lids. As they entered the lounge Anita Chvalkovsky sprang to her feet and the box of chocolates fell to the floor, still unopened. She went to her father and with a gesture of extreme tenderness stroked his temples with her two hands. For a moment father and daughter looked at one another, and then, without saying a word, they went up to their rooms.

It was a sad episode in the life of our hotel, and I think there can have been no one who did not feel deep sympathy for the gentlemen from Prague, whose fate was sealed that night.

At the beginning of June 1939 Prince Paul of Yugoslavia and his wife paid a State visit to Berlin. They stayed at the Schloss Bellevue, of which the domestic arrangements were, as usual, in the hands of the Adlon; but for members of their entourage, and of the German diplomatic corps appointed to attend them, accommodation had to be found in the hotel. This party included a number of leading members of the German Embassy in Belgrade. Princess Olga, Prince Paul's wife, was a Greek princess, one of the two sisters of the Duchess of Kent. The third sister, Elisabeth, was the wife of a member of the old Bavarian nobility, Count Törring-Jettenbach, and this pair, too, were stopping at the Adlon.

Great pomp attended the proceedings. The Government, the armed forces and heavy industry, in the persons of Hitler, Goering and Herr Krupp von Bohlen, mingled with the cream of European aristocracy and diplomacy at a gala performance of the 'Meistersinger', given in the State Opera's most lavish style. The Adlon prepared the cold buffet for this occasion, and Hermann Goering was afforded a handsome opportunity to indulge his fondness for decorative display.

Louis Adlon and I were among the invited guests, occupying our usual seats in the stalls. The auditorium was a glittering spectacle of jewellery, gold, silk and purple, and when the royal pair appeared with Hitler in the centre box the entire audience rose to its feet. Princess Olga was as beautiful as her sisters, Marina of Kent and Elisabeth von Törring. She looked exquisitely lovely, standing within the frame of the box, and her jewels outshone all others. But this was no surprise to anyone who knew where they came from. They had been a part of the Romanov jewellery, brought to Athens by her mother, a Russian princess, as her dowry.

I must confess that we at the Adlon scarcely knew whether we were on our head or our heels. The State visit lasted until the 5th

June, to conclude with the military parade at which for the first time parachute troops and the new German heavy artillery were displayed for the benefit of the foreign military attachés. The passage of huge guns shook not only the streets of the town and the foundations of our hotel, but also the spirits of the visiting diplomats. As usual, the Adlon was the place where the foreign visitors principally foregathered, and it was not hard for the hotel staff to guess, from chance-heard words, what they were talking about. The gun-carriages thundered through their conversation as they had thundered down Unter den Linden, and the commotion was not abated when the advance-party arrived which heralded the return of the Condor Legion from the Spanish civil war.

The Yugoslav royal pair and their entourage had not yet left, and with the coming of this contingent the hotel began to resemble an army camp. The gold braid of high-ranking Spanish and Italian officers, and the German officers escorting them, filled our public rooms, together with the click of their spurs and the gleam of their monocles. Wallenstein's camp can scarcely have been more colourful or adventurous in aspect than was the lounge of the Adlon during those June days, twelve weeks before the outbreak of war.

In August that year the Anglo-German Society held a literary function at the Adlon. If I remember rightly a lecture was delivered by Sir Philip Gibbs, but of this I am no longer sure, for Sir Philip often stopped at the Adlon. When the official part of the proceedings was over, English and German members of the society sat chatting in informal groups in the lounges, resembling those of a club, between the ball-room and the Raphael gallery.

Political tension throughout the world was rising to its climax, but that evening the Adlon presented a last picture of international understanding. Laughter and friendly voices were to be heard, and there seemed to be nothing to disturb the prevailing tranquillity.

Suddenly Herr Schmidt appeared, a member of the Press

Section of the German Foreign Office. All heads turned to look at him. He seemed as imperturbable as ever, but everyone felt that there must be some particular reason for his late arrival.

'I'm sorry I couldn't get away sooner,' he said. 'We've been awaiting news from Moscow.'

'From Moscow?' repeated one of the secretaries of the British Embassy, and smiled faintly. 'Good news, I trust, Herr Schmidt?'

'It depends how you look at it,' said Herr Schmidt. He sat down, glanced at the Englishman, and said: 'The signing of a pact with Russia is now assured.'

'Well, that's excellent,' said the Englishman, his mind naturally turning at once to the long-drawn-out negotiations between Britain and Russia. He leaned back in his chair, sipping champagne. 'That should greatly improve the situation. It was nice of you to tell me.'

Herr Schmidt said with an expressionless face:

'We think it's good news too. The German Foreign Minister will be flying to Moscow tomorrow——'

The Englishman sat bolt upright.

'——to sign a Russo-German pact,' Herr Schmidt concluded. 'The news was broadcast just twenty minutes ago.'

Everyone now looked with intent interest at the member of the British Embassy. But by this time he had pulled himself together. He rose slowly from his chair, made a little bow, and walked quietly and composedly out of the room. But once he was in the hall his pace increased. To the astonishment of the staff he darted out of the hotel almost at a run, leaving his hat and coat behind.

A few days later we had a first-hand glimpse of how it had all come about. A gala dinner was held by Herr Schnurre, another high official of the German Foreign Office, his guests being the Soviet Trade Delegation in Berlin, under the leadership of a certain Comrade Atanasov. Atanasov and the leading members of the delegation were stopping in the hotel, and so it came about that history was again made under the Adlon roof.

Q

It was whispered of Atanasov that he was a prominent member of the G.P.U., the Russian secret police. However this may be, those silent Russians were evidently very capable men, or they could scarcely have paved the way for the Russo-German pact as skilfully as they did.

Atanasov had been stopping at the Adlon since the spring, and the Russo-German trade negotiations had been dragging on all this time without getting anywhere, while the negotiations in Moscow, with the Anglo-French delegation, pursued an exactly similar course. The Russians, as the world eventually discovered, coolly 'stalled' with both sides while making up their minds which side it would suit them to join.

According to what we saw and heard in the hotel, a largely unwitting go-between in the preliminaries to the Russo-German Pact was a member of the Bulgarian Embassy, a Colonel Dragonoff. This dapper little ex-army officer was one of the permanent guests at the Adlon and was reputed to be very friendly to Germany. At the same time all the Bulgarians were on excellent terms with the Soviet representatives, and the Bulgarian Embassy in Berlin had the reputation of being better informed about Russia than any other.

It happened one day that the Russian, Atanasov, and Dragonoff met in the hotel. The encounter was apparently quite accidental, but in the light of subsequent events one may assume that Atanasov had deliberately contrived it. The gentlemen lunched together, and in the course of their conversation Atanasov remarked, merely in passing, that it was time Russia and Germany settled their differences. A hint of this sort, in diplomatic circles, constituted a minor sensation, and Dragonoff must instantly have passed it on to his government.

As to how he did so, and whether a cipher was used which the German Secret Police could be relied upon to break, I cannot say. But there is no doubt that Atanasov's remark eventually reached the German Chancellery. And the next move in the game also took place at the Adlon. Herr Schnurre of the Foreign Office invited Atanasov to have lunch with him at the hotel. Thus the first contact was established which led to the exchange of tele-grams between Berlin and Moscow and eventually to the signing of the Pact.

The successful conclusion of the tortuous business was finally celebrated at the gala dinner at the Adlon, to which the Russians contributed vodka, smoked salmon and grey caviar from Astrakhan.

24

The War-days

THUS was war prepared, and a few days later war came. I may mention two of its first manifestations at the Adlon.

On the afternoon of the 3rd September the manager handed every waiter a small pair of scissors with a chain attached. These were destined to become a kind of symbol, during the years ahead, of all matters connected with food. They were intended for cutting the coupons off ration cards.

The other happening was the arrival of a large party of British subjects from the Embassy in the Wilhelmstrasse, which was to be sealed in the presence of the Swiss Minister, who thereafter took charge of British interests in Germany. The distance from the door of the British Embassy to the Adlon's Wilhelmstrasse entrance was only a matter of a few yards, but the removal to the hotel took four days. The last to come to us was the Embassy Councillor, Sir George Ogilvie-Forbes.

Seven members of the French Embassy followed the British. These representatives of the two enemy Powers remained at the Adlon, on parole, as it were, until they could be taken from Berlin to Bad Nauheim, whence they were exchanged through Switzerland with their opposite numbers in England and France.

Such were two of the first tokens of the coming war to the Adlon. But there was a third which deserves to be recorded, a recurrent phenomenon that took place whenever Hitler made an important speech.

These speeches, besides being prepared in advance, were also translated in advance into a number of languages, and for the purpose of this task the entire Foreign-language Section of the Foreign Office was transferred to the Adlon. They amounted to about 150 people, who were housed on two floors and kept in a state of close confinement under an armed guard supplied by the Secret Police. The most elaborate security measures were enforced. All telephone lines to the third and fourth floors of the hotel were disconnected. No official of the Foreign-language Section was allowed during these occasions to have any contact with the outside world. Waiters and chambermaids doing duty on the third and fourth floors were searched at regular intervals. In short, everything conceivable was done to ensure that not a syllable of the forthcoming speech was allowed to leak out before it was delivered.

The head of the Foreign-language Section was a certain Dr. Gautier, of the Foreign Office. He, too, was hermetically sealed in the hotel. And anyone passing along the adjoining streets must have been struck by the large number of men in civilian clothes who appeared to be strolling aimlessly up and down, all with their eyes glued to the third- and fourth-floor windows of the Adlon. They were members of the Secret Police whose job was to ensure that no attempt was made to communicate with the outside world by this means.

Until their work was completed, and the speech delivered, the 150 interpreters, translators, secretaries and typists were marooned in the Adlon as though on a desert island. They themselves referred to these occasions as the big 'campaign days', but the hotel staff called them 'paper warfare days', on account of the endless bundles of sheets spewed out by the duplicating machines, and the huge quantity of litter which had to be tidied up when the party was over.

For reasons which I do not now remember Emil Jannings was at that time stopping at the Adlon. He was a friend of the surgeon, Dr. Sauerbruch, who for a long time had occupied a suite in the hotel. In those days of petrol rationing Jannings had to get about the town on foot, or by the underground, whereas Sauerbruch, by reason of his calling, was still able to travel by car. So Jannings took particular note of the times when Sauerbruch left the hotel in order to be able whenever possible to ride with him.

One day, however, Sauerbruch told Jannings that he was

unable to take him, because, he said briefly and almost rudely, he had 'something else to do'.

Jannings was annoyed. He, too, had something particular to do, and he had counted on getting a lift from Sauerbruch. Swallowing his ill-humour he went out into the street and walked uncertainly up and down, hoping for a taxi, although these were now very rare. None came in sight, but Sauerbruch's car was standing parked at the corner of the Pariser Platz. As though drawn to it by a magnet, Jannings drifted in that direction, and continued gloomily to pace up and down beside it.

This occurred on one of those occasions when the Foreign-language Section was incarcerated in the Adlon and the Secret Police were patrolling the streets. As Jannings, still waiting for a taxi, stood gazing abstractedly at the hotel a man came up to him and said:

'Boring job, isn't it? Nothing ever happens. Got a fag?'

Jannings gazed at him in some astonishment, for the moment quite failing to understand. However, he produced a cigarette, and the man went on:

'It would be nice if something did happen, but what a hope! Those Foreign Office people have all been screened a dozen times over—you can't expect them to try any funny business.'

A light now dawned on Jannings. Pulling a solemn face, and with an admonishing gesture, he said:

'That's not the right way to look at it. There can be traitors anywhere—fifth columnists.'

'Ah,' said the other. 'Well, you're right there.'

Jannings was about to build the thing up a bit more when Dr. Sauerbruch appeared, walking towards his car. The sight of him gave Jannings an idea.

'What about that fellow?' he said. 'Travels by car, it seems. Who is he anyway? What's he doing here? Perhaps we'd better look him over.'

Before his new-found colleague could reply he had seized him by the arm and led him towards the car, which Sauerbruch was in the act of entering.

'Secret Police!' he snarled, and put a hand up to the lapel of his coat. His 'colleague' did the same, but he genuinely displayed the metal shield of the Secret Police.

'Is this your car?' Jannings demanded. 'Will you kindly show me your permit?'

Privately-owned vehicles which were still allowed to be used had a corner of the number-plate blocked out in red, in addition to the written permit which the owner carried. Dr. Sauerbruch, in a state of some confusion, produced a wallet containing his permit and driving-licence and handed them over to the genuine police official. He passed them on to Jannings, who studied them with care and then said in a tone of deep respect:

'Professor Sauerbruch! We must apologize, sir, for having troubled you. We should have recognized you.' He then closed the wallet and slipped it into his own pocket, to Sauerbruch's further consternation. 'As it happens,' he said, partly to his colleague, 'I have to pay a call at the Charité Hospital to attend to a small matter. I'm sure the Herr Professor won't mind taking me.'

He got into the car without waiting for a reply. And then Sauerbruch understood. As they drove off together he said:

'I'd like my papers back, if you don't mind. How the devil did you manage that?'

'Necessity,' said Jannings, handing over the wallet, 'is the mother of invention. I really have got something rather important to do. You'll take me part of the way, won't you?'

Sauerbruch laughed.

'It looks as though I'd better, if I don't want to be arrested as a spy by Emil Jannings.'

After the ending of the Polish campaign the armies were withdrawn from the east and concentrated in the west. Many of the commanding officers took the opportunity of visiting Berlin, and many stopped at the Adlon. Thus it happened that after a long interval we again saw General von Rundstedt, who came accompanied by his aide-de-camp, Captain von Salviati. The latter, a most able cavalry officer, had often represented Germany at foreign riding tournaments, and had successfully led a number of international teams. Rittmeister von Salviati was connected by marriage with the Hohenzollern family, his sister being the wife of the eldest son of the former Crown Prince, Wilhelm of Hohenzollern.

The Crown Prince had sent a message to Captain von Salviati asking to see him; in order not to create difficulties he proposed to do so at the Adlon, because his apartment at the royal palace was kept under observation. His son, Prince Wilhelm, was a company commander in the Army, and the Crown Prince was anxious to discover from General Rundstedt, by way of von Salviati, what appointment he might expect to receive for the forthcoming campaign in the West.

But it happened unfortunately that a large number of generals were present in the hotel that evening. Gathered together at dinner in the small room behind the main restaurant were men destined to play a great part in the battles lying ahead—and perhaps to be shot or hanged for conspiracy in 1944. Von Rundstedt was there, and Generals von Beck, von Kleist, Warlimont and Stülpnagel; and seated slightly apart was Admiral Canaris, with the light of the candles, at which the gentlemen lit their cigars, drawing gleams from the broad gold bands on his sleeves.

Hemmed in as he was by this illustrious company, it was not easy for von Salviati to get away to attend to a private matter, but he had had no chance to send word to the Crown Prince telling him how he was placed. The Prince came to the Adlon in civilian clothes, and in order not to attract notice went at once to the Goethe garden, where Louis Adlon hurried to welcome him when he heard that he had arrived.

My own opinion of the Crown Prince, a woman's opinion of a man, quite unconnected with political circumstances, is that he was the most distinguished and truly aristocratic figure I ever saw. He listened quietly as Louis told him of von Salviati's dilemma. Louis offered to go himself and ask the captain to come to the

Goethe garden for a few minutes, but the Crown Prince restrained him with a hand that was shaking slightly, so Louis said.

He walked through the restaurant with Louis at his side, and stood for a few moments in the doorway of the adjoining room, gazing with an expression of great unhappiness at the brilliant scene, the red and gold and field-grey of the uniforms, the lustre of high office and great reputation, while he himself remained outside that magic circle, in civilian clothes.

'I know them all,' he said, looking at the faces assembled round the table. Then abruptly he turned away. 'I can't do it,' he said to Louis. 'I can't go in there, much as I would like to have news of my son. Better not.'

His erect figure and graceful stride as he left the Adlon remain for me an unforgettable memory. A prince and a deeply unhappy man, obliged to go in fear for himself and for others, because he had been born a prince.

Thanks to the big 'campaign days' we were on terms of close friendship with members of the Foreign-language Section of the Foreign Office. It was owing to this that we learned of an incident that set all official Berlin in turmoil at the time of the opening of the offensive in the West.

On the 9th May 1940, that is to say, twenty-four hours before the attack was due to begin, the Section was again summoned to action stations. This time, however, it was not mustered in the Adlon but, owing to the increasing fear of espionage, in the presidential palace. The work of translation and duplication had to be rushed through at high pressure in a few hours during the night. Our restaurant-manager knew all about it because he had the task of ensuring that adequate supplies of coffee, brandy and sandwiches were provided. By this time the palace, being so near the Foreign Office, had become the Foreign Minister's official residence. In the apartments where Ebert and Hindenburg had lived, the same where Mussolini had unavailingly turned on the hot-water taps, the language specialists were gathered together and the duplicating machines installed. As had happened at the

Adlon, all telephones were cut off, windows sealed and doors guarded, and anyone entering the building during this time was not allowed to leave.

A police cordon surrounded the palace, as our staff had no difficulty in perceiving, and we knew that military action of the highest importance was impending. But as to its nature and direction we could only guess.

At midnight a party of Gestapo officials arrived at the Adlon demanding to be taken to the third and fourth floors, where the Foreign-language Section had been installed on previous occasions. The leader of the party asked to see a list of all hotel-guests who had occupied rooms on these floors since the Section had first made use of them. Furthermore, all guests at present sleeping on the two floors had to be aroused and turned out of their rooms. There were fortunately not many, for the war was making itself felt at the Adlon. The Gestapo men then proceeded to a thorough scrutiny of all the rooms. Furniture was shifted, carpets raised, walls tapped, every inch meticulously examined.

What had happened? None of us could conceive of a reason for this upheaval, and our questions were not answered. Armed guards stood at the head of the stairs, denying all access to the floors.

Some light was shed the next day when the Government Proclamation was broadcast—the first of the Army Command 'Special Bulletins'—announcing the start of the western campaign; but it did not really explain why the Adlon should have been subjected to that drastic visitation. In the prevailing excitement, however, the matter was rather lost sight of, and it was not until some time later, when the Foreign-language Section again came to make use of our premises, that we learned what had brought it about.

It seems that on the night of the 9th May the telephone-monitoring service of the Gestapo had tapped a highly disturbing conversation between the Dutch military attaché in Berlin and someone in The Hague. Beginning with the words, 'It looks as though the weather will be stormy over Holland tomorrow . . .'—

that is to say, in disguised but perfectly intelligible language—the military attaché had warned the Dutch Army chiefs of the exact time of the German attack on the Low Countries.

Within an hour the conversation had been reported to Hitler, who, roaring with fury, ordered the most stringent security measures to be taken. It was clearly a case of treachery somewhere, since the Dutch officer could only have got the information from someone in the know.

Apparently assuming that all members of the armed forces were beyond suspicion, the authorities at once leapt to the conclusion that a civilian must be responsible; and of the comparatively few civilians having foreknowledge of the operation, a large proportion were members of the Foreign-language Section. Hence the raid on the Adlon, while the presidential palace was being similarly treated. Subsequently all the members of the Section, who had, of course, already been carefully 'screened' in the ordinary way, were subjected to a further rigorous examination and kept under close observation for a long period.

But all without result. No culprit could be discovered, and not until after the war did the truth become known. Then it was learnt that the leak had come, not from the Foreign Office or any civilian, but through Colonel Oster, deputy head of the Counterespionage Service under Admiral Canaris. Like his chief he was a member of the underground opposition to Hitler.

But although nothing at all could be traced to the Adlon, the authorities took advantage of the event to make certain alterations to the hotel. Without our agreement or connivance, a party of technicians one day descended upon us, sent by order of the Gestapo to install hidden microphones and wiring in the restaurant and elsewhere. Once again we had to submit to the presence of armed guards. The work was carried out under the supervision of Gestapo officers, and no one connected with the hotel was allowed anywhere near while it was going on.

None of us, in short, knew exactly where all these infernal devices were concealed. But here and there we came upon a microphone hidden behind a cupboard or under a table, and we

developed a warning system for the safeguarding of guests who
were known to us. Louis Adlon would say, with a slight flicker of
one eye:

'Don't you find it rather warm, so close to the radiator? Let me
move your chair a little farther away.'

Everyone knew what this meant. The secret language of those
days called for no dictionary or interpreter.

Although all kinds of textiles had been strictly rationed since
the beginning of the war, we contrived to make certain improve-
ments in our upholstery. Louis was particularly concerned for the
comfort of the prominent guests, both German and foreign, who
occupied the larger suites, where, no doubt, very interesting conversations sometimes took place. We furnished these with new,
large cushions, so designed that they might be used, for example,
to smother a microphone. This innovation met with much ap-
proval, and here again the secret language was employed. The
guest might say upon departing:

'My dear Herr Adlon, I have been most comfortable, and I
found your new cushions particularly soothing to the nerves.'

The capitulation of France, and the great session of the Reichstag at which numerous generals were promoted to the rank of
Field-marshal, once again brought the glitter of uniforms to the
hotel; and on the 18th July the triumph of the German Army was
symbolized by the march of the Brandenburg Regiment through
the Brandenburger Tor.

The events and achievements of those months brought a flood
of foreign visitors to Berlin. Spanish, Roumanian, Japanese,
Yugoslav, Italian, Bulgarian and Swedish parliamentarians, together with trade delegations from many neutral countries, filled
our public rooms with the stir and hubbub of the conferences held
at that time. But of all the many public figures who visited us there
is only one of whom I retain any particular memory.

In November 1940 a special train adorned with the Red Flag
and the hammer-and-sickle arrived at the Anhalter Bahnhof,
bringing Foreign Minister Molotov to Berlin. Molotov and his

staff were accommodated at the Schloss Bellevue, and we should
have seen little of his visit had not a noteworthy contretemps
caused him to pass through the Adlon.

At the conclusion of Molotov's talks with Hitler a banquet was
held at the Russian Embassy, which was only a few doors away
from the Adlon, at No. 11 Unter den Linden. Ribbentrop was
the principal guest at this affair; but while he and Molotov were
engaged in what was, no doubt, the liveliest and most amicable of
conversations, a third party elected to join them. The wail of
sirens announced that the R.A.F. had arrived.

Most of those attending the banquet at once left the Embassy,
which had not yet been prepared for such emergencies. However,
Ribbentrop invited Molotov and the other gentlemen to accompany him to the Adlon, and the party walked the short distance
along the avenue.

He had good reason for doing so. Beneath the flat expanse of
the Pariser Platz the Todt organization—the Nazi Military
Labour Force—had built an enormous air-raid shelter. It was
divided into two parts, both deep underground. The further section, towards the Brandenburger Tor, was intended for the use of
foreign diplomats, Foreign Office officials from the Wilhelmstrasse, and distinguished visitors to the hotel, while the lesser hotel
guests, and the staff, were to be accommodated in the nearer
section, adjoining the hotel.

The shelter could be entered from the basement of the Adlon
by way of the barber's shop. One passed through an 'air cham-
ber' into a maze of passages and cell-like rooms where a stranger
would have had some difficulty in finding his way. The part
intended for the 'high ups' was comfortably furnished with carpets, armchairs, radio receivers, typewriters and all that was need-
ful in the way of glass and crockery. The other cells, however,
were fitted out simply with wooden benches, in order to accommodate as many people as possible.

We spent very many nights in this shelter, which had another
outlet beyond the Brandenburger Tor, in case the hotel entrance
should be blocked. Louis Adlon had big, mellow-sounding gongs

installed in the hotel, and they served throughout the war to warn the guests of an alert and to notify them of the all-clear. Needless to say, the division of the shelter into sections for 'high ups' and 'non-high ups' could not in the long run be maintained. The common danger had its inevitable levelling effect, and people crowded in wherever they could find room.

However, on the occasion of Molotov's visit the farther section was, of course, reserved for him and Ribbentrop. It was in the shelter, so it is said, that Ribbentrop became finally convinced of the impossibility of reaching any lasting agreement with Soviet Russia, and it was from this moment that war with Russia became inevitable.

A bad thing happened in June 1941 shortly before the attack on Russia.

The foreign press correspondents, who were accustomed to meet regularly in the Adlon bar, were in close and friendly contact with a certain official of the Propaganda Ministry, Dr. Karl Bömer, an alert, friendly man who was much liked by everyone who had dealings with him, even those hard-boiled journalists. With his pleasant, humorous manner he had succeeded in smoothing out many difficulties which they encountered in the course of their work.

This was at the time when Hitler's deputy, Rudolf Hess, flew to Britain and the German Government adopted the unhappy expedient of proclaiming him to be mad.

Bömer, who had hitherto kept his end up very well in his informal dealings with the foreign press, now found himself in an awkward corner, assailed by blistering questions from all sides.

'So now even Hitler admits that Germany is run by lunatics!' was the gist of the pressmen's remarks. And to this there was no very easy answer. Bömer could only raise his glass and say dryly:

'Well, here's luck to you!'

Naturally the foreign correspondents knew about the redeployment of Germany's forces in the east, which could only be aimed at Russia. But despite all their efforts they had not been able to discover when the attack was to be launched. Security arrangements this time functioned really well. The knowledge was confined to a very small number of people in Germany; but one of this inner circle, as the correspondents rightly suspected, was Dr. Bömer.

In June, a week or so before the decisive Sunday, Bömer had another session with his foreign friends, nearly all of them Americans. Seated with them in the usual corner of the Adlon bar he had to contend with the usual barrage of quips and questions.

But this time the talk followed a more precise pattern, as though the Americans had put their heads together and decided upon a plan of campaign. They tossed the ball from one to another in an effort to trap Bömer into giving them some clue to the secret of secrets, the actual date of the attack.

Neither the barman nor the waiter could later say exactly how the conversation reached its critical point, but it seems that they arrived at it by reviving the subject of Hess.

'Heard the latest about Hess, Bömer?'

'No, what is it?'

'The British asked him if he wanted to go back to Germany. Know what his answer was? He said, "I'm not mad!"'

There was a burst of laughter, and Bömer was ruffled out of his usual calm. Half-angrily and half in jest he answered quickly—too quickly:

'Thank God I shan't have to listen to your jokes much longer.' At this they pricked up their ears.

'Why? Do you mean you're going to another job? Where? Are you going to join the Army?'

'No,' came the ill-judged answer. 'Next week I shall be Permanent Secretary under Rosenberg.'

At any other time this might have been treated as a joke, and indeed that is perhaps how Bömer intended it. Dr. Goebbels, to whose Ministry he was attached, and Alfred Rosenberg were known to be on terms of bitter rivalry. But just then, with the attack on Russia so evidently impending, shrewd minds could

read into the remark an especial significance, for Dr. Rosenberg
was Hitler's personal adviser on all matters relating to Russia.

The laughter of the journalists died down. They exchanged
glances and then looked hard at Bömer.

'You're going to be Permanent Secretary under Rosenberg in
a week?' one of them repeated slowly.

Bömer might perhaps still have saved the situation with a flip-
pant reply—anything to persuade them that he had only been
joking. But for once, perhaps because he had drunk a little too
much, or simply because he was angry, his quickness of wit deserted him. Instead a look of horror came over his face as he met
their eyes and realized the full implications of what he had said.
A Permanent Secretary could only be attached to a Minister.
Rosenberg was not yet a Minister. If he was due to become one
within a week, the acknowledged expert on Russia, it could only
mean that a Ministry for Russian Affairs was to be created, and
this fact furnished the strongest possible pointer to the date of the
attack on Russia. Bömer's momentary change of countenance, as
he gazed at them, was all the confirmation the foreign correspondents needed.

And then began the personal tragedy of Dr. Bömer. Unobtrusively, one by one, the journalists slipped away to rush to their
offices and draft their cables. Bömer presently found himself alone.
Now fully aware of what he had done he let his head sink on to
his arms on the table and sat there groaning.

I do not know how the authorities came to establish his responsibility for the story that appeared in the foreign press. He was
arrested and a widespread investigation was held, rendered more
difficult by the fact that foreign press correspondents were beyond
the reach of the Gestapo. Members of our staff were interrogated.
They said nothing, naturally; but no one could deny that Bömer
had been in company with the foreign correspondents that evening.

He had many friends who did their best to protect him, but
unfortunately for him he was an officer on the active list, a captain of artillery seconded for special duties to Army High Com-

mand in order that he might continue to work at the Foreign Office. He had therefore to be tried by court-martial according to the severe code governing the conduct of officers.

The sentence passed on him was as mild as regulations permitted. He was not imprisoned but was degraded in rank and sent to the front—the Russian front!—as an ordinary bombardier.

But Bömer remained the brave man he had always been. He volunteered for a succession of dangerous missions and was steadily promoted. He had already reached the rank of full lieutenant when his leg was shattered by high explosive; and as he lay in hospital, desperately wounded, he received news that he had again been promoted captain, which implied his full rehabilitation. A few days later he died.

With the declaration of war on the United States, in December 1941, the last of our American guests, the foreign correspondents, departed. From the very beginning the Adlon had been the German hotel most favoured by Americans. This had become a tradition maintained and cherished on both sides. People in the States talked of 'America House on Unter den Linden'.

We had always been on terms of warm friendship with our American patrons, and the list of distinguished names was a very long one—from 'Teddy' to Franklin Roosevelt (who visited Berlin as a young man), from Mary Pickford to Doris Duke, from Herbert Hoover to Sumner Welles. For Louis Adlon and me it was one of the most painful moments of our lives when we took leave of the last of them. We went with them to the cars, with grey-uniformed drivers, which were to carry them away from Berlin.

This time there could be no cheerful 'Auf Wiedersehen' or 'I'll be seeing you!' and as things turned out there was to be no return. It marked the end of an epoch for the Adlon, the proud hotel, as it did for the great city in which it had played so notable a part.

Before turning back into the hotel we stood for a little while at the doorway looking up and down Unter den Linden. Little now remained of the avenue's former elegance. The clouds of war

R

hung over the bare trees. The sands were running out, and the sound was almost to be heard. The broad streaks of white on the corner houses, designed to assist pedestrians to find their way in the black-out, were like shrouds made ready for the death of the town. Beyond the Brandenburger Tor great nets were suspended above the Charlottenburger Chaussee. They were designed to veil that thoroughfare, running like a broad pathway through the forest of houses, from the sight of enemy aircraft—grey testimony to our impotence in the air.

We turned with heavy hearts and walked hand in hand into the hotel. Neither of us said a word, but we were filled with foreboding.

Into the deserted rooms of the Adlon came other guests, for the most part from those European States whose destinies, for better or for worse, were linked with that of Germany.

Only rarely did we receive visitors from more distant lands. But one came to us in 1942, an exotic permanent resident who stayed at the hotel until the bitter end. His full name was Mohammed Haji Amin al Husseini, but he was always known as the Grand Mufti, the title designating his religious office.

This strange man was the sworn enemy of Britain, and it was this enmity that had brought him to the side of Hitler. Apart from his exalted priestly state he was a person of high temporal rank in the Islamic world, and was treated by the members of his entourage, which included two Arab officers in German Army uniforms, with the utmost ceremony and respect. He was very often visited by Admiral Canaris, and it was said that he had organized a spy-network in the Middle East to assist the German counter-espionage service and had raised a number of Arab volunteer contingents to serve with the German Army.

He would sweep through the hall of the Adlon with his robes flowing and his head held high, and whenever I saw him thus I would think of the value of that head. The British had put a price of £50,000 on it, dead or alive.

This we knew from the radio. The British radio, naturally—for who could resist the temptation, in the evenings when one was alone, to turn the knob a little farther and listen to the ghostly voices of the B.B.C.?

We had to be very cautious about this, since we ran the risk of a long prison sentence. One of our guests, a certain Dr. Ghuenzer, listened to London one night and was denounced by his neighbour in the next room, who had overheard the familiar call-signal. He was hauled off to police-headquarters and subjected to a rigorous cross-examination; but in default of further evidence, and in face of his strenuous denials, it seemed that the police were bound to let him go. As he was in the act of leaving the room one of the officers who had been interrogating him held out his hand and said in the friendliest way:

'My dear Herr Doktor, of course we all listen to foreign broadcasts. But it doesn't do to be caught. You must be more careful in future.'

Warmly grasping the extended hand, and sighing with relief, the doctor answered:

'Yes, I'll certainly be more careful next time!'

Whereupon he was promptly re-arrested, having fallen a victim to one of the oldest tricks in the police repertoire.

25

The End

THE winter of 1943–44 brought the turning-point, and we all found ourselves in a hideous dilemma of hope and fear. Were we to pray for a quick ending, even though it meant the victory of the Red Army, or should we hope that our land and nation might be spared this ultimate disaster? But that would imply the victory of a régime for which we had not the smallest sympathy.

The times grew steadily more mad. A state of total war was proclaimed, clearing the way for all the despots, petty and great alike, and giving free rein to denunciation, humiliation, all forms of personal malice.

A new system of transport control was introduced at the same time. Yellow, blue and red cards were issued, dividing the public into three different categories. By this means the use of private cars was still further restricted, only the small number of persons belonging to the first category being allowed to travel in them. The underground railway remained the principal means of transport in Berlin, and the crowds were appalling, particularly when there was an alert.

As many people as possible were evacuated from Berlin to save them from the increasing, hideous severity of the air attacks. A protective wall was built round the Adlon, reaching from ground-level to the height of the first-floor balconies. It lent the building, of which the graceful architecture had been so essential a part of Unter den Linden and Berlin, a strangely remote and repellent aspect, as though, from being an hotel world-famous for its warmth and hospitality, it had become a fortress where no one might enter. Could there be any greater paradox?

The first big night-attacks did fearful damage to Berlin. To walk down Unter den Linden was to feel a constant tightening of the heart. The fine dome of the Hedwig's Church had vanished, and its great cross, seven metres high, had shattered the wall in its fall and was itself broken to fragments. The charred remnants of curtains fluttered in the burnt-out windows of private houses, and here and there a stark chimney-stack, rising above the rubble, remained to show where a fine building had stood.

The old Habel Hotel, the Kaiserhof and the Bristol were no more; but still the Adlon remained intact amid the ruins and portents of defeat. Since the building of the protective wall no daylight had penetrated to the great reception-hall with its lofty marble walls, its bronze ornaments reflecting the splendour of a vanished age and its beautiful and unique Chippendale furnishings. No one seemed any longer to have eyes for such things. Food, a bed and the use of a telephone were all our guests demanded, for who was there in those days who could claim to possess an unscathed dwelling or a functioning telephone of his own?

The town was transformed into a lunar landscape where not even the most exalted beings, not even the foreign embassies, could be guaranteed immunity from destruction. The Foreign Office had arranged for the removal of all members of the diplomatic corps to villas and castles outside the immediate danger area. Only the Chancellery remained in Berlin, since the status of the capital as the seat of Government had at all costs to be maintained.

The action of the Foreign Office had its repercussions in the Adlon, where it led to a sort of ghostly reflection of the life of former days. Wednesday became a regular 'at home' day, when the Foreign Minister collected the foreign diplomats around him, and on those nights the Adlon was the scene of a cosmopolitan gathering as it had been in the past. Meals were eaten at small, round tables, and our waiters served them in long coats and white gloves as though the world had never changed. Something at least of the old elegance and luxury was for a few hours recovered; and what was more there was always something 'off ration' to eat. 'Il y aura quelque chose,' Louis Adlon would say in response to murmured inquiries or beseeching looks.

People prominent in the former life of the town would come to dine on these occasions, happy at the thought of drinking a glass of good red wine after their meal—Professor Sauerbruch, the great surgeon, and Wilhelm Furtwängler, the conductor, leading actors such as Paul Wegener, Gustaf Gründgens and Elisabeth Flickenschild, the directors of the Ufa and Tobis film companies and such theatre-managers as Kirchoff and Baky. And round other tables would be seated young Luftwaffe officers, most of them decorated with the *Ritterkreuz*, lean, hard young men with taut faces and tired eyes. They were the fighter-pilots whose task was to defend Berlin. They were off duty every other day, and then they came to the Adlon, to enjoy life where it still seemed attractive and worth defending. The most serious of them was the ace of the night-fighter pilots, Prince Sayn zu Wittgenstein. He crashed after his eighty-seventh victory, while attacking an approaching bomber squadron.

The many-coloured pattern woven by the lives of these different people was something one came to know intimately when the soft banging of the Adlon gongs gave warning of an alert. They sat together in the big shelter, indiscriminately mingled according to the order in which they had arrived, the fighter-pilot beside the Spanish count, the beautiful blonde actress beside the Swedish banker, the Foreign Office official, the company director, the film-producer, the surgeon from the Charité Hospital. And as though by an unspoken compact, the horrors of the time were left outside. The talk was of art and literature and music, and travel in foreign lands.

Terrible as those nights were, I would not wish to forget them. Now as I recall them they seem to me like the last flicker from a happier past: the flicker of a candle whose shrinking light was drowned in the flames that roared up from the town.

There is one date which I particularly remember, because for me it summed up that last winter of the war. As from the 1st October all theatres and other places of public amusement in Berlin were closed down. Actors and musicians were either enrolled in the armed forces or drafted to war-work of one kind or another.

Many young actresses were sent to work in munition factories, but most of the men went into one or other of the reserve formations, 'Volkssturm' or 'Volksgrenadier-Divisionen', which were intended to supply a last line of defence against the advance of the Allies.

When this happened I found myself remembering certain words uttered by Dr. Goebbels in one of the many speeches which, as the 'protector of German art', he had delivered before the war. He had said in effect: 'A nation which abandons its art ceases to be civilized . . .'

But although the theatres stopped, the Foreign Office 'At Homes' did not. Every Wednesday the ghostly gathering assembled at the Adlon. The Russians had reached the Oder, but not a word was spoken in that circle that had any bearing upon the hideous reality. Often the guests were hours late in arriving, because the succession of day and night raids was now almost uninterrupted. But this was treated merely as an occasion for matter-of-fact apology, as though it were due to nothing more serious than a late train or a flat tyre.

Not until the spring of 1945 did this macabre entertainment come to an end. Reality forced its way at length even into the diplomatic corridors, and the last dinner was served on the day on which the first Allied troops crossed the Rhine.

In April 1945, the Foreign Office was transferred to Bad Gastein. A long column of cars and trucks stood waiting in the roadway outside the hotel to take what was left of Ribbentrop's Ministry out of the dying town. Their silhouettes stood out in sharp relief as they passed under the one archway of the Brandenburger Tor that remained open. The other archways had already been barricaded with paving stones. Only the central one, the 'Kaiser's archway', was left clear.

As the last of the procession vanished from our sight the hall-porter remarked:

'Off they go—to Germany's air-raid shelter!'

He meant the Austrian Salzkammergut, some five hundred

miles south of Berlin. It was to this region, bordering the Alps, that the central administrative machinery of Germany withdrew, carrying out a 'strategic retreat', to use the current military phrase.

The foreigners were all gone, and the Foreign Office with them. There were no more official visitors to Berlin, for all contacts and conferences now took place at that grisly hide-out in East Prussia which was known as the 'Wolf's Lair'. It afforded more safety from the Allied bombers than did the capital. But this immunity was of short duration. When the advancing Russians threatened the Führer's headquarters, the occupants of the Wolf's Lair were forced to return to Berlin.

And now there were new guests in the Adlon. With the burning of the Eden Hotel a group of scientists came to us, known to the staff as the 'atom investigators'. As to the real nature of their work I know nothing, but all their documents and files were heavily imprinted with the word 'Secret'.

During the very last weeks we ourselves did not live entirely in the Adlon. We spent the nights at our country house in Neufahrland, near Potsdam, returning to Berlin by day in order to keep things in order, so far as that was still possible. But it did not really serve much purpose, for during that last period the Adlon seemed scarcely to belong to us. It passed increasingly into the hands of large and well-armed organizations using it for administrative purposes.

Passing through the heavy steel door of the protective wall into the reception-hall, one found oneself in the midst of a strange commotion. There were soldiers and uniformed people everywhere—civilians with steel helmets and rifles, women in air-defence uniform carrying gas-masks, Russians, Ukrainians, men of the Volkssturm. And here and there stood sinister-looking S.S. men in their black uniforms, giving loud-voiced orders. These were the real masters of the hotel.

And through all this our waiters continued imperturbably to perform their duties, generally silent amid the prevailing racket and seeming almost unconscious of it. They went on wearing their black coats until the last days of April, although the meals they served were only what came out of a field-kitchen.

But during these visits to Berlin we met many old friends for whom the Adlon had become a last place of refuge. The hotel's independent lighting and water systems, at a time when many districts of the town were entirely without light or water, bore witness in a way that had never been intended to the foresight of old Lorenz Adlon.

Among those living in the hotel at this time was Dr. Morell, who for ten years had been Hitler's medical adviser. His consulting-room was in the Kurfürstendamm, and he had gained a great reputation in certain intellectual and political circles for his treatment of severe cases of nervous exhaustion and sexual neurasthenia. Seated with the other guests in the air-raid shelter he would talk in guarded terms of Hitler's physical condition since the attempt on his life on the 20th July 1944. He walked, his body bent, with the aid of a stick, his hands and legs trembling, his face bloated and grey with the subterranean life he lived, so that it was shocking to see him.

'Is it true that you're giving him injections?' someone asked.

The doctor, whose reserve had been steadily breaking down since the beginning of the collapse, admitted that for years he had been treating Hitler with testis-hormones. His ailment—Parkinson's Disease, according to Dr. Morell—had nevertheless grown steadily worse. It was the delayed outcome of a severe cold in the head or influenza, which he had contracted in Vinniza in 1943. Probably a brain-tumour had developed after the influenza had seemingly cleared up, and it was to the growth of this that the fainting-fits, the trembling of the hands, the stumbling gait and the mask-like fixity of Hitler's expression were all to be attributed.

This account, by the doctor who for years had been responsible for Hitler's health, made a deep impression on me. Indeed, it was what finally decided us to avoid Berlin and get away to Neufahrland as often as we could. The end could not be far off, and it seemed to us that we had a better chance of surviving the onrush of the Red Army in the country than on the Pariser Platz. We overlooked the fact that Neufahrland was very near Potsdam, the military town *par excellence*. But how could we have foreseen the tragedy that was to overtake us?

During the last weeks before the capitulation the frequency of air-attacks rose to as much as seventeen in a day. The life of the Adlon was lived almost wholly underground, and many of the guests took up permanent quarters in the cellar.

Yet the well-tried apparatus of the hotel continued to function with a smoothness such as only a long-established and deeply-rooted tradition could instil in each individual member of the staff. Hot meals were regularly served at midday and in the evening. Hot water flowed from the taps as it had always done. There were baths, clean beds and, almost to the very end, full hotel service.

Something of the sort must have happened on board the *Titanic* as the great ship slowly sank beneath the waters of the Atlantic. In that half-way house, when men have abandoned the hope of life and prepared themselves for death, simple, everyday matters acquire an especial significance. The love of life, mingling with the clear-eyed acceptance of the fact that it must end, confers upon each small act and gesture a wholeness and integrity which may otherwise be lacking.

Such was the impression I received during my last visit to the Adlon, and I write these lines to express my most heartfelt gratitude to all members of the staff who, to the very end—to the moment, that is to say, when the building collapsed in flames—remained loyal to the hotel, rendering service as faultless and devoted as in the days of imperial splendour.

It was on the 21st April that the first shells exploded in Unter den Linden. The Adlon was now within the zone of Russian artillery fire, which was directed at the Chancellery building.

This day was marked by two other events: the Adlon stopped presenting accounts to its guests, and the Allies stopped presenting their own account from the air. With the Red Army at the outskirts of Berlin they could not run the risk of hitting their own side.

With the end in sight, the hotel served meals without asking for money or ration-coupons, and moreover every guest received a glass of wine. The Adlon still possessed a very well-stocked cellar, and thanks to the Wednesday gatherings held by the Foreign Office there were large supplies of food-stuffs and tobacco. The building was one of the few remaining intact within a wide area. Two shells exploded in the roof, but the ensuing fires were extinguished by the united efforts of everyone available.

The circle of steel drawn by the Russians round the city grew daily smaller, until the final battle was concentrated upon the Government quarter. Dead bodies lay on the pavements, the wounded cried out for help but there was no longer anywhere to take them. The Adlon was hastily converted into a field dressing-station. The barber's shop in the basement served as an operating theatre. Post-operational cases, and those whose wounds had been attended to, were taken into the air-raid shelter, and the bodies of the dead were laid out in the Goethe garden, covered over by the staff with hotel blankets.

By day and by night the artillery bombardment continued, while the earth trembled and the lights went out and then came on again. Low-flying Russian aircraft screamed down Unter den Linden, the rattle of their machine-guns audible even in the depths of the shelter. At the end of April the Academy of Art, on the Pariser Platz, went up in flames. The fire threatened to spread to the Adlon but was fought and finally repelled by our tireless staff and such hotel-guests as remained.

Next day the Ministry of Propaganda crumbled to dust and ashes, and on that same day the Adlon staff witnessed the last manifestation of the Third Reich—the passing of the aeroplane which bore Field-Marshal Ritter von Greim, the newly appointed 'Commander-in-Chief of the Luftwaffe', away from Berlin.

The tocsin was sounding for the last hours of the German capital. The Pariser Platz, with the bullets whipping across it, was emptied of human life, and the hotel itself was like a place of the dead. Only the wounded, those for whom no room could be found down in the shelter, lay in the reception-hall, in the bar, in all the lounges and public rooms. Those who were conscious might study the numerous placards bearing in large letters the admonition of Dr. Goebbels—'Berliners, be on your guard against enemy agents in German uniform! Their objective is the capitulation of Berlin!'

On the 30th April the Red Flag was hoisted above the dome of the burnt-out Reichstag. On the night of the 2nd May Russian tanks rattled under the Brandenburger Tor, and at eight o'clock the next morning the first Russian soldiers appeared in the Adlon. They came cautiously into the reception-hall, tommy-guns at the ready, and looked about them. Seeing nothing but the prostrate, groaning forms of the wounded, they went away again.

By now the bombardment had ceased, and the dwellers in the basement and cellars ventured to return to daylight. The shattered town presented an appalling spectacle, and many, peering through the hotel windows, burst into tears. The chariot on the Brandenburger Tor had been destroyed by a direct hit, its four horses twisted out of shape. Brown uniforms swarmed over the Pariser Platz and along Unter den Linden, while Soviet tanks proceeded along the central lane of the avenue and dark clouds of smoke swirled above the ruins.

But there was little time for gazing. Russian labour detachments rounded up everyone who could walk, and put them to work clearing away the rubble from the Wilhelmstrasse-Linden crossing. At the same time other parties of soldiers made a tour of inspection of the hotel, in the course of which a great many articles of value disappeared. The real trouble began, however, when a party in search of loot found the entrance to the wine-cellars. The same evening a string of Russian trucks drove up and the entire stock of wines was removed.

It seemed as though the end of that famous wine-cellar betokened the end of the hotel, for it was in the cellar that fire broke out. There could have been no better kindling than the piles of empty crates and packing-straw that were left behind. The flames, fanned by the draught from open windows, roared upwards from floor to floor at a tremendous rate; and so, having survived all the bombing, all the vicissitudes of war, the house met its end after the fighting was done.

No one could deal with the sudden, violent outbreak. The panic cry of 'Fire!' drove everyone out into the street, the wounded limping or crawling through the narrow steel door in the surrounding wall. Some managed to drag themselves to the middle of the avenue, out of reach of the flaming débris that came raining down, but others remained prostrate on the pavement.

Fate decreed that no colour should be lacking from that gruesome scene. At the height of the conflagration there was a sudden blaring of klaxons and shouting of orders. Trucks drove up, cameras were unloaded, and a Russian news-reel contingent filmed the dying hotel. Searchlights and lenses were turned upon the blazing roof, the glowing façade, the wounded lying near the entrance, the corpses amid the debris. Such were the last pictures taken of the Adlon, later to be included in the Russian film of 'The Battle for Berlin'. To me it was the most terrible documentary I have ever seen on the screen.

The flames utterly destroyed all the lavish fabric and appurtenances of the hotel, but when they had died down the framework still remained, a great skeleton of iron girders and blocks of marble. The ruin was left in this state for seven years, and foreigners returning to Berlin could stroll through the Tiergarten, bereft of its trees, under the damaged Brandenburger Tor and across the ravaged Pariser Platz to pause in contemplation at that corner of Unter den Linden—Number One. The Adlon! There must have been many, gazing at what remained, who conjured up in their mind's eye a picture of gaiety and luxury and civilized hospitality not readily to be forgotten. The name has outlived the house, and all over the world there are people for whom the word 'Adlon' has an especial meaning.

Not until 1952 was the burnt-out part of the building finally

demolished. The girders were used, so I have heard, in the con-
struction of the new luxury-thoroughfare in East Berlin which was
named the Stalin-Allee. The part that remained, the annex giving
on to the Wilhelmstrasse, once known as the 'Courier's wing',
has become a new 'Hotel Adlon', conducted under the auspices
of the German Democratic Republic. The former messengers'
room in the entresol is now the restaurant.

The avenue of Unter den Linden vanished with the Adlon. The
ruined houses were blown up and the sites levelled. Only those
buildings that seemed to the Occupying Power to be of value were
rebuilt. Among others, a vast new structure now stands on the
site of the Former Russian Embassy.

Only in one respect has the lovely street been partly restored:
the shattered lime-trees were replaced by new saplings. And to
these young trees I pin my hope of a new Hotel Adlon, one which
I may conceivably live to see, but not Louis Adlon. A few days
after the fire he met his own tragic end.

Exactly how it happened will probably never be known. But I
know only too well what made it possible. We took too little heed
for our own lives.

During the last phase of the war we had many messages from
friends in Western Germany urging us to leave Berlin and join
them in the west, where we might at least hope to escape being
caught by the Red Army. We did not do so because it seemed to
us impossible to abandon the hotel. We thought ourselves safe
enough in Neufahrland, whence we could quickly reach the Adlon
at any time. To have gone farther away for the sake of our personal safety would have been a betrayal, not merely of the hotel
itself but of our staff and patrons.

I have taken great pleasure in reading and quoting the writings
of Confucius. He taught that there are three ways to wisdom: the
way of reflection, which is the noblest; the way of imitation,
which is the easiest; the way of experience, which is the bitterest.
We thought to choose the noblest way, but found the bitterest
instead.

When all communications with the town were cut there remained nothing for us to do but helplessly await our fate. On the morning of the 25th April the Russians came. Our house was searched and looted. Fresh relays of troops constantly arrived, and we were exhaustively interrogated by one commissar after another.

And then the fearful thing happened. A further batch of leather-jacketed men burst into the house. They tramped about brandishing their weapons and shouting at us:

'Dokumenta! Dokumenta!'

The wife of a member of the hotel-staff, who had taken refuge with us a few days before, went up to them crying, 'Nix Dokumenta!'

She pointed to Louis Adlon and added by way of explanation:

'Da—Generaldirektor.' (In English, 'That is the managing director.')

The Russians, only understanding the word 'general', instantly seized hold of my husband. Louis Adlon, who had so often extolled Russian culture and hospitality, and who had shown the representatives of Soviet Russia, when they visited the Adlon, precisely the same consideration as in earlier times he had shown members of the Czarist nobility, was dragged off unresisting by the men of the Red Army. They first locked him in a near-by cellar, then took him on to Nedlitz and Krampnitz, and lastly to Seeburg, where the end came.

Why? It is useless to ask, because there can be no rational answer. I followed him for days along the roads and through the woods. I had to discard my shoes on that agonizing journey because my feet were bleeding. I had no thought except to keep on his trail, which I constantly lost and laboriously picked up again by means of countless inquiries. But at the end I found nothing but my beloved husband's dead body.

All that remained for me to do was to arrange for a coffin and a suitable grave. In order that he might be buried alone I bought a temporary plot in a quiet corner beneath a birch-tree, which he especially loved.

As often as was possible in those disordered times I went to visit the grave; but on many occasions I could only do so by going a long way round, since the cemetery was in the Russian Zone and I was constantly molested. Later, when the curtain came down and all ways were barred to me, I contrived to get the body removed to Berlin. It is in the Cemetery of St. Hedwig, beside his parents and his sister, that Louis Adlon has his last resting-place.

The one-time Hotel Adlon no longer exists. The establishment now bearing that name is no more than the botched-up remnant of a ruin, used by the East Berlin authorities as a sort of overnight hostel for State employees.

In recent years it has been proposed to me in many quarters that I should rebuild the Adlon, either in West Berlin or elsewhere in Western Germany. The necessary capital has been forthcoming.

I have refused all these offers.

Most certainly I would like to see the house rise again, to the honoured memory of my husband and Lorenz Adlon. I would like to rebuild the Adlon. But only when there is no more talk of West or East, and only on the site where it always stood, and where I passed the happiest years of my life—in the very heart of Berlin, at Number One, Unter den Linden.